Deaf and Hard of Hearing Multilingual Learners

Foundations, Strategies, and Resources

Edited by Joanna E. Cannon, Caroline Guardino, and Peter V. Paul

Routledge
Taylor & Francis Group
NEW YORK AND LONDON

Cover image: Getty Images/DrAfter123

First published 2022
by Routledge
605 Third Avenue, New York, NY 10158

and by Routledge
4 Park Square, Milton Park, Abingdon, Oxon, OX14 4RN

Routledge is an imprint of the Taylor & Francis Group, an informa business

© 2022 selection and editorial matter, Joanna E. Cannon, Caroline Guardino, and Peter V. Paul; individual chapters, the contributors

The right of Joanna E. Cannon, Caroline Guardino, and Peter V. Paul to be identified as the authors of the editorial material, and of the authors for their individual chapters, has been asserted in accordance with sections 77 and 78 of the Copyright, Designs and Patents Act 1988.

All rights reserved. No part of this book may be reprinted or reproduced or utilised in any form or by any electronic, mechanical, or other means, now known or hereafter invented, including photocopying and recording, or in any information storage or retrieval system, without permission in writing from the publishers.

Trademark notice: Product or corporate names may be trademarks or registered trademarks, and are used only for identification and explanation without intent to infringe.

Library of Congress Cataloging-in-Publication Data
Names: Cannon, Joanna E., editor. | Guardino, Caroline, editor. | Paul, Peter V., editor.
Title: Deaf and hard of hearing multilingual learners : foundations, strategies, and
    resources / edited by Joanna E. Cannon, Caroline Guardino, and Peter V. Paul.
Description: New York, NY : Routledge, 2022. | Includes bibliographical references and index.
Identifiers: LCCN 2021044827 (print) | LCCN 2021044828 (ebook) | ISBN 9781032194400
    (hardback) | ISBN 9781032155654 (paperback) | ISBN 9781003259176 (ebook)
Subjects: LCSH: Deaf—Education. | Hearing impaired—Education. | Multilingual education.
Classification: LCC HV2430 .D39 2022 (print) | LCC HV2430 (ebook) |
    DDC 371.91/2—dc23/eng/20211208
LC record available at https://lccn.loc.gov/2021044827
LC ebook record available at https://lccn.loc.gov/2021044828

ISBN: 978-1-032-19440-0 (hbk)
ISBN: 978-1-032-15565-4 (pbk)
ISBN: 978-1-003-25917-6 (ebk)

DOI: 10.4324/9781003259176

Typeset in Garamond Pro
by Apex CoVantage, LLC

Access the support material: www.routledge.com/9781032155654

Deaf and Hard of Hearing Multilingual Learners

This critical resource provides foundational information and practical strategies for d/Deaf or hard of hearing (d/Dhh) multilingual learners. These learners come from backgrounds where their home languages differ from the dominant spoken or sign languages of the culture. This book is a one-stop resource for professionals, interventionists, and families, helping them to effectively support the diverse needs of d/Dhh multilingual learners by covering topics such as family engagement, assessment, literacy, multiple disabilities, transition planning, and more. The book provides vignettes of learners from 25 countries, discussion questions, and family-centered infographic briefs that synthesize each chapter. *Deaf and Hard of Hearing Multilingual Learners* is a groundbreaking step towards better supporting the many languages and cultures d/Dhh students experience in their lifetimes through strength-based and linguistically responsive approaches.

Joanna E. Cannon is an Associate Professor in the Department of Educational and Counselling Psychology and Special Education, and is coordinator of the Education of the Deaf and Hard of Hearing graduate program at the University of British Columbia in Vancouver, Canada.

Caroline Guardino is a Professor of Exceptional and Deaf Education at the University of North Florida in Jacksonville, Florida.

Peter V. Paul is a Professor of Special Education, emphasis on d/Deaf Education, at the Ohio State University. Paul is the current editor of the *American Annals of the Deaf*.

Contents

Preface   vii
Peter V. Paul

Acknowledgments   xii

Contributors   xiv

1   Learners Who Are d/Deaf or Hard of Hearing and Multilingual: Perspectives, Approaches, and Considerations   1
Joanna E. Cannon and Caroline Guardino

2   Family Engagement: Developing Partnerships for d/Deaf and Hard of Hearing Multilingual Learners   30
Sandy K. Bowen and Sharon Baker

3   Developing a Comprehensive Language Profile to Support Learning: The Assessment of d/Deaf and Hard of Hearing Multilingual Learners   67
Lianna Pizzo and Laurie Ford

4   Language Development, Assessment, and Intervention for d/Deaf and Hard of Hearing Multilingual Learners   106
Kathryn Crowe and Mark Guiberson

5   d/Deaf and Hard of Hearing Multilingual Learners and Literacy Instruction   142
Jessica Scott, Chidinma Amadi, and Terynce Butts

6	Leadership and Collaboration in School Settings for d/Deaf and Hard of Hearing Multilingual Learners *Lianna Pizzo*	175
7	d/Deaf and Hard of Hearing Multilingual Learners With Disabilities: A Case Study of a Learner Who Is Deaf With Autism Spectrum Disorder and From an Immigrant Family *Eun Young Kwon, Caroline Guardino, and Joanna E. Cannon*	219
8	Transition for d/Deaf and Hard of Hearing Multilingual Learners: Guiding Principles and Planning Tools *John L. Luckner and Joanna E. Cannon*	264
Index		300

Preface

Peter V. Paul

This book focuses on d/Deaf and hard of hearing (d/Dhh) students who are multilingual learners (DMLs), which refers to an increasing cohort of d/Dhh students throughout many predominantly English-speaking countries. In fact, as asserted in the first chapter, this broad cohort of individuals represents one of the fastest-growing groups in PreK-12 schools in the United States, constituting, at present, more or less a third of the population of learners. This is, indeed, one of the fastest growing groups in the larger general student population. Students who are multilingual learners with disabilities have also increased substantially over the last quarter century.

What do we the editors mean by DMLs? Basically, these multilingual learners are those whose home languages differ from the language of the dominant culture, that is, English, in the United States. Or the home languages might also be different from the dominant sign language in the USA, that is, American Sign Language. Similar to the cohort in our first volume (d/Dhh learners with disabilities [DWD]), DMLs is a group with diverse complex education and social needs. DMLs who also possess disabilities present even more challenges for theorists, researchers, and practitioners.

There are eight chapters in this volume, which synthesizes research and provides a toolkit of educational strategies and procedures. The range of topics includes the engagement of families, the general assessment of multilingual learners, and the assessment of language and literacy as well as the development of these constructs. Other topics include transition to post-secondary settings, and the facilitation of and need for collaboration across school settings to meet the needs of learners and their families. There is even a chapter that contains a case study on a deaf learner with autism spectrum disorder as well as strategies and other information for working with DMLs with disabilities (i.e., DML-D).

Chapter 1 presents the overall purposes of the book and an overview of the socio-demographics and intersectionality of d/Deaf and hard of hearing multilingual learners. It highlights the fact that it is necessary to examine research from the broader fields of bilingual and special education. Similar to the main themes discussed in our volume on DWD (Guardino et al., 2022), this chapter discusses the merits of utilizing collaborative, asset-based approaches that emphasizes the strengths of learners—a concept which permeates the entire book. The authors assert that it is important for practitioners to not only understand the complexities of working with DMLs and their families, but also implement linguistically and culturally responsive practices to improve the education and social lives of DMLs. This requires, at the least, for professionals to ascribe to the Radical Middle construct that encourages the examination of implicit biases in resolving conflicts and challenges.

There is little doubt that families are critical to the development of all learners, and in particular d/Dhh multilingual learners. This is the topic of Chapter 2. As mentioned in this chapter, the crux is to encourage the engagement of families—that is, to utilize family-centered practices, especially for early intervention and throughout the school years. Educators need to be aware of the challenges for families; nevertheless, families should be partners in this process. Families are diverse, representing a range of international cultures. Chapter 2 provides strategies for engaging families to support the mainstream language and literacy development of their children who are either bilingual or multilingual while, at the same time, respecting the home language and culture.

The next three chapters cover critical topics related to the assessment and development of language and literacy. Chapter 3 addresses the general issues and techniques related to selecting and interpreting assessments of DMLs, particularly the development of a "comprehensive language profile." As noted in this chapter, it is difficult to provide adequate instructional services and render appropriate instructional decisions without results of high-quality language proficiency measures. And, of course, families should be involved in the assessment process.

Chapters 4 and 5 delve deeply into language and literacy acquisition, advocating a strength-based approach, providing evidence-based practices and strategies, and emphasizing development and maintenance. The authors reiterate that it is a challenge to describe and address the complexities of multilingual language and literacy acquisition. Educators, parents/caregivers, and other stakeholders need relevant knowledge about the various language and communication modes such as spoken, signed, and written.

Chapter 5 recognizes the limited research with respect to understanding and supporting literacy development for multilingual learners. The authors synthesize research on literacy for all d/Dhh learners and for non-d/Dhh English learners with the intent to apply strategies and practices that might be relevant for DMLs. Time-honored concepts such as explicit instruction, background knowledge, metacognition, and others are discussed. The authors conclude with recommendations for further research and instruction.

The *Essential Instructional Supports Framework* provides the groundwork for the discussion of leadership and collaboration strategies in Chapter 6. The author explores concepts that can be implemented to support linguistically and culturally responsive instruction. Also mentioned is the need to provide strategies and practices for constructing a supportive learning environment for DMLs. There is little doubt that strong and diverse leadership is needed to ensure the success of programs and practices for DMLs and their families. Leaders themselves must also reflect on their practices— and this process is similar to the tenets of the Radical Middle concept.

Understanding DMLs is challenging and addressing the needs of DMLs with disabilities (i.e., DML-D) may be more demanding, as discussed in Chapter 7. Similar to the discussion of DWDs, it is difficult to obtain reliable and valid estimates of the prevalence and the incidence of DML-Ds. There is limited research available; however, it seems to be clear that this cohort of school-age individuals is growing. Although there might be a tendency to emphasize the "disability" of DMLs, the authors argue that it is more productive to focus on the learners' assets and to consider the sociocultural variables such as culture, identity, and language. Clearly, DML-Ds possess intersectionality, which must also be considered in planning instruction and curriculum, as well as in developing and utilizing assessments. In addressing the needs of this cohort, the authors proffer and elaborate on a familiar sociocultural construct, discussed in the DWD volume: *Tenets of Effective Practice for Learners who are DWD*. This culturally responsive construct contains "four pillars": collaboration, asset-based approach, Zone of Proximal Development, and the Radical Middle. Readers should appreciate the use of a case study on a deaf individual with Autism Spectrum Disorder, which—within reason—can be viewed as a starting point for addressing the concerns and needs of DML-D learners and their families. There is a strong need for additional research on identifying and examining individuals who are DML-D.

No text on DMLs is complete without a discussion of transition, which is the topic of the final chapter, Chapter 8. Planning for transition to postsecondary employment or educational environments should commence as early as possible to ensure that DMLs receive familial and social supports to eventually lead productive adult lives in the community. The authors provide guiding principles and research-based strategies, including those for engaging families in the transition process as well as procedures for involving agencies such as vocational rehabilitation. In addition to discussing several transition assessments, readers will become familiar with person-centered planning practices that are culturally and linguistically responsive. It is no surprise that families need to be actively involved in the transition planning process, which entails trust and open communication. Understanding and respecting the culture and identities of families is a point that has been made throughout this text. Transition is another area that is in need of additional research.

We the editors hope that this text serves as a comprehensive and accessible resource for addressing the needs of DMLs and their families, especially in predominantly English-speaking countries (e.g., United States, Canada, Great Britain, and Australia). Attractive features include learning objectives at the beginning of each chapter and discussion questions at the end to stimulate dialogue and debate, as well as to provide fodder for further instruction and research. The vignettes sprinkled throughout each chapter should enhance the understanding of the various concepts associated with DMLs.

The book features vignettes of families from 26 countries: North America (Canada, including the Algonquin community; US, including the Cherokee community; Mexico), Central America (Guatemala, El Salvador), Africa (Cameroon, Cape Verde, Ethiopia, Ghana, Kenya), the Asian-Pacific region (Australia, New Zealand), Eurasia (Russia), Southeastern Asia (Myanmar, Philippines, Thailand), Europe (Netherlands, Portugal, Poland, Iceland), Asia (China—Hong Kong, Mainland China, Japan, Korea, Nepal), India, the U.K. (Scotland, England), and Palestine (Gaza/West Bank). The families described within the vignettes use 25 languages spoken and written languages: Amharic, Arabic, Burmese, Cantonese, Cherokee, Creole, Dutch, English, Filipino, French, Gujarati, Hindi, Korean, Mandarin, Nepali, Polish, Portuguese, Punjabi, Q'anjob'al, Russian, Shona, Spanish, Swahili, Thai, and Twi. In addition, the families discussed in the chapters use 11 sign languages: American Sign Language (ASL), Australian Sign Language (Auslan), British Sign Language (BSL), Icelandic Sign Language, Lengua de Señas Mexicana (LSM; Mexican Sign Language), Lengua de Señas Salvadoreñas, (LESSA; El Salvador Sign Language), Mayan Sign Language (K'iche), Modern Standard Thai Sign Language, New Zealand Sign Language (NZSL), Sign Language of the Netherlands (SLN), and Zimbabwe Sign Language (ZSL). The book also provides four vignettes of multilingual and multicultural families with d/Dhh children with disabilities: cerebral palsy, autism spectrum disorder, developmental delays, and Down syndrome. The authors also include several vignettes of learners using assistive devices (e.g., augmentative alternative communication), applications, and a motorized wheelchair.

For further study and information, there is a list of resources (e.g., publications, websites, and organizations) at the end of the chapters. It is our hope that this information can be used to improve the educational and social lives of individuals who are d/Deaf and hard of hearing multilingual learners, including those with disabilities.

Reference

Guardino, C., Cannon, J. E., & Paul, P. V. (2022). *Deaf and hard of hearing learners with disabilities: Foundations, strategies, and resources*. Routledge.

Acknowledgments

The journey from proposing this book to witnessing it in print has allowed us to gain knowledge about our own privilege with respect to understanding: intersectionality, culturally responsive pedagogy, multilingual development, culturally and linguistically diverse perspectives, and theories and frameworks that support culturally and linguistically diverse learners and their families. This process has helped us further develop our cultural competence while acknowledging our own biases and inherent beliefs. As editors, we had the honor of working with 18 diverse experts who served as authors and external reviewers. Together we have grown to better understand and strategize how professionals in the field of deaf education can provide more effective services for d/Deaf or hard of hearing multilingual learners and their families.

We thank the following external reviewers that assisted in improving and clarifying the content: Drs. Sharon Becker, Megan Farnsworth, Danielle Guzman-Orth, Chris Hiers, Soonyang Kim, Tia Kimball, and Pam Luft. We want to express our appreciation of your expertise, time, and the detailed feedback. The family-centered briefs were designed by Dr. Bonita Squires from the University of British Columbia. Thank you for your willingness to work with us through several versions to create practical infographic handouts for families and community members working with these learners. We are pleased that you were able to bring to life our vision of providing a resource for families that offers them a summary of the information from each chapter in an accessible format.

We would be remiss without recognizing all of the professionals working with d/Dhh multilingual learners and their families, as well as the students who are d/Dhh multilingual themselves. We encourage professionals to expand upon this resource by engaging in coaching opportunities and research studies that test the recommended strategies. Distribute the family-centered briefs freely and with confidence knowing they are translated into eight languages (Spanish, French, Mandarin, Punjabi, Arabic, Tagalog, Korean, Vietnamese) to provide accessibility for families that you work with. To the families of d/Dhh multilingual learners, we honor your distinctive backgrounds, cultural practices, and the rich diversity you bring to our educational settings. You are a critical component to helping professionals working with your child(ren) to be culturally competent and highly effective teachers who use culturally responsive teaching strategies. And finally, to the learners who are d/Dhh and multilingual, you are the inspiration for this book. Working with you was the impetus for creating this resource that may allow your family members, professionals, and community members to understand culturally responsive practices to better meet your needs.

Contributors

Chidinma Amadi
Doctoral Student
Georgia State University
Atlanta, GA

Sharon Baker
Program Developer, Oklahoma School for the Deaf
University of Tulsa
Tulsa, OK

Sandy K. Bowen
Professor
University of Northern Colorado
Greeley, CO

Terynce Butts
Doctoral Student
Georgia State University
Atlanta, GA

Joanna E. Cannon
Associate Professor
University of British Columbia
Vancouver, BC, Canada

Kathryn Crowe
Postdoctoral Scholar
University of Iceland
Reykjavík, Iceland

Laurie Ford
Associate Professor
University of British Columbia
Vancouver, BC, Canada

Caroline Guardino
Professor
University of North Florida
Jacksonville, FL

Mark Guiberson
Professor
University of Wyoming
Laramie, WY

Eun Young Kwon
Doctoral Candidate
University of British Columbia
Vancouver, BC, Canada

John L. Luckner
Professor
University of Northern Colorado
Greeley, CO

Lianna Pizzo
Associate Professor
University of Massachusetts Boston
Boston, MA

Jessica Scott
Assistant Professor
Georgia State University
Atlanta, GA

1
Learners Who Are d/Deaf or Hard of Hearing and Multilingual: Perspectives, Approaches, and Considerations

Joanna E. Cannon and Caroline Guardino

LEARNING OBJECTIVES

The reader will:

1. Understand the characteristics, and demographics of d/Deaf and hard of hearing multilingual learners (DMLs).
2. Recognize the complexities of multilingual development that may be present for DMLs as they progress through schooling.
3. Examine their personal perspective on multilingual acquisition and cultural competence, and identify how this reflective practice can support the success of DMLs in a linguistically and culturally responsive way.
4. Comprehend the benefits of a collaborative, strength-based/positive approach, considering the intersectionality of the DML population.
5. Consider how approaches such as asset-based, linguistically and culturally responsive, and family-centered can guide instruction and engagement to better serve DMLs and their families.

Learners across educational systems in countries where English is the primary language (e.g., United States, Canada, United Kingdom, and Australia) come from diverse backgrounds, both linguistically and culturally. These backgrounds offer tremendous academic and social benefits for those acquiring multiple languages. d/Deaf and hard of hearing (d/Dhh) learners who are multilingual (DML) include learners with a home language that varies from the dominant culture's spoken language (e.g., English) or sign language (e.g., American Sign Language [ASL] or British Sign Language). Families, schools, and communities should offer linguistically enriching experiences crucial for language and literacy development, as well as the social and emotional well-being of DMLs.

For teachers of the d/Dhh in the United States, DMLs constitute approximately 18.4–35% of the population of K-12 learners (Gallaudet Research Institute, 2013). Statistics indicate that the culturally and linguistically diverse learners are the fastest-growing group across the general population of learners (US Department of Education, National Center for Education Statistics [NCES], 2019). The identification of students with disabilities who are English Learner(s) (EL) has significantly increased over the past 20 years (NCES, 2019). The population growth for ELs and DMLs means that more professionals within the schools will need information about the best ways to support these learners. Many general education certification bodies in the United States and other countries require EL endorsements and/or coursework to prepare teachers to support the linguistic needs of all learners in the classroom.

d/Deaf and Hard of Hearing Learners Who Are Multilingual

With the ever-changing, transient, and global society in which we live, DMLs and their families may include those who: (a) are born in their country of residence but utilize a minority language from their ethnolinguistic community (e.g., Algonquian; see Box 1.5); (b) are born in a country and relocate to another country where the majority language of the ethnolinguistic community does not match that of the home language (e.g., Amharic; see Box 1.4); (c) are a d/Dhh child who is an immigrant and already has a foundation in his or her native language (e.g., Spanish), as well as the sign language of their home country (e.g., Lengua de Señas Mexicana [LSM], Mexican Sign Language; see Box 1.2); (d) a d/Dhh child adopted and raised in a different country with a foundation in their home language (e.g., Mandarin; see Box 1.1); or (e) d/Dhh child born in an English-speaking country of parents who immigrated and use a native spoken language at home (e.g., Filipino; see Box 1.3). DMLs are students who are bilingual, trilingual, or at times quadrilingual, sometimes across modalities. DMLs refer to a variety of learners who experience exposure to multiple languages both in and outside of the school setting, including learners who: (a) enter school without a language base and no formal schooling, (b) enter school with a foreign language base (native sign language or listening and spoken language) and formal schooling, (c) enter school with a language base that is incomplete, or (d) enter school with interrupted age ranges in formal education.

We also know that children who are immigrants and/or refugees have a variety of experiences during the transition process between countries that may impact their language acquisition and schooling. While families who emigrate to a new country may have planned this transition, those who are refugees may have fled unexpectedly from their home. For children who are refugees and are d/Dhh, they may have experienced trauma leaving their home, country, people who know how to communicate with them in their native sign language, unexpected separation from family members, and/or exposure to information in multiple languages and contexts unfamiliar to them (Akamatsu & Cole, 2000).

Statistics and Demographics

There are over 7,117 spoken languages and 144 sign languages throughout the globe (Eberhard et al., 2021) and half of the world population is multilingual (Grosjean, 2013). These statistics are expected to rise in the upcoming decades, with students who are ELs constituting 40% of the US school-age population by 2030 (Grosjean, 2013). Currently over 400 languages are utilized in homes in the United States, with statistics of students who are ELs in the current school system ranging from 9.6–20% depending on the state (Migration Policy Institute, 2019).

There has been an increase in immigration to predominantly English-speaking countries (e.g., Canada, Australia, and Great Britain; Leigh & Crowe, 2020) in the past decade, with predictions of further increases in the next decade (Counts et al., 2018). One in seven (14%) individuals in the United States are born in other countries; whereas, approximately 20% are born in Canada, Australia, and the United Kingdom (Leigh & Crowe, 2020). The demographics for learners who are d/Dhh appear to be similar, but accurate statistics are difficult to ascertain. A recent study in Canada found over 11 languages other than English or ASL utilized in the home across 37 d/Dhh participants (Cannon et al., 2019).

Purpose

The purpose of this book is three-fold. First, to expand upon concepts discussed in the 2016 Special Issue of the *American Annals of the Deaf* (Cannon et al., 2016), which focused on students who are DMLs. Second, to provide a comprehensive, accessible resource across languages for parents and practitioners working with DMLs. Third, to collaboratively write with a strengths-based/positive approach across all chapters, considering the intersectionality of the DML population, practitioners, and families that support their education.

Although the Special Issue focused on broader categories (i.e. early intervention, assessment, and teacher preparation), this text contains chapters on language and literacy, collaboration across school settings, transition to postsecondary settings, and students with disabilities who are also multilingual learners. The content is more specific to previous research and strategies and the focus of this book is to provide beneficial information to anyone working for DMLs who are in predominantly English-speaking countries (e.g., United States, Canada, Great Britain, and Australia), enrolled in the school systems, and receiving specialized services.

Through the expansion of concepts, we hope to increase the awareness of the potential unique language and communication support for these learners (e.g., cultural brokers, transdisciplinary approaches, multiple interpreters, and videos of strategies for parents). Furthermore, our goal is to increase the available materials for practitioners, families, researchers, and professionals to conduct research and embed culturally and linguistically responsive content into coursework and professional development. Each chapter in this book contains learning objectives that are related to the discussion questions posed at the end of each chapter to spur critical discourse of the concepts presented. Vignettes of fictitious DMLs are also embedded throughout each chapter to illustrate snapshots of learner characteristics and demographics beyond those offered by the examples within the text. A family-centered brief synthesizes the main ideas of each chapter and are translated into multiple languages: Spanish, French, Mandarin, Punjabi, Arabic, Tagalog, Korean, and Vietnamese. We hope these briefs will provide families and community members with accessible information to supplement the text. A list of resources, including books, articles, websites, and organizations follow each chapter to present the reader with additional helpful information.

There is an overall dearth of research regarding students who are d/Dhh compared to other areas of education, especially regarding students who are d/Dhh and diverse (i.e., those with a disability and those whose are multilingual learners; Guardino & Cannon, 2015; Guardino & Cannon, 2016). Therefore, another purpose of this book is to examine research from the broader fields of bilingual and special education. We challenged the authors of this co-edited volume to critically analyze the literature beyond the field of the Education of the d/Dhh and expand into the general special education and bilingual fields. This knowledge may serve as a foundation to increase future research that includes case studies of DMLs, their families, and supports that may be beneficial to them, in addition to conducting replication studies of existing research (e.g., Cannon et al., 2010; Cannon et al., 2016; Guardino et al., 2014) and expanding the scope of other research (Guiberson, 2013). We challenged the contributing authors to synthesize the literature and examine their own personal biases and cultural competences. This required self-reflection of their cultural values, beliefs, and perceptions and how those lenses clarify concepts of DMLs. The information throughout each chapter offers researchers, practitioners, and parents with an overview of the research from the broader fields applied to DMLs and encourages a continuation of the discourse on the best practices for success with these learners.

Multilingual Development

Theorists provide frameworks to better understand the complexities of language acquisition in multilingual development. For example, basic interpersonal communication skills (BICS; Cummins, 1984) are surface-level skills used in conversation during social interactions, including gestures, pronunciation, intonation, and vocabulary. BICS are context-embedded, not cognitively demanding, and does not require specialized language, but takes approximately two years to acquire if immersed in the language and culture. Yet BICS is not sufficient for learners to acquire new knowledge until the learner acquires cognitive academic language proficiency (CALP; Cummins, 1984). This is the level of language that students must achieve to understand higher order concepts and complete academic work in the classroom. CALP is the foundation of all academics and includes reading comprehension, expressive writing skills, and text-embedded vocabulary knowledge. School-related tasks are typically context-reduced and cognitively demanding because they include comparing, contrasting, synthesizing, inferencing, and other higher order thinking skills. Due to the complexity of CALP, it takes approximately five to seven years to acquire; although the acquisition of both BICS and CALP are interconnected and not linear, with a combination of the two occurring across multiple languages (Aukerman, 2007). Depending upon when a DML enters school in their new country, support of multilingual acquisition may be more critical for educators to consider when working with this population.

The Qualitative Similarity Hypothesis (Paul et al., 2013) supports bilingual acquisition via a bimodal (visual and/or auditory) pathway exhibiting cognitive, social, and cultural benefits to learning multiple languages. The benefits of multilingualism are qualitatively similar for d/Dhh learners and support the development of cultural identity. The development of identities within cultures of the hearing, deaf, Deaf, or hard of hearing communities is particularly relevant to the intersectionality DMLs may experience throughout their lifespan (Crenshaw, 1989).

Additional considerations in multilingual development include whether the individual is experiencing simultaneous or sequential language acquisition, as well as additive (i.e., gaining linguistic competence in languages over time) or subtractive multilingualism (i.e., losing linguistic competence in a language over time). Gathering information about the type of multilingual development a DML experiences is crucial to gaining a complete language profile to plan for language and literacy instruction (see Crowe & Guiberson, 2022, Chapter 4; and Scott et al., 2022, Chapter 5 for further discussion). It is important to make these distinctions because different interventions work with different levels of language and generalizations about language levels and abilities will not meet the unique learning needs of DMLs.

Cultural Considerations

Multilingual vs. Monolingual Perspective

An historical myth in the field of educating learners who are d/Dhh is that multilingualism interferes with language acquisition, yet studies reveal and parents believe that bilingualism has advantages (Guiberson, 2013). Bilingual d/Dhh students outperformed monolingual d/Dhh peers on language tasks and have exhibited increased executive functioning, metalinguistic awareness, and literacy skills for learners with and without disabilities (Bunta et al., 2016; Guiberson & Crowe, 2018; Sininger et al., 2010; Thomas et al., 2008). Brain-imaging research reveals that, with accessible language input, d/Dhh learners can acquire multiple languages across modalities (Kovelman et al., 2009; Petitto & Kovelman, 2003; Petitto et al., 2000). These advantages can be capitalized on by providing support in the home language (e.g., Spanish) as well as the majority culture language (e.g., English) to increase English language outcomes rather than providing English-only support (Bunta et al., 2016). In Box 1.1, we are introduced to Jiao's family who understand the benefits of bilingualism, as they use both Mandarin and English in a variety of ways to highlight the importance of both languages. Furthermore, Jiao's family demonstrates how cultural and family connections can be maintained through bilingualism.

Multilingual benefits can be documented and further expanded upon when practitioners measure DML learning using a comprehensive language profile (Hoover et al., 2018; see Pizzo & Ford, 2022, Chapter 3 for more discussion). For example, in Box 1.2, we meet Juanita, who has LSM

Box 1.1 Jiao

Jiao has a mild, bilateral hearing level and was born in Guilin, a city in North Guangxi, China. A Chinese British family adopted her when she was 4 years old. Minimal information was available regarding when her hearing level was discovered, or if she received any early intervention services for speech and language. The family has one other child, a son, and they all use Mandarin as the primary language in the home, although the parents are bilingual and also fluent in English. Upon Jiao's arrival to Bristol, England, the family continued to expose her to Mandarin, although when she responded she was very quiet and rarely spoke above a whisper. The parents contacted The Bristol Deaf Children's Society who provided information about family play groups, a teacher of the deaf and hard of hearing, a speech-language pathologist for early intervention, and parent support groups. The family continued to expose Jiao to Mandarin and English by: (a) participating in a play group twice a week, (b) taking her to early intervention and speech-language therapy sessions in English, (c) video chatting with their family in China twice a month, (d) attending events at the Chinese Community Centre in Bristol, and (e) reading Mandarin stories before bedtime. Combining activities across languages and cultures shows respect for each and continues to increase overall language skills.

Box 1.2 Juanita

Juanita is nine years old and deaf with deaf parents. The family lived in Mexico City, Mexico until they migrated to the United States of America when Juanita was eight years old. They all use Lengua de Señas Mexicana (LSM; Mexican Sign Language) as their primary language for communication, and Spanish to read and write. Juanita has a profound, bilateral hearing level that was identified at birth due to the family history of deafness. Juanita attended the Instituto

> Pedagogico Para Problemas de Lenguajes (School for the Deaf), the same school her parents attended. Juanita's grandparents (both hearing and fluent in LSM) moved to Santa Fe, New Mexico and the family often visited them on holidays and birthdays. When her mother died suddenly in an accident, Juanita and her father moved into his parents' home in Santa Fe. Her father began work in her grandfather's company. Both grandparents used Juanita's home language (LSM), provided childcare, and nurtured her social-emotional well-being. Juanita's father took her to visit the New Mexico School for the Deaf where she was introduced to American Sign Language (ASL) and English through the LSM interpreter the school provided for their visit. The teachers and administration explained that many teachers within the school knew some LSM and many were fluent in Spanish. The teachers would use cues and visual supports for Juanita as she acquired ASL and English. The school also has a counselor who offers activities and groups to support Juanita's social-emotional well-being during her transition and time of grieving. The school personnel and students that they met during the tour were excited about Juanita becoming a member of the school community.

as her first language, Spanish as her second language, and is now being exposed to ASL and English. Given her strong foundation in her first language, family members who use LSM in the home, and the supports available in LSM and Spanish at the New Mexico School for the Deaf, Juanita has the potential to be quadrilingual with an intersectionality of multiple cultural identities.

Understanding that learners have vertical (i.e., those from within the family culture) and horizontal (i.e., those outside their immediate family culture) identities (Solomon, 2014) helps educators understand multiple student perspectives when planning instruction. The intersectionality of all identities forms one's core personality and character (Crenshaw, 1989; Hoover et al., 2018). Meaningful engagement with learners and their families includes a multilingual perspective that exhibits respect for all aspects of a family's linguistic and cultural identity. This perspective can enhance educational planning if one considers cultural features (e.g., cooperative versus competitive learning, views regarding the concept of time, community/public behavioral expectations, adjustment to new environments, understandings of race, sexual orientation, and identity; Denninger, 2017; Hoover et al., 2018) that may impact outcomes for learners. Considering the cultural features is more productive than the use of "normative expectations" or assumptions. Awareness of how these cultural features can increase linguistic awareness assists in planning instruction. This instruction may include using experiential learning to tap into prior knowledge, enhancing learners' CALP, and creating opportunities for mapping concepts across a DML's linguistic and cultural repertoire.

Examining Our Cultural Awareness, Competence, and Identity

The Radical Middle (TRM; Easterbrooks & Maiorana-Basas, 2015; Maiorana-Bases, 2018) is a project created by professionals and parents in deaf education that challenges people to examine their personal biases regarding communication modalities when working with d/Dhh learners. We also challenge professionals in the field to self-reflect and examine their cultural competences and linguistic biases in order to increase their multicultural awareness to better serve diverse populations such as DMLs. When we are cognizant of our own cultural competences, we become aware of the unconscious influence these may have on our ability to understand a learner's, or their family's, perspectives. The components of cultural awareness, including competence and identity, will be explored to improve our understanding of how to best support DMLs and their families.

Cultural Awareness

Culture is a complex and individualized concept that encompasses both superficial and in-depth aspects of the society and environment in which we live. Figure 1.1 illustrates this multifaceted concept through the metaphor of an iceberg (Hall, 1976; Multicultural Council of Saskatchewan, 2017). The iceberg metaphor can be utilized to reflect upon one's own

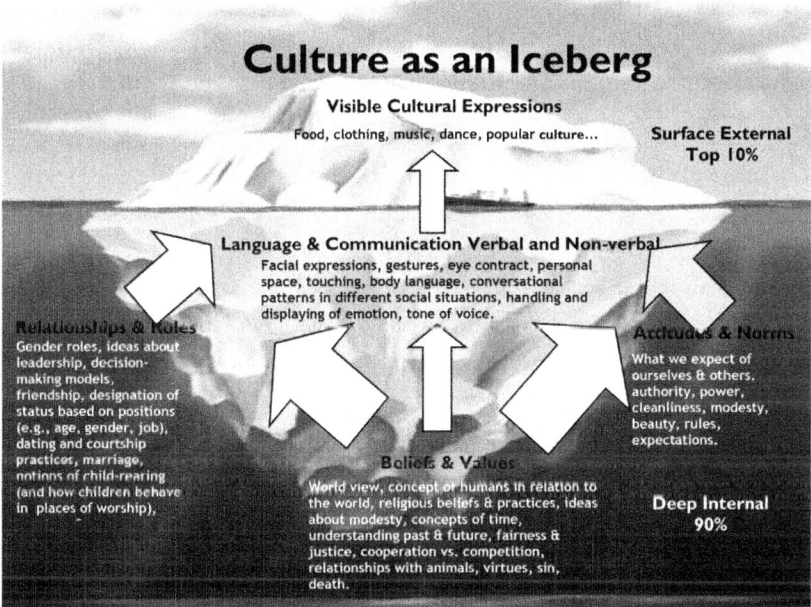

FIGURE 1.1 Cultural Iceberg Model
Source: Adapted from Edward T. Hall's Cultural Iceberg Model (1976)
© Copyright Multicultural Council of Saskatchewan (2017)

beliefs, attitudes, and experiences at the surface and deeper levels, and increase cultural awareness of oneself and one's dominant culture (McCain & Farnsworth, 2018). Self-reflection of one's cultural biases, beliefs, and norms increases cultural awareness of oneself and allows educators to better meet the needs of learners who are culturally and linguistically diverse. There is often a cultural mismatch between professionals and learners and developing the knowledge of our cultural selves can mediate the gap with the potential to enhance the services provided (McCain & Farnsworth, 2018). The low percentage of culturally and linguistically diverse teachers of the d/Dhh can also cause a mismatch between teachers and students (e.g., the majority of teachers are Caucasian, female, and hearing; Luckner & Ayantoye, 2013), and reveals why a focus on cultural competence is vital for current educators in addition to increasing the diversity of teachers of the d/Dhh (Cannon & Luckner, 2016; Leigh & Crowe, 2015). Having more deaf, Deaf, and hard of hearing teachers of the d/Dhh who serve as role models and represent their native cultures to their students is imperative.

Cultural Competence. Having cultural competence means an individual recognizes how culture, language, family structure, socioeconomic status (SES), and perceptions of social values impact student opportunities and access to supports (e.g., educators with specialized expertise, community resources, and cultural brokers; Jozwik et al., 2018). Cultural competence includes understanding culture-specific and general knowledge, skills, and attitudes necessary to communicate and interact with various cultures (McCain & Farnsworth, 2018). One aspect of cultural competence is self-examination and understanding of our own biases, beliefs, and attitudes. Another aspect is how culture intertwines with cognition and impacts social interaction. Some examples such as individualism versus collectivism can be explored further in materials provided in the Resources section of this chapter (e.g., McCain & Farnsworth, 2018). One's understanding of these concepts and self-examination can shape the educational experiences of learners (Leigh & Crowe, 2015). Strategies for building cross-cultural competence are provided in Table 1.1 (Jozwik et al., 2018).

Cultural Identity. Cultural identity includes language background, ethnicity, age, gender, disability, SES, and religion, as well as social, historical, and political factors of the country and/or culture in which one participates (McCain & Farnsworth, 2018). This intersectionality of identities includes attitudes, abilities, interests, beliefs, skills, and dispositions from dominant and minority cultures in an individual's environment (Crenshaw, 1989). An individual's agency (i.e., ability to act independently and make choices) is therefore fluid through the lifespan and may differ from their family's and/or that of the dominant ethnolinguistic community and culture in which they live (McCain & Farnsworth, 2018). How these cultural identities intersect and overlap with the horizontal and vertical identities of each individual varies (e.g., Deaf culture, Latina culture and Feminist culture; see Box 1.5). Identities and languages can also be fluid across cultures. For example in Box 1.3, Gerard moves between Filipino, Deaf, and a new high school culture that he will have to navigate using three languages.

TABLE 1.1 Strategies for Building Cross-Cultural Competence (from Jozwik et al., 2018, p. 142)

Strategies for Building Cross-Cultural Competence
1. Recognize that a constellation of factors interacts to shape the development of one's cultural identity (e.g., age, ability, gender, religion, language, and socioeconomic status). Avoid making generalizations and strive to understand cultural complexity on an individual level.
2. Recognize variances in preferred communication styles. Critically reflect on and examine your own preferred style of communication (e.g., be mindful of wait time and monitor your tone and body language).
3. Be willing to tolerate ambiguity and discomfort while you are in the ongoing process of learning and developing cross-cultural competence.
4. Read books, attend conferences, and attend webinars that center on the theme of building cross-cultural competence.
5. Hold events so that you can interact with families and learn from them about their cultural backgrounds.
6. Strive to learn about and guard against stereotype threat and implicit bias.
7. Educate yourself about the concept of color blindness and the ways in which a culture-free approach may send a message that is incongruent with your intention.
8. Interact with other educators whose cultural identities differ from your own.
9. Be willing to listen and learn by considering multiple perspectives.
10. Find and establish a network of support (e.g., professional learning communities) with whom you can share in learning about this topic.

Cultural Brokers. Cultural brokers advocate for understanding of cultural practices between parents and educators (Cannon & Luckner, 2016; see Chapters 3 & 8; Bowen & Baker, 2022; Luckner & Cannon, 2022). Community service providers can serve as cultural brokers and assist

> Box 1.3 Gerard
>
> Born in Honolulu, Hawaii, Gerard is a 14-year-old male who is entering his first year of high school. Gerard was identified as deaf at birth, with a bilateral, severe hearing level, and uses hearing aids. Both his parents have typical hearing, with no family history of hearing loss. They emigrated to Honolulu from Manila, Philippines five years before Gerard was born. The family's primary language is Filipino, although they began using American Sign Language (ASL) in the home during Gerard's early intervention years. They also use listening and spoken language when speaking Filipino and English to provide Gerard with as much language exposure as possible.
>
> Gerard and his family visit the Philippines at least once a year, have extended family visit them frequently, and attend a nearby Catholic church with many other Filipino families. Gerard attended the Hawaii School for the Deaf and Blind on the island until he was in sixth grade, when he transferred to the local middle school. Gerard is trilingual, using primarily listening and spoken Filipino and ASL at home, Filipino at church and local community events, and ASL and English in his school and other community settings. Now, in ninth grade, he is moving to his local high school where he will continue to receive support from a Teacher of the d/Dhh, Ms. Kekoa, two days per week. Gerard will also have a full time ASL interpreter, Mr. Watanabe, while he attends general education classes. Being trilingual allows Gerard to: (a) learn from his close Filipino family and communities, (b) foster his friendships from the school for the deaf and within the Deaf community of Oahu, and (c) expand his concept of culture and community with new relationships and experiences in his inclusive high school educational setting.

professionals and family members in gaining cultural competence and understanding each other's cultural identities (e.g., hard of hearing, African, and male). Educators can use the information learned from brokers to teach concepts from multiple perspectives to assist DMLs who experience home languages and cultural differences. See Box 1.4 for an example of how a cultural broker was used during Abel's transition to a new country's school system, as well as ideas for exposing him to as much language as possible to reduce deprivation and increase acquisition.

Professionals must consider a family's cultural background when providing them information and resources. Cultural brokers can help ensure interpreters and/or materials are culturally appropriate so that family engagement is not impeded with substandard materials and information (Bowen & Baker, 2022; see Chapter 2). They ensure that the information

> ### Box 1.4 Abel
>
> Abel is an eight-year-old male with a moderate unilateral hearing level who grew up in Ethiopia and uses spoken Amharic to communicate with his family. Abel wears hearing aids and received speech and language therapy since his parents discovered his hearing level at 15 months old. When Abel was six years old, his father's civil engineering job transferred the family to Brisbane, Australia. His parents have two other children, one older (14 years old) and one younger (five years old). Although none of the children know English, both parents are fluent, as this is the language taught in secondary schools in Ethiopia. In preparation for the move, the family began exposing their children to more spoken and print-based English at home. After arriving in Brisbane, Abel's mother contacted their neighborhood school to gather information about enrolling the children. The school personnel connected her with one of the school district's cultural brokers, Ms. Abimbola. After meeting with the cultural broker, Abel's mother was able to understand how the school system in Australia differed from Ethiopian schools, especially for Abel. According to his previous teachers, Abel was experiencing some language delays in Amharic. His mother was concerned about the transition to a new country, culture, language, and school for all of her children and wondered if becoming bilingual would be a challenge for Abel. Ms. Abimbola told his mother to expose

> Abel to as much language as possible to reduce language deprivation and increase acquisition. She encouraged her to continue to use Amharic in multiple ways at home (e.g., reading storybooks, telling stories, and video chatting with friends and family in Ethiopia), as well as use English in a variety of ways (e.g., labelling items to practice vocabulary, attending community events, watching television together, and helping with homework). These activities and routines support acquisition and growth across both languages, while respecting cultural values and traditions in their new environment.

provided is translated into the recipient's preferred language and is culturally appropriate (Steinberg et al., 2003).

Approaches

Asset-Based Approach

An asset-based approach examines the strengths and interests that the learner exhibits and scaffolds learning to maximize them at an individual level (see Guardino & Cannon, 2022). Reducing deficit-view statements may positively inform our attitudes, beliefs, and practices when working with diverse learners, particularly those who are DMLs (Crowe & McLeod, 2014). One strategy is to expose students to role models who are d/Dhh and multilingual, as well as to the multiple spoken and sign languages throughout the world. Role models can be selected according to individual interests and can be introduced in a number of ways, such as books (e.g., with a character who is a deaf artist from Brazil; a biography of a Korean-American professor who uses Korean Sign language, spoken Korean and English, and ASL), multimedia (e.g., recording of a chat with a deaf Squamish elder; movies and/or television with a character who is deaf from India), or interactive activities (e.g., a teacher who is Deaf and from Mexico visits the class; an electrical engineer who is hard of hearing and uses four languages video chats with students who are interested in engineering).

A multi-tiered system of support (MTSS) is another collaborative asset-based approach that supports teachers in scaffolding instruction and monitoring progress for DMLs in general education settings (Hoover et al., 2018). The MTSS approach provides core instruction (Tier 1) to the entire class, while implementing progress monitoring to document students' strengths and needs. For those who need more individualized support, supplemental instruction (Tier 2) is provided to increase skills. This approach incorporates behavioral and social support in the identification of learners who require extra assistance, documents student progress, and is a collaborative decision-making model (Hoover et al., 2018). Paired with linguistically and culturally responsive approaches, MTSS may provide useful information about a DML that can guide their Individualized Education Plan.

Linguistically and Culturally Responsive Approach

Linguistically and culturally responsive approaches are a mindset rather than a list of strategies (McCain & Farnsworth, 2018) that challenges educators to consider multiple perspectives by connecting concepts to a student's identity, regardless of the content. This requires a growth mindset philosophy about the learner and the benefits of multilingualism, as well as an understanding of language acquisition and cultural competence. All of these components of a growth mindset are needed to successfully scaffold learning. Examples of linguistically and culturally responsive activities include: (a) encouraging families to engage in language-rich experiences; (b) understanding the characteristics of disabilities and/or cultural backgrounds; (c) providing experiences to enhance language learning; (d) using child-guided conversational approaches; and (e) systematic, scaffolded instruction (Pizzo, 2016; for more information see Pizzo, 2022; Chapter 6). Further examples of school-wide linguistically and culturally responsive practices that may engage DMLs and their families can be seen in the vignette of Nuna in Box 1.5. Nuna's school actively shows respect for her Algonquian community and culture through engagement with elders and events. These activities may enhance Nuna's vertical and horizontal identities and should include others within

> **Box 1.5 Nuna**
>
> Nuna is a 12-year-old female who was born in a small community on the Pikwakanagan Indian Reserve in Ontario, Canada. This Algonquian community consists of over 400 residents who are bilingual in Algonquian and English. Nuna experiences a mild-to-moderate, bilateral hearing level that was identified at birth, utilizes hearing aids and Communication Access Real-Time Translation (CART) services in her school setting, and prefers listening and spoken language as her primary mode of communication. Nuna is fluent in Algonquian and English. She is currently on grade level with her peers both academically and socially, with an average grade of "C" in most academic courses. Nuna's teacher of the d/Deaf and hard of hearing, Ms. Almanza, visits her once a week and is targeting study skills to increase Nuna's classroom grades. Nuna attends a middle school in a nearby school district, which utilizes culturally and linguistically responsive practices to engage families and provide effective language and communication supports for their learners.
>
> Some of the culturally and linguistically responsive practices that the school has implemented include: (a) acknowledging the school's presence on the traditional unceded territory of the Algonquin Anishnaabeg people at the beginning of every school day and at events and gatherings, (b) adopting curriculum and presenters who are elders in the community that address the history and reconciliation of Aboriginal Peoples in Canada and beyond, (c) having cultural brokers from the Algonquin community to support families in school meetings and procedures, (d) incorporating the art and language of the Algonquin people throughout the grounds of the school, and (e) engaging and providing sponsorship to the annual Powwow celebration.

and beyond the community that are DMLs as role models and as elders to spread their wisdom.

Another avenue to a linguistically and culturally responsive approach is incorporating dimensions of multicultural education into the curriculum.

English (2018) recommends embedding multicultural education to increase cultural competence and allow learners to appreciate multiple cultures, including their own. This can be accomplished through five dimensions: content integration, knowledge construction, equity pedagogy, prejudice reduction, and empowering school culture (English, 2018). These dimensions challenge educators to consider how they are incorporated within their curriculums, particularly in science and math courses. For example, content integration should consider that ASL is only one of 144 sign languages in the world, and that exposure to other sign and spoken languages throughout the globe are important for those DMLs in class. The dimension of knowledge construction reminds us as educators to discuss cultural bias and how it may influence information, thus increasing critical thinking among DMLs. Equity pedagogy enacts strategies that will include all students, regardless of their language ability (e.g., allowing partners to respond to questions and randomly selecting students for responses), while prejudice reduction may use cooperative learning activities with a social justice lens to surface equity issues. Finally, empowering the school culture by critically analyzing how the community is involved and asking for their perspective are some avenues to incorporating linguistically and culturally responsive approaches and multiculturalism into the school climate and curriculum.

Family-Centered Approach

A component of linguistically and culturally responsive approaches is that families are an integral part of a transdisciplinary team. Some governments and agencies have mandated family engagement in the educational planning process for learners with special needs, especially those from culturally and linguistically diverse backgrounds (Calderon, 2000). A family-centered approach highlights the importance of establishing trust with a learner's family through meaningful engagement that recognizes and embraces cultural and language differences. This family-centered approach may increase the learner's academic and social success, as well as their overall school experience and should include linguistically and culturally responsive practices (see Chapter 2; Bowen & Baker, 2022 for further information).

Conclusion

The introduction chapter to this text sets the stage for a collaborative, asset-based approach across all chapters, by considering the intersectionality of the DML population, the practitioners, and families. This chapter also introduced the characteristics and demographics in the education of DMLs by examining the literature and providing vignettes (Boxes 1–5). The benefits of multilingual development, as well as collaborative, asset-based, family-centered, and linguistically and culturally responsive approaches, were reviewed. The use of these approaches in combination with examining our own cultural competences and identities through reflective practice can support the success of DMLs. Recommendations of models that may be effective for DMLs and their families are discussed below.

Overall recommendations include: (a) engaging in culturally responsive practices; (b) encouraging parents to raise multilingual d/Dhh children through exposure to all languages to increase awareness, options, vocabulary, and social-emotional well-being; (c) recruiting and mentoring culturally diverse providers, including members who are DML; (d) decreasing subtractive bilingualism to encourage language exposures and experiences within and among the multiple cultural influences of a learner's linguistic environment; (e) increasing additive bilingualism; (f) developing case studies to gain an understanding of the unique characteristics of these learners and their families (see Chapter 7; Guardino et al., 2022 for an example); and (g) increasing single case design research to build upon the minimal studies conducted in the field with this unique population.

Classroom-based research using qualitative and/or quantitative designs with linguistically and culturally responsive models that are effective for DMLs and their families should be also explored. This could be accomplished by recording teachers who are d/Dhh and multilingual using these techniques in action to document native strategies they find effective with DMLs. Collaboration across researchers is vital to tackle these recommendations, as expertise from across deaf education and linguistically and culturally responsive teaching techniques would benefit any research studies. Forming research clusters of diverse stakeholders (Singleton et al., 2014) may be beneficial to: (a) examine the questions that remain, (b) have enough participants to analyze data sets, and (c) be an avenue for funding opportunities. Acquiring more accurate and detailed national and regional demographic data would enable teachers and administrators to support requests for increased support for DMLs, as well as provide researchers with valuable background information to guide research questions.

Discussion Questions

1. What are the characteristics and demographics of d/Deaf and hard of hearing multilingual learners?
2. Did anything surprise you regarding the complexities of multilingual development for DMLs and what further questions do you have?
3. What is your personal perspective on multilingual acquisition, cultural competence, and identity?
4. What are the benefits of a collaborative, strength-based/positive approach?
5. What activities would you do to embed approaches such as asset-based, linguistically and culturally responsive, and family-centered with DMLs and their families?

Resources

Websites

- Aceves, T. C., & Orosco, M. J. (2014). Culturally responsive teaching (Document No. IC-2; https://ceedar.education.ufl.edu/wp-content/uploads/2014/08/culturally-responsive.pdf).
- ASL Connect, Gallaudet University (www.gallaudet.edu/asl-connect) provides a venue for families and professionals to learn basic ASL for free.
- Collaboration for Effective Educator Development, Accountability, and Reform (CEEDAR, https://ceedar.education.ufl.edu/about-us/) supports students with disabilities in transition by working with teachers to ensure evidence-based practices and MTSS are implemented.
- Family Guide to At-Home Learning (https://ceedar.education.ufl.edu/family-guide-to-at-home-learning/): this CEEDAR guide is offered in Spanish and English to provide families with tools they can use at home.
- Innovation Configurations (https://ceedar.education.ufl.edu/innovation-configurations/): information at CEEDAR regarding evidence-based practices, universal design for learning, and culturally responsive teaching.

- Implicit Social Attitudes Association Test: Project Implicit (https://implicit.harvard.edu/implicit/): find out your implicit associations about race, gender, sexual orientation, and other topics.
- Institutes of Educational Sciences and What Works Clearinghouse Practice Guides:
  - Effective Literacy and English Language Instruction for English Learners in the Elementary Grades (https://ies.ed.gov/ncee/wwc/PracticeGuide/6)
  - Teaching Academic Content and Literacy to English Learners in Elementary and Middle School (https://ies.ed.gov/ncee/wwc/PracticeGuide/19)
  - Teaching Elementary School Students to Be Effective Writers (https://ies.ed.gov/ncee/wwc/practiceguide/17)
- Understanding Deafness and Diversity (http://understandingdad.net/): Website for teachers and families of learners who are d/Dhh and have a disability and/or come from homes with culturally and linguistically diverse learners.
- Spread the Sign (www.spreadthesign.com/en.gb/search/): This website hosts videos of numerous sign languages from around the world. The user can select words or phrases from a particular language and see how these terms are signed. The site also displays selected signed languages side by side for the viewer to compare and learn new signs and sign languages.
- Multicultural Considerations, Laurent Clerc National Deaf Education Center (https://clerccenter.gallaudet.edu/national-resources/info/info-to-go/multicultural-considerations.html): The Center provides extensive resources in English as well as other languages. Resources include books, websites, organizations, and handouts.

Books

- Christensen, K. (Ed.). (2017). *Educating deaf students in a multicultural world*. Dawn Sign Press.
- Gonzalez, M. (2014). *50 strategies for communicating & working with diverse families* (3rd ed.). Pearson.
- McCain, G., & Farnsworth, M. (2018). *Determining difference from disability: What culturally responsive teachers should know*. Routledge.

Perspectives, Approaches, Considerations 23

Family-Centered Brief

FAMILY-CENTERED BRIEF

CHAPTER 1
Learners who are d/Deaf and Hard of Hearing and Multilingual:
Perspectives, Approaches & Considerations

by Joanna E. Cannon & Caroline Guardino

PURPOSE

This **BOOK** explores the unique abilities and intervention approaches of d/Deaf and hard of hearing multilingual learners.

These **FAMILY-CENTRED BRIEFS** provide brief summaries of school-related information from the chapter on how families can support their child who is a DML.

KEY TERMS

d/Deaf and hard of hearing multilingual learners (DMLs)
d/Deaf or hard of hearing learners with a different home language than the dominant culture's spoken language (e.g., English) or sign language (e.g., American Sign Language [ASL]).

Cultural competence
Ability to effectively interact with people across different cultures

Vertical identity
Identity within family culture

Horizontal identity
Identity outside family culture

Intersectionality
One's core personality and character at the intersection of **vertical** and **horizontal** identities

BOOK CHAPTERS

- Chapter 2 — Family Engagement
- Chapter 3 — Assessment
- Chapter 4 — Language Development
- Chapter 5 — Literacy Instruction
- Chapter 6 — Leadership and Collaboration in School Settings
- Chapter 7 — DMLs with One or More Disabilities
- Chapter 8 — Transition Planning

MULTILINGUAL DEVELOPMENT

We need to know if the child's languages are being learned

SIMULTANEOUSLY or **SEQUENTIALLY**
Language A / Language A
Language B / Language B

We need to know if the child's language learning is

ADDITIVE or **SUBTRACTIVE**
Language A / Language A
Language B / Language B

RESOURCES
Spread the Sign www.spreadthesign.com
Family Guide to At-Home Learning https://ceedar.education.ufl.edu/family-guide-to-at-home-learning/

R 📖 Deaf and Hard of Hearing Multilingual Learners: Foundations, Strategies, and Resources (2022)

References

Akamatsu, C. T., & Cole, E. (2000). Meeting the psychoeducational needs of deaf immigrant and refugee children. *Canadian Journal of School Psychology, 15*(2), 1–18.

Aukerman, M. (2007). A culpable CALP: Rethinking the conversational/academic language proficiency distinction in early literacy instruction. *The Reading Teacher, 60*(7), 626–635.

Bowen, S. K., & Baker, S. (2022). Family engagement: Developing partnerships for d/Deaf and hard of hearing multilingual learners. In J. E. Cannon, C. Guardino, & P. V. Paul (Eds.), *Deaf and hard of hearing multilingual learners: Foundations, strategies, and resources* (pp. 30–66). Routledge.

Bunta, F., Douglas, M., Dickson, H., Cantu, A., Wickesberg, J., & Gifford, R. H. (2016). Dual language versus English-only support for bilingual children with hearing loss who use cochlear implants and hearing aids. *International Journal of Language & Communication Disorders, 51*(4), 460–472.

Calderon, R. (2000). Parental involvement in deaf children's education programs as a predictor of child's language, early reading, and social-emotional development. *Journal of Deaf Studies and Deaf Education, 5*(2), 140–155.

Cannon, J. E., Fredrick, L. D., & Easterbrooks, S. R. (2010). Vocabulary acquisition through books in American Sign Language. *Communication Disorders Quarterly, 31*, 98–112. https://doi.org/10.1177/1525740109332832.

Cannon, J. E., Guardino, C., & Gallimore, E. (2016). A new kind of heterogeneity: What we can learn from d/Deaf and hard of hearing multilingual learners. *American Annals of the Deaf, 161*(1), 8–16.

Cannon, J. E., Guardino, C., Antia, S., & Luckner, J. (2016). Single-case design research: Building the evidence-base in the field of education of Deaf/hard of hearing students. *American Annals of the Deaf, 160*(5), 440–452. https://doi.org/10.1353/aad.2016.0007

Cannon, J. E., Hubley, A., O'Loughlin, J., Phelan, L., Norman, N., & Finley, A. (2019). A technology-based intervention to increase reading comprehension of morphosyntax structures. *Journal of Deaf Studies and Deaf Education*, enz029, 1–14. https://doi.org/10.1093/deafed/enz029

Cannon, J. E., & Luckner, J. (2016). Increasing cultural and linguistic diversity in Deaf education teacher preparation programs. *American Annals of the Deaf, 161*(1), 89–103.

Counts, J., Katsiyannis, A., & Whitford, D. K. (2018). Culturally and linguistically diverse learners in special education: English learners. *NASSP Bulletin, 102*(1), 5–21.

Crenshaw, K. (1989). Demarginalizing the intersection of race and sex: A black feminist critique of antidiscrimination doctrine, feminist theory and antiracist politics. *University of Chicago Legal Forum*, 139.

Crowe, K., & Guiberson, M. (2022). Language development, assessment, and intervention for d/Deaf and hard of hearing multilingual learners. In J. E. Cannon, C. Guardino, & P. V. Paul (Eds.), *Deaf and hard of hearing multilingual learners: Foundations, strategies, and resources* (pp. 106–141). Routledge.

Crowe, K., & McLeod, S. (2014). A systematic review of cross-linguistic and multilingual speech and language outcomes for children with hearing loss. *International Journal of Bilingual Education and Bilingualism, 17*(3), 287–309.

Cummins, J. (1984). *Bilingualism and special education: Issues in assessment and pedagogy* (Vol. 6). Taylor & Francis Group.

Denninger, M. (2017). Lesbian, gay, bisexual, and transgender deaf students: Invisible and underserved. In K. Christensen (Ed.), *Educating deaf students in a multicultural world.* (pp. 271–294). Dawn Sign Press.

Easterbrooks, S. R., & Maiorana-Basas, M. (2015). Literacy and deaf and hard of hearing students In H. Knoors & M. Marschark (Eds.), *Educating deaf learners: Creating a global evidence base* (pp. 149–172). Oxford University Press.

Eberhard, D. M., Simons, G. F., & Fennig, C. D. (Eds.). (2021). *Ethnologue: Languages of the world* (24th ed.). SIL International. www.ethnologue.com.

English, A. (2018). ASL is just the beginning: A plea for multicultural deaf education. *Odyssey: New Directions in Deaf Education, 19*, 44–48.

Gallaudet Research Institute. (2013). *Annual survey of deaf and hard of hearing children and youth* [State Summary Report of Data from 2011–2012]. Gallaudet Research Institute, Gallaudet University.

Grosjean, F. (2013). Bilingualism: A short introduction. In F. Grosjean & L. Ping (Eds.), *The psycholinguistics of bilingualism* (pp. 5–26). Blackwell.

Guardino, C., & Cannon, J. E. (2015). Theory, research, and practice for students who are deaf and hard of hearing with disabilities: Addressing the challenges from birth to post-secondary education. *American Annals of the Deaf, 160*(4), 347–355. https://doi.org/10.1353/aad.2015.0033

Guardino, C., & Cannon, J. E. (2016). Deafness and diversity: Reflections and directions. *American Annals of the Deaf, 161*(1), 104–112. https://www.jstor.org/stable/26235254

Guardino, C., & Cannon, J. E. (2022). Approaches and frameworks that support students who are d/Deaf or hard of hearing with disabilities. In C. Guardino, J. E. Cannon, & P. V. Paul (Eds.), *Deaf and hard of hearing learners with disabilities: Foundations, strategies, and resources* (pp. 1–24). Routledge.

Guardino, C., Cannon, J. E., & Eberst, K. (2014). Building the evidence-base of effective reading strategies to use with deaf English language learners. *Communications Disorders Quarterly, 35*(2), 59–73. https://doi.org/10.1177/1525740113506932.

Kwon, E. Y., Guardino, C., & Cannon, J.E. (2022). d/Deaf and hard of hearing multilingual learners with disabilities: A case study of a learner who is deaf with autism spectrum disorder and from an immigrant family. In J. E. Cannon, C. Guardino, & P. V. Paul (Eds.), *Deaf and hard of hearing multilingual learners: Foundations, strategies, and resources* (pp. 219–263). Routledge.

Guiberson, M. (2013). Bilingual myth-busters series: Language confusion in bilingual children. *Perspectives on Communication Disorders and Sciences in Culturally and Linguistically Diverse Populations, 20*(1), 5–14.

Guiberson, M., & Crowe, K. (2018). Interventions for multilingual children with hearing loss. *Topics in Language Disorders, 38*(3), 225–241. https://doi.org/10.1097/TLD.0000000000000155

Hall, E. (1976). *Beyond culture*. Doubleday.

Hoover, J. J., Erickson, J. R., Herron, S. R., & Smith, C. E. (2018). Implementing culturally and linguistically responsive special education eligibility assessment in rural county elementary schools: Pilot project. *Rural Special Education Quarterly, 37*(2), 90–102.

Jozwik, S. L., Cahill, A., & Sánchez, G. (2018). Collaboratively crafting individualized education program goals for culturally and linguistically diverse students. *Preventing School Failure: Alternative Education for Children and Youth, 62*(2), 140–148.

Kovelman, I., Shalinsky, M. H., White, K. S., Schmitt, S. N., Berens, M. S., Paymer, N., & Petitto, L. A. (2009). Dual language use in sign-speech bimodal bilinguals: fNIRS brain- imaging evidence. *Brain & Language, 109*, 112–123.

Leigh, G., & Crowe, K. (2015). Responding to cultural and linguistic diversity among deaf and hard-of-hearing learners. In H. Knoors & M. Marschark (Eds.), *Educating deaf learners: Creating a global evidence-base* (pp. 69–92).

Leigh, G., & Crowe, K. (2020). Evidence-based practices for teaching learners who are deaf or hard-of-hearing in regular schools. In U. Sharma (Ed.), *Oxford research encyclopedia of education: Inclusive and special education*. Oxford University Press. https://doi.org/10.1093/acrefore/9780190264093.013.ORE_EDU-01258.R2

Luckner, J. L., & Ayantoye, C. (2013). Itinerant teachers of students who are deaf or hard of hearing: Practices and preparation. *Journal of Deaf Studies and Deaf Education, 18*(3), 409–423. https://doi.org/10.1093/deafed/ent015

Luckner, J., & Cannon, J. E. (2022). Transition for d/Deaf and hard of hearing multilingual learners: Guiding principles and planning tools. In J. E. Cannon, C. Guardino, & P. V. Paul (Eds.), *Deaf and hard of hearing multilingual learners: Foundations, strategies, and resources* (pp. 264–299). Routledge.

Maiorana-Bases, M. (2018). A shift to the middle: Redefining the community of practice for deaf educators. *Odyssey: New Directions in Deaf Education, 19*, 4–9.

McCain, G., & Farnsworth, M. (2018). *Determining difference from disability: What culturally responsive teachers should know*. Routledge.

Migration Policy Institute. (2019). *ELL information center*. www.migrationpolicy.org/programs/ell-information-center

Multicultural Council of Saskatchewan. (2017). *Culture as an iceberg*. https://mcos.ca/

Paul, P. V., Wang, Y., & Williams, C. (2013). *Deaf students and the qualitative similarity hypothesis: Understanding language and literacy development*. Gallaudet University Press.

Petitto, L. A., & Kovelman, I. (2003). The bilingual paradox: How signing-speaking bilingual children help us to resolve bilingual issues and teach us about the brain's mechanisms underlying all language acquisition. *Learning Languages, 8*(3), 5–18.

Petitto, L. A., Zatorre, R., Gauna, K., Nikelski, E. J., Dostie, D., & Evans, A. (2000). Speech-like cerebral activity in profoundly deaf people processing signed languages: Implications for the neural basis of human language. *Proceedings of the National Academy of Sciences, 97*(25), 13961–13966.

Pizzo, L. (2016). d/Deaf and hard of hearing multilingual learners: The development of communication and language. *American Annals of the Deaf, 161*(1), 17–32.

Pizzo, L. (2022). Leadership and collaboration in school settings for d/Deaf and hard of hearing multilingual learners. In J. E. Cannon, C. Guardino, & P. V. Paul (Eds.), *Deaf and hard of hearing multilingual learners: Foundations, strategies, and resources* (pp. 175–218). Routledge.

Pizzo, L., & Ford, L. (2022). Developing a comprehensive language profile to support learning: The assessment of d/Deaf and hard of hearing multilingual learners. In J. E. Cannon, C. Guardino, & P. V. Paul (Eds.), *Deaf and hard of hearing multilingual learners: Foundations, strategies, and resources* (pp. 67–105). Routledge.

Scott, J., Amadi, C., & Butts, T. (2022). d/Deaf and hard of hearing multilingual learners and literacy instruction. In J. E. Cannon, C. Guardino, & & P. V. Paul (Eds.), *Deaf and hard of hearing multilingual learners: Foundations, strategies, and resources* (pp. 142–174). Routledge.

Singleton, J. L., Jones, G., & Hanumantha, S. (2014). Toward ethical research practice with deaf participants. *Journal of Empirical Research on Human Research Ethics, 9*(3), 59–66.

Sininger, Y. S., Grimes, A., & Christensen, E. (2010). Auditory development in early amplified children: Factors influencing auditory-based communication outcomes in children with hearing loss. *Ear and Hearing, 31*(2), 166.

Solomon, A. (2014). Far from the tree: Parents, children and the search for identity. *Vintage*, 976. ISBN 0099460998. www.farfromthetree.com/

Steinberg, A., Bain, L., Li, Y., Delgado, G., & Ruperto, V. (2003). Decisions Hispanic families make after the identification of deafness. *Journal of Deaf Studies and Deaf Education, 8*(3), 291–314. https://doi.org/10.1093/deafed/eng016

Thomas, E., El-Kashlan, H., & Zwolan, T. A. (2008). Children with cochlear implants who live in monolingual and bilingual homes. *Otology & Neurotology, 29*(2), 230–234.

US Department of Education, National Center for Education Statistics (NCES). (2019).

2
Family Engagement: Developing Partnerships for d/Deaf and Hard of Hearing Multilingual Learners

Sandy K. Bowen and Sharon Baker

LEARNING OBJECTIVES

Readers will:

1. Describe the components of family engagement and relate them to practice.
2. Examine research in family engagement for d/Deaf and hard of hearing multilingual learners (DMLs) in early intervention and school age populations.
3. Identify challenges and possible solutions to enhance family engagement for DMLs.
4. Explore the resources available to DML families.
5. Learn ways to help parents provide activities that support their children's bilingual and multilingual language acquisition in both spoken and signed languages.

Parents and/or caregivers are often a child's first teacher. They are integral to the development and learning for their young child. In fact, parents are so crucial that the federal government has recognized family engagement in some federal legal mandates. For example, in the United States, parent participation is listed as a key component in Individualized Education Program (IEP) meetings in the most recent

DOI: 10.4324/9781003259176-2

revision of the Individuals with Disabilities Education Act (IDEA, 2004). Parent participation includes being a central part of the child's IEP team and providing meaningful feedback on educational decisions, including goals and objectives, placement considerations, and communication choices (IDEA *FEDC Issue Brief*, 2012). Furthermore, the importance of family engagement was recognized in the United States with the expansion of Family Engagement in Education Programs in the Every Student Succeeds Act (ESSA, 2015), which is the most recent reauthorization of the Elementary and Secondary Education Act (ESEA, 2015).

Throughout this chapter, the term "parents and families" is used to describe any and all caregivers of a child who is d/Deaf or hard of hearing (d/Dhh). Turnbull and colleagues characterize a family as "two or more people who regard themselves as family and who perform some functions that families typically perform" (Turnbull et al., 2015, p. 30). In this definition, family is a functional construct that goes beyond blood or marriage relationships and can include extended family members and even friends. This definition of family is essential in understanding cultural differences and family dynamics among multigenerational households, role flexibility and kinship, and child rearing practices in culturally and linguistically diverse (CLD) families.

Family Engagement

Family engagement is an interactive process involving professionals, families, and children in developing and maintaining a positive goal-oriented relationship (National Center on Parent, Family, and Community Engagement [NCPFCE], 2011). "Family engagement in schools is defined as parents and school personnel working together at the classroom, local, and system level to support and improve the learning, development, and health of children and adolescents" (Centers for Disease Control and Prevention, 2015, p. 1). Family engagement may look different for every family but it shares a commitment to actively supporting their child's learning and development. In addition, schools and professionals are committed to engaging parents in meaningful ways such as: (a) providing parents with information and skills, (b) encouraging parents to be part of decision making at the school, (c) offering a wide variety of volunteer opportunities, (d) training staff to work with parents, and (e) solving conflicts in scheduling and transportation (Centers for Disease Control and Prevention, 2015). A critical component of family engagement is that it must be culturally and linguistically responsive to diverse families, including multilingual and multicultural Deaf families.

As communities and schools become increasingly more CLD, it is essential to consider what is meant by family engagement and how professionals support families to become more involved in their children's development and education. Traditional definitions of parent involvement include school-initiated activities, such as attending school sponsored events, helping with homework, and volunteering in the schools (Bower & Griffin, 2011). However, this limited view defined by schools does not honor differing perspectives from CLD families (Bower & Griffin, 2011). Parents who do not engage in these activities may be seen as uninvolved in their child's education. Brewster and Railsback (2003) suggest, "rather than assuming families are unwilling to become more active partners with schools, educators would do well to examine closely the specific causes of poor school-family relationships and low levels of involvement in their community. By examining these barriers, schools can begin to develop solutions for gaining support and trust" (p. 1). One way to bridge this gap is to develop culturally responsive behaviors and practices. According to Grant and Ray (2016):

> the culturally responsive family engagement approach involves practices that respect and acknowledge the cultural uniqueness, life experiences, and viewpoints of families and draw on those experiences to enrich and energize the classroom curriculum and teaching activities, leading to respectful partnerships with students' families.
>
> (p. 5)

In this model, family engagement is about building trust, developing respect, and reaching out to parents and families from diverse cultures in meaningful ways to overcome language and cultural obstacles.

There are numerous studies and reports on the advantages and benefits of family engagement (Baker et al., 2016; Hoover-Dempsey et al., 2005). Research over the past two decades has confirmed that students with engaged families are more likely to: (a) earn higher grades and test scores, (b) enroll in higher-level academic programs, (c) be promoted on time and earn more credits, (d) adapt better to school and attend more regularly, (e) have better social skills and behaviors, and (f) graduate and go on to postsecondary opportunities (Hoover-Dempsey et al., 2005). However, achieving effective family engagement, particularly for families from diverse cultures, may present barriers (Hornby & Lafaele, 2011). Baker et al. (2016) identified both barriers that hinder families' engagement and solutions that schools can employ to improve family engagement. Some of the most common barriers identified include poor school-to-home communication, the parents' own previous negative experiences with school, and logistical issues or current life contexts (e.g., transportation problems, work schedules, childcare needs, and finances).

Families from CLD backgrounds have reported issues with timeliness of communication, quality, and clarity of information from schools (Baker et al., 2016). Many times, the communication comes at the last minute or serves only to report a problem. For families who speak a language other than English, communication challenges can be confounded with difficulties accessing qualified and available interpreters which leads to less access to written and verbal communication. In a study by Baker and colleagues (2016), parents indicated that when teachers communicated with them more frequently, they felt more involved and had a better understanding of what was expected in their child's classroom.

Another obstacle is the degree to which parents feel welcome in their child's school. Baker and colleagues (2016) noted "school actions and attitudes send a clear message that parents are or are not welcome in school" (p. 172). When parents feel a sense of belonging, they are more likely to participate in school-sponsored events and activities. One way to address this issue for families from diverse backgrounds is by establishing a Newcomers Program (Short & Boyson, 2012). Newcomer Programs are generally for immigrants and newly arrived students from other countries who speak a language other than English. Newcomer Programs help them navigate and acclimate to the local school system, typically during the first year in the district, by providing academic, social, and emotional support (NCELA, n.d.). Welcoming diverse parents and community members to school demonstrates respect and understanding of diverse cultures and opens doors to full integration of the community into the school system. This process can be seen in Maria's vignette (see Box 2.1), in which her family was invited to learn English and participate in school and community bilingual events. Whereas, with Myitzu (Box 2.2), her family was able to access the Family Resource Center housed within Myitzu's school.

Box 2.1 Maria

Maria immigrated to the US from Mexico with her family when she was five years of age. The fifth child in a family of six children, she is the only deaf child in the family. Maria's profound hearing loss was due to an illness and high fever at ten months old, prior to developing spoken language skills. All of Maria's family members speak Spanish and use some Mexican Sign Language (Lengua de Senas Mexicana, LSM [Mexican Sign Language]) to communicate with Maria. The family immigrated to the US to provide better educational opportunities for Maria and her siblings. The family moved into a neighborhood with other Spanish-speaking families. The neighborhood school provides bilingual programming for Spanish-speaking students and social services including English classes to Spanish-speaking parents. Maria's parents have taken advantage of the services offered including attending these classes, as they want to learn English, but they also want their children to retain their heritage languages (Spanish and LSM). The school district offered a center-based program for d/Dhh students that uses American Sign Language (ASL), which was located about 30 minutes by bus from Maria's home. The family and the IEP team discussed why this school may provide language models and peers for interaction to increase Maria's ASL skills. Through a collaborative effort, the district provided transportation for Maria to the center-based school, informed her family that they would begin receiving weekly intervention sessions focusing on increasing their ASL from the nearby university speech and hearing clinic via teleconferencing in their home, and that the family may continue to attend their neighborhood school's bilingual classes and social events to provide family engagement across the school and community settings with opportunities to retain their heritage language.

> ### Box 2.2 Myitzu
>
> Myitzu is a young refugee from Myanmar (formerly Burma) who emigrated to Australia when she was approximately 12 years old. She lives with a multigenerational family, with her mother and father, paternal grandparents, two aunts and uncles, and several siblings and cousins. She does not distinguish between biological siblings and cousins. She calls them all brothers and sisters. The family primarily speaks Burmese, but the grandparents also speak an indigenous language and the children also speak English at school. The family does not have an accurate record of when she was born or when she lost her hearing. She has a moderate to severe hearing loss. She wears binaural hearing aids and attends her neighborhood school along with many other refugee children. Myitzu is learning English and using Burmese to help her translate text and make connections between the two languages. She receives services from an itinerant teacher of the deaf and hard of hearing three times a week who checks on her auditory equipment and works with her teacher to provide opportunities to increase Myitzu's English skills and academic knowledge. There is a well-established Newcomer Program with a Family Resource Center housed within the school. The school works closely with the community's Immigrant and Refugee Center which provides cultural liaisons and family resources, including English classes for parents. The school employs a full-time Burmese interpreter, who is a young adult from Burma and whose family also lives in the community. Myitzu's parents and family members are invited and encouraged to come to school as often as they want. Myitzu's mother, and many others with younger children, gather in front of the school each morning as they walk their older children to school. They are often greeted by community members and school personnel.

The benefits of family engagement have been well documented. However, as indicated before, there are still considerations to ensure that all families, particularly those from diverse backgrounds and with multicultural Deaf learners, are fully engaged. In order to foster this understanding of engagement, professionals need to be aware of the fundamental components of collaborative family partnerships.

Models of Family Engagement

Models of family engagement seek to identify ways parents can be involved to support student academic performance. However, some (Arias & Morillo-Campbell, 2008; Tarasawa & Waggoner, 2015) argue that these traditional models "give insufficient attention to family-centered practices among marginalized populations and perpetuate the myth of noninvolvement among minority parents" (Tarasawa & Waggoner, 2015, p. 1). This section will briefly explore traditional models and nontraditional approaches to family engagement to increase practices that are culturally and linguistically appropriate.

Epstein's Spheres of Influence

Epstein's theory of family engagement described the shared responsibility between the home and the school as the most important aspect of meaningful parent involvement (2010). Epstein identified six types of involvement: Type 1: *Parenting*; Type 2: *Communicating*; Type 3: *Volunteering*; Type 4: *Learning at Home*; Type 5: *Decision Making*; and Type 6: *Collaborating with Community* (2010). Type 1 focuses on creating supportive home environments through school programs, family education, and home visits to support student learning. Type 2 emphasizes regular school-home communication about student progress and school programs. Type 3 highlights schools providing a wide variety of parent volunteer opportunities and welcoming parents into the school setting. Type 4 emphasizes how schools encourage parents to assist their children in learning, including family activities at home and at school. Type 5 recommends that parents and schools share in making decisions that affect children and families by encouraging involvement in parent organizations and school committees. Type 6 promotes accessing community resources and services to bolster family support and school programs.

Hoover-Dempsey and Sandler

Hoover-Dempsey and Sandler (1995, 1997) developed a model for parental involvement that focused on why and how parents become involved in their child's education. This model suggests that parental involvement is motivated by two belief systems: how the parents view their role in relationship to their children's success in school; and the parents' own sense of efficacy to help their children succeed in school. These views are often shaped by the parents' own personal educational experiences and their cultural views of what their role should be. Walker et al. (2005) modified Hoover-Dempsey and Sandler's model, suggesting that "life contexts" function as a third indicator of parent involvement. These life contexts include the knowledge, skills, time, and energy parents have; in other words, what parents have to offer, as well as when and how they can be involved in their child's education.

Non-Traditional Models of Parental Involvement

Arias and Morillo-Campbell (2008) advocate for a non-traditional model of parental involvement that is based on the cultural strengths of the families and the community. They support a reciprocal school-parent relationship that highlights parental empowerment. Cultural reciprocity is the process of becoming aware of and understanding the values in our personal and professional beliefs and systemic practices, in order to explain them to families from culturally and linguistically diverse backgrounds who might not share these same values and ideas, as well as to change practices in our school systems that inherently perpetuate these beliefs (Kalyanpur & Harry, 2012).

In addition to upholding culturally and linguistically appropriate practices, schools also develop CLD parental involvement by "supporting families, promoting communication and advocacy for empowerment" (p. 11). Parents feel empowered when the school considers the family's logistics and modifies meetings to accommodate the parents' work schedules, arranges transportation to facilitate student involvement in afterschool activities, and provides childcare for parents to attend school functions. They further feel empowered when the school acknowledges the parents' cultural values by understanding and respecting differences and similarities, and by striving to provide bilingual access to school personnel and school communications.

Family Engagement for Students Who Are DMLs

There is no current research on family engagement for DMLs. In an effort to understand what this might look like, research from other related fields, including d/Dhh, English Learners (EL), and special education, will be explored. The following sections outline what we currently know about family engagement in early intervention and at the school level, and what we still need to discover for DMLs.

The Importance of the Deaf Community in Fostering Family Engagement for DMLs

It is well documented that in order to develop positive self-identities in d/Dhh children, they and their families should have frequent and ongoing interactions and relationships with Deaf adults, Deaf role models, and Deaf mentors (Benedict et al., 2015, Calderon & Greenberg, 2012; Hamilton & Clark, 2020). In particular, early intervention and school-age programs should invite Deaf adults from diverse cultural and linguistic backgrounds to serve as role models for DML children and their families. This is important for multilingual and multicultural Deaf families in addition to culturally or linguistically diverse families who have a child who is d/Dhh.

Family Engagement in Early Intervention

In an International Consensus Statement (Moeller et al., 2013), experts in the field of early intervention and deafness identified ten principles to guide FCEI for children who are d/Dhh and their families. Principle Two focuses on family/provider partnerships, stating: "A goal of FCEI is the development of balanced partnerships between families and the professionals supporting them. Family—provider partnerships are characterized by reciprocity, mutual trust, respect, honesty, shared tasks, and open communication" (p. 432). Within this guiding principle, the focus is on the family. Service providers work in partnership with the family on family-identified goals and priorities. Paramount to this partnership is that service providers "recognize the diversity within cultural groups (i.e., spiritually, views on health and disability, child rearing, help seeking, and family structure)" (p. 432) and seek support when their own cultural background differs from the cultural background of the family. These two principles are critical for DMLs in early intervention.

Early intervention is by definition focused on the family and requires some level of family engagement and participation. In the United States, IDEA (2004) assures that infants and toddlers with disabilities and their family members receive family-centered early intervention (FCEI) in a natural environment. The goal of FCEI is to build capacity around the parents and family to support and enhance the overall development of a child with disabilities or at risk for developing a delay. An Individualized Family Service Plan (IFSP) is developed outlining the services necessary to facilitate the child's overall development and to enhance the family's capacity to facilitate the child's development. The IFSP pinpoints the family's concerns, priorities, and available resources needed to facilitate the child's development.

There is a growing body of evidence that links family involvement in d/Dhh early intervention programs with later positive outcomes. Moeller (2000) investigated the relationship between child language outcomes and family involvement. She concluded that although early intervention was beneficial to all children, the most successful children were those with families of high levels of involvement in the early intervention process.

DesJardin (2006) examined parental self-efficacy, parental involvement, and children's language skills in early intervention programs for children who are d/Dhh. The mothers' self-efficacy beliefs related to developing their children's speech and language were positively associated with higher-level facilitative language techniques. Perceived parental involvement was also positively related to lower-level language techniques, including imitation and closed-ended questions (DesJardin, 2006). These findings were corroborated by Roy (2013) in the *Birth of a Word* project at Massachusetts Institute of Technology. Roy and his team identified the techniques that caregivers use as a child with typical hearing attempts to say his or her first word. Roy found that as the child babbled approximations of the word, the caregiver repeated the word slowly, breaking the word down into phonemic segments so that the child could imitate the sounds he or she was hearing. Research has also shown that Deaf mothers modify their communication with their babies by using lower-level language techniques such as signing slower, repeating the sign, making signs larger, and emphasizing the sublexical aspects of the sign (Andrews & Baker, 2019).

Zaidman-Zait and Young (2008) conducted a case study with two young children with cochlear implants to investigate the parents' habilitation involvement after surgery. They found, among other things, that parental involvement is important because both the child and the parent engage in a meaningful, active relationship that builds upon each other's behaviors across time. Specifically, "both mothers demonstrated a strong commitment to pursuing their goals, which included investment of time and efforts in 'working' with their child on [spoken language] skills" (p. 208).

More recently, parental involvement has been explored in the context of telehealth (also known as teleintervention, teletherapy, or telepractice). Telehealth uses some form of electronic technology (i.e. videoconferencing, streaming media) to deliver long-distance health-related education (NCHAM, 2018). Telehealth is used to provide therapies and early intervention to families who do not have access to a qualified interventionist in their area. Several studies have documented both provider skills and parent engagement through telehealth for families of children who are d/Dhh.

Stredler-Brown (2017) investigated early intervention providers' use of FCEI strategies when intervention was delivered via telehealth. Results demonstrated that three provider behaviors (i.e., observation, parent practice with feedback, and child behavior with provider feedback) occurred in telehealth more frequently than in-person conditions reported in the literature. Two studies have compared telehealth visits to in-person home visits with families of children who are d/Dhh (Behl et al., 2017; Blaiser et al., 2013). The studies found that parents in the telehealth group were more engaged during intervention sessions than the comparison in-person group and that families in telehealth had at least the same if not better outcomes than those with in-person visits. These three studies suggest that an unforeseen benefit of telehealth is greater parent engagement. The absence of the interventionist in the room with the parent and child may instinctively force the provider to coach the parent on using the strategies discussed, naturally enhancing parent engagement and allowing the parent to use culturally and linguistically appropriate resources.

Proponents of telehealth mention its numerous benefits for CLD families: it provides access to highly qualified interventionists and spoken language interpreters, as well as access to families when the professional or therapist uses a language that differs from the home language of the family (Poole et al., 2020). There are a variety of interpretation services such as remote three-way videoconferencing and phone interpretation. However, just like in-person settings, schools and agencies should provide appropriate high-quality interpreters who can not only translate the message but also provide cultural understanding in context of the therapy. A further advantage is that it provides these services in more rural areas where access to qualified interpreters and early intervention professionals may be limited (Cole et al., 2016; NCHAM, 2014). However, there are some potential challenges for teleintervention with DML families. High-quality internet connection may be unavailable in areas where CLD families reside or may be too costly for families to purchase. In addition to internet fees, the cost of the equipment, if not provided by the agency, may be outside of the family budget (Behl et al., 2010). Furthermore, more research is needed to investigate cultural competence in providing teleintervention to families from CLD backgrounds. The medical field (SAMHSA, 2016; Tirado, 2011) is also looking at these issues for telehealth care; d/Dhh professionals should closely monitor this research to learn how to best serve DMLs and their families using teleintervention. Utilizing community resources (e.g., free internet at the public library, the local university/college branch, or the community centers) may be one way to overcome some of the barriers to service access.

Family Engagement in School-Age Populations

Most of the studies with school-age families of children who are d/Dhh focus on parental involvement, rather than parental engagement. As we have demonstrated, parent involvement may look different than parent engagement, but it can still provide the foundation for what is known about parents of children who are d/Dhh. Powers and Saskiewicz (1998) compared the classroom involvement of parents of children with typical hearing and of parents of d/Dhh children and found that there were no significant differences in the level of involvement for these two groups. However, they did note that parents of children who are d/Dhh observed more than participated in the classrooms. They hypothesized that the parents may have felt uncomfortable interacting with other deaf children because they did not necessarily share the same mode of communication as the other children in the class.

Kluwin and Corbett (1998) interviewed 105 parents of children who are d/Dhh from a diverse pool (41% African American and 38% Hispanic). One interesting finding was that many families viewed their child's education as important and valuable, but lacked sufficient time or resources to contribute to their education. Parents living in lower socioeconomic conditions may have to focus more on providing the basic necessities for the family's survival as a unit, which may in turn limit the time they have to engage in their d/Dhh children's education.

Calderon (2000) examined parental involvement as a predictor of language, reading, and social-emotional outcomes for young d/Dhh children. Calderon asked teachers to rate parents' involvement in d/Dhh classrooms on 14 indicators (e.g., attends IEP meetings, volunteers in the classroom, and attends school events) and then compared the ratings to child outcomes. Results from the study suggest that school-based parental involvement predicted early reading skills.

In a study looking at the role of parents of children who are d/Dhh in academic achievement, Reed et al. (2008) identified the factors that facilitated achievement and the factors that detracted from achievement. Specific to parental involvement, they found that high family expectations, the families' ability to support homework, and good school-home communication were among the facilitators of academic achievement.

Culturally responsive family involvement and engagement has been explored in the general special education literature. As expected, researchers agree that parent involvement is one factor that improves academic outcomes for all students, regardless of race or ethnicity (Baker et al., 2016; Brown et al., 2019). However, this literature also shows that CLD parents exhibit lower levels of participation when measured against traditional views of involvement. The literature suggests one approach for parents to be more involved in the special education process is for schools to implement culturally responsive IEP practices. Some practical examples are: (a) using interpreters (spoken and sign) at IEP meetings; (b) enlisting cultural brokers and Deaf Mentors to understand disability views, health beliefs, and parenting styles; and (c) helping CLD families understand advocacy for themselves and their child (Brown et al., 2019; Zhang & Bennett, 2003). Many of these strategies can be seen in the vignettes provided about Maria (Box 2.1), Myitzu (Box 2.2), Aleksei and Evelina (Box 2.3), and Nancy (Box 2.4).

Box 2.3   Aleksei and Evelina

Aleksei and Evelina are hard of hearing siblings born three years apart, both with mild-to-moderate hearing losses. They wear binaural hearing aids consistently. Their mother Ivana, who is bilingual in Russian and English, moved to Canada from Russia as a young adult. Today she is a stay-at-home mother, with a strong desire for her children to be bilingual in Russian and English and to identify with Russian culture. To assist in bilingual development, Ivana ordered children's books written in Russian and recited Russian nursery rhymes. The early interventionist, who is a listening and spoken language specialist, worked collaboratively to support bilingual language development for the girls: the early interventionist spoke English while the mother repeated the message in Russian. During this process, the children learned to listen and speak in two languages. The early interventionist modeled early reading strategies with children's books written in English. After the modelling process, the mother employed the strategies to read a children's book in Russian while the early interventionist observed. The interventionist used English-based fingerplays and nursery rhymes, but they did not attempt to translate them into Russian; rather, the mother followed with Russian nursery rhymes and children's songs.

> ### Box 2.4 Nancy
>
> Nancy, the child of a Cherokee family, was born in the United States where a newborn hearing screening identified that she had a hearing loss. The audiologist at the hospital later confirmed that her hearing loss was in the mild-to-moderate range and fitted Nancy with hearing aids at three months of age. Nancy's parents, who lived in a rural area, were unsure about having a home interventionist from the city—someone they had never met—come to their home. When the early interventionist (Brian) contacted them by phone, he suggested that they have their first meeting in the local community center and asked if it would be okay to bring a cultural broker. Prior to contacting the family, the interventionist had contacted a local cultural broker who was Cherokee and had experience in the family's community. The family was relieved after this conversation and felt their language and culture were respected in the interaction. During the initial session with the family Brian and the cultural broker worked together to explain the purpose of the sessions and ways they could use both Cherokee and English to communicate with Nancy and increase her language skills. Through their discussion it was decided that Nancy would participate in intervention sessions at the local community center once a week. After six months of sessions Nancy's parents decided to invite Brian into their home for sessions so that more family members could participate and because they now trusted him. The family also invited Brian to attend their community storytelling event, which expanded his understanding of the culture, language, and community members in Nancy's life.

Finally, the use of technology has recently been studied as a way to positively engage parents and share school experiences. Technology (e.g., smartphones, email, web-based apps, websites, and digital portfolios) allows parents and teachers/school personnel to communicate without a common meeting time (Thompson et al., 2015). Although technology-based communication approaches offer new opportunities for parents to be engaged, schools need to be aware of potential gaps for CLD families and provide opportunities for families to have access, learn, and use the technology (Machado-Casas et al., 2014).

Family Engagement for DML Populations: What We Still Need to Discover

Although there are a few studies that have investigated parental involvement for d/Dhh children, there are still many things we do not know for parents of children who are DMLs who come from culturally and linguistically diverse backgrounds. There are a number of factors in this area that need more attention and research. These are described in the next sections along with some ideas for how to overcome these barriers.

Early Intervention DML Parent Engagement Needs and Concerns

Bowen (2016) emphasizes that, since early intervention is built on the partnership of the professional and the family, "understanding the cultural influence of families' beliefs and expectations" (p. 34) is essential in providing FCEI. "When a family speaks a language other than English, parents' abilities to interact with the interventionist may be noticeably limited by language barriers as well as restricted in more obscure ways by cultural differences" (Wieber & Quiñonez-Sumner, 2016, p. 78). It is not simply using the same language but understanding the cultural differences in views of disability, child-rearing practices, playtime behaviors, and cultural resources that may improve the relationship (Bowen, 2016; Wieber & Quiñonez-Sumner, 2016). Professionals who are not culturally attuned may overlook language learning opportunities in and outside the home. In order to optimize parent engagement and child outcomes, intervention must be provided within the framework of the family's specific culture. This includes using culturally appropriate songs, nursery rhymes, games, books, and activities within the family's daily routines and understanding and respecting the family's beliefs, values, and traditions (Wieber & Quiñonez-Sumner, 2016). While there is a paucity of research documenting the use of traditional songs and stories in early intervention, there is evidence to support increased parent engagement in preschool programs that include parent-generated literacy activities (Purcell-Gates et al., 2014). In an informal observation of this practice, Wieber and Quiñonez-Sumner (2016) noted that when interventionists began using culturally appropriate songs, games, and activities, families responded positively, demonstrated greater engagement during sessions, and continued to use the strategies at home.

The best approach to meet the needs of diverse families is to employ CLD providers (Bowen, 2016; Yoshinaga-Itano, 2014). However, in the absence of qualified professionals, it is important to have skilled oral language interpreters and cultural brokers involved in the early intervention process (Bowen, 2016; Wieber & Quiñonez-Sumner, 2016). A cultural broker is defined as a "go-between" or one who advocates on behalf of another individual to reduce conflict or produce change (Georgis et al., 2014; Jezewski & Sotnik, 2001). In early intervention, cultural brokers serve as a bridge between the parents and the professional to bring an understanding of the cultural practices to the early intervention process. These individuals need more than linguistic proficiency in both languages; they also need "culturally based communication strategies" (Bowen, 2016, p. 39) to support family engagement during early intervention services (see Figure 2.1). Culturally based strategies indicate a knowledge of values, beliefs, and child-rearing practices of both cultural groups as well as an understanding of traditional and indigenous wellness and cultural medical practices. Ideally, but not always, the cultural broker is a member of the family's culture, but if not, should have extensive involvement in the family's culture (NCCC, 2004). We can see the importance of early intervention and understanding the cultural perspective of hearing loss in Nancy's vignette (Box 2.4). The parents were unsure of what hearing loss was and needed guidance in their own language from individuals who understood their views and perceptions of hearing loss. We can also see the use of cultural brokers in Myitzu's story (Box 2.2) for school age children.

In addition to providing cultural brokers and interpreters, professionals should strive to develop cultural competence in order to establish meaningful relationships with families. There are several steps professionals can take to develop cross-cultural competence. Some of these include reflecting and assessing your own cultural identity and beliefs, being aware of the cultural perspectives and views of the community with whom you work,

TABLE 2.1 Educational Considerations for DML Family Engagement

Participation Intent	Strategies to Engage Families	References
Sharing of Information	• Provide access to high-quality interpreters. • Employ cultural brokers or guides. • Explore alternative options (text, apps, video messages, etc.).	Baker et al. (2016); Brown et al. (2019); U.S. Department of Education. Office of English Language Acquisition (2016a); U.S. Department of Education. Office of English Language Acquisition (2016b)
Attending School Events	• Consider alternative meeting schedules and different community locations. • Invite parents to attend events and to visit the classroom. • Provide childcare.	Baker et al. (2016); Epstein et al. (2002); Hoover-Dempsey and Sandler (1997); U.S. Department of Education. Office of English Language Acquisition (2016b)
Supporting Homework	• Give detailed information on how to help. • Technology-based homework support. • Specific activities that can be done at home. • Support home experiences that benefit student overall development (e.g. responsibility for chores, extended family involvement, and social functions). • Recognize home learning activities that are more congruent with their cultural values.	Anderson and Minke (2007); Baker et al. (2016); Epstein et al. (2002); Thompson et al. (2015); U.S. Department of Education. Office of English Language Acquisition (2016b)

(Continued)

TABLE 2.1 (*Continued*)

Participation Intent	Strategies to Engage Families	References
Parental Advocacy	• Teach parents what advocacy means and support them to advocate in culturally acceptable ways (recognize that educational advocacy is not a universal construct).	Arias and Morillo-Campbell (2008); Brown et al. (2019); Gonzales and Gabel (2017); U.S. Department of Education. Office of English Language Acquisition (2016b)
Welcoming School Environment	• Invite families to share their knowledge, cultural beliefs, and traditions (i.e. cultural capital). • Employ multicultural staff and volunteers. • Engage in culturally responsive practices (respect for differing values and perspectives). • Integrate cultural traditions of families throughout the school.	Arias and Morillo-Campbell (2008); Baker et al. (2016); Breiseth (2011); Brown et al. (2019); Gonzales and Gabel (2017); Grant and Ray (2016); U.S. Department of Education. Office of English Language Acquisition (2016b)
Partnering with Community Groups	• Build strong communities by partnering with businesses, faith-based organizations, and cultural community centers. • Technology partnerships.	Brown et al. (2019); Epstein et al. (2002); Machado-Casas et al. (2014); Rodriguez-Valls and Torres (2014); U.S. Department of Education. Office of English Language Acquisition (2016a)

learning about a specific culture including contrasting and similar values and beliefs, and finally, acknowledging and respecting differences (Lynch, 2011). Furthermore, it is important for professionals to consider moving beyond cultural competence to embrace cultural humility. Cultural humility is a lifelong process that focuses on personal self-reflection to not only acknowledge one's own biases, but to also continually move beyond a basic understanding of culture and realize we are never done learning (Tervalon & Murray-Garcia, 1998). Furthermore, it strives to correct the imbalances in power and develop true partnerships to create positive changes (Tervalon & Murray-Garcia, 1998).

Parents of children who are DMLs have many complex choices regarding communication options used by the child and family including: (a) spoken home language, (b) spoken English, (c) signed home language and/or American Sign Language (ASL). Recent research has shown that a growing number of families from CLD backgrounds with children who are DMLs desire their children to be bilingual (Bowen, 2016; Guiberson, 2014). If a child has access to the sounds of a spoken language (through appropriate amplification), parents who speak a language other than English in the home may feel as though they must choose if their child will learn both the spoken language of the home and spoken English. However, professionals should encourage families to use and foster the development of both languages. Furthermore, many DMLs use sign language as their primary mode of communication, including the sign language of their native country (e.g., Lengua de Señas Mexicana, LSM [Mexican Sign Language]; 日本手話 or Nihon Shuwa, Japanese Sign Language, JSL). For these children, providing opportunities for parents to learn their native country's sign language as well as ASL is critical to the child's overall development. The complexities of language choice and use can be seen in each of the four vignettes provided for Maria (Box 2.1), Myitzu (Box 2.2), Aleksei and Evelina (Box 2.3), and Nancy (Box 2.4). Each of these vignettes represents different choices families make for their children.

Depending on the age of the child, one way to facilitate signing skills with families who speak a language other than English is through using simple handshape stories (Gietz et al., 2020; Lin & Ku, 2020). Handshape stories are stories that are signed using the letters of the alphabet, numbers, or other handshapes, tend to have strong iconicity, and are easy to learn.

Parents may also use nursery rhymes with their children (Andrews & Baker, 2019), which manipulate the sub-lexical or phonological structure of language and provide children with playful language experiences. Whether DMLs are using listening and spoken language and/or sign language, service providers could engage with families by teaching them English-based nursery rhymes and in turn having the family teach the service provider nursery rhymes from their heritage language, as demonstrated with Aleksei and Evelina (Box 2.3). This type of engagement is beneficial to both parents, service providers, and the DML in terms of increasing communication and language skills while valuing and learning from each other. Encouraging parents to promote the bilingual development of their child is crucial for the DML to participate in family, social, and community activities, in both English as well as their heritage language and culture.

Emergent Literacy. Parents of DMLs, regardless of whether their children are learning to sign and/or to listen and speak more than one language, should take advantage of the language(s) they already know to facilitate emergent literacy in their DMLs. One strategy for supporting emergent literacy is learning to fingerspell common words used in their home environment (Baker, 2010). In addition, orthographic manipulatives (e.g., magnetic letters of the alphabet) can be used to teach children to recognize printed words. Parents could post written labels (in English and the family's heritage language) and pictures (of the signs associated with an object) at the child's eye-level (i.e., refrigerator door, wall with large white magnetic board, or bulletin board) to encourage the identification and use of new vocabulary within their environment. Furthermore, children and caregivers can draw and label pictures to depict an upcoming event (e.g., going to grandma's house, going to the park to play, or going to the store to buy milk). They could use the bilingual strategy of chaining: point to a real object, write the name of the object, fingerspell it, and sign (and/or say) the name of the object in one or both languages. This helps to facilitate communication and improves children's memory and vocabulary retention, which are important for emergent literacy (Humphries & MacDougall, 1999).

Early Intervention programs should encourage parent engagement by providing opportunities for them to understand and make decisions regarding language choice in both spoken and signed languages. The National ASL and English Bilingual Consortium for Early Childhood Education recognized the need for a *Sign Bank* of specific vocabulary used by families representing diverse cultures. Family members and service providers will be able to access the *Sign Bank*, currently under development, in a variety of ways including with an application on a mobile phone (personal communication L. Simms, April 13, 2019). This organization has many early childhood educators who are deaf persons of color from different cultural backgrounds and experiences.

School Age DML Parent Engagement Needs and Concerns

Once a child enters school there are several factors that need to be considered to enhance and enrich family engagement and participation, including: (a) communication choice, (b) educational systems and placement options, and (c) child and family characteristics.

Communication Choice. Communication is a central concern for DML family engagement in two aspects: the parents' ability to communicate with their child and school-to-parent communication. Similarly, as discussed under early intervention, the parents' ability to communicate with their DML child fluently, particularly if the child uses sign language, is a critical need (Clark et al., 2020). Even at the most basic level of school involvement, the parents need to be able to communicate in the child's primary language (e.g. ASL or spoken language) well enough to discuss school related activities, help with homework, and understand what is happening at school (Cawthon et al., 2015). Learning sign language, however, can be challenging for hearing parents of DML children. Fortunately, new technologies have been created that make learning signs easier such as the SMARTSign app, which teaches ASL vocabulary (Xu, 2013), television programs such as *Signing Times* (Azevedo Brown & Coleman, 2002), and online ASL classes, which provide learning opportunities for children and parents alike. Some of these new technologies provide opportunities in other languages (e.g. Signing Fiesta).

An equally important aspect of communication is school-to-home and home-to-school communication. From previous research, we know that regular and clear communication is one of the most essential factors of successful parent engagement. Schools can encourage communication by providing access to competent spoken language interpreters and cultural brokers. Information should be communicated to parents in their preferred language and in multiple ways by: (a) phone, (b) email, (c) text message, (d) app-based communication, (e) video calls/conferencing, and/or (f) handouts. Communication should be ongoing, not only when there is a problem or concern.

Educational Systems and Placement Options. For parents who are new to the country and to its educational system, there is a lot to learn, and the learning process can be complicated. Furthermore, parents may have a different cultural view of the purpose of education and their role in their DML child's education. Some cultures view the teacher as the expert and as a result may be reluctant to offer their own ideas or question the decisions made, even when asked to. Particular cultures see the role of the school as to teach general world knowledge and skills and the role of the parent to teach personal and moral development (e.g., the difference for many Latino families between *education* [what students learn in school] and *educación* [personal and moral development learned at home]; Zarate, 2007).

Furthermore, there are many legal considerations particularly for students with disabilities, including hearing loss. In the United States, IDEA provides for students with disabilities to be educated in the least restrictive environment (LRE), as determined by the IEP team. For students who are DMLs, this opens several placement possibilities including a continuum of options for d/Dhh students (i.e., full inclusion in their neighborhood school, self-contained or resource classes in center-based programs, and residential and charter schools for the deaf) and a continuum of programs for bilingual learners (i.e., ESL pull-out, content-based Sheltered English, and transitional or maintenance bilingual programs). We saw how this decision was made in Maria's (Box 2.1) and Myitzu's (Box 2.2) stories.

Regardless of where the child is educated, schools need to provide an accepting atmosphere where parents feel their involvement and participation is expected and welcomed (Hoover-Dempsey et al., 2005). Because the school climate sets the foundation for family engagement, schools should define parent engagement and invite parents to be engaged. Box 2.3 provides several ways schools and educators can establish trust and build relationships for parental engagement.

If children are placed in a school that is not located near the family's home (i.e., residential schools for the deaf), considerations must be made to assist parents in becoming active participants at school. For example, parents can be involved via teleconferencing, virtual events, and teletutoring to work with schools to support their child's education. Organizations such as the Clerc Center have prioritized family engagement and school partnerships, in part because current models of family engagement may not be sufficient for families with d/Dhh children or DMLs. Researchers are currently engaged in finding evidence and developing resources to support family engagement and advocacy (Clerc Center, n.d.). Schools need to widen their definition of parental involvement and engagement beyond what is currently recognized and observable (e.g., attending school events, volunteering in the classroom, and fundraising) and consider that many families are involved in "less visible" or traditionally defined ways (e.g., teaching cultural values and beliefs, attending cultural events, and sharing oral stories and traditions; Gonzales & Gabel, 2017).

Child and Family Characteristics. Individual and family characteristics may cause challenges to family engagement. As was presented earlier, Hoover-Dempsey and Sandler's revised model of family involvement lists the parents' life contexts as a critical element to consider (Hoover-Dempsey et al., 2005). The parents' life contexts include the knowledge, skills, time, and energy they bring to a request for involvement. One important area that encompasses life contexts is socioeconomic status (SES).

SES has been researched in relation to family engagement, with mixed results. Hoover-Dempsey and her colleagues (2005) explain that "SES does not generally explain why parents become involved, nor does it explain why parents in similar or identical SES categories often vary substantially in involvement practices or effectiveness" (p. 114). They suggest that the differences in involvement actually occur because of availability of resources which often accompany SES. The relationship between SES, race, and ethnicity is intimately intertwined. Research has shown that race and ethnicity are often common indicators of a person's SES, "those most likely to be poor are African American, Latino, and Native American children, children in single-mother families, children of immigrant parents, and children younger than 5 years of age" (Cheng et al., 2015, p. e225). Voss and Lenihan (2015) looked at factors of poverty related to SES and the availability of resources for young d/Dhh children and families. They suggest that early intervention can have a positive influence on stability for families living in poverty by providing resources that increase resiliency against the impacts of poverty. Hoover-Dempsey et al. (2005) echo this sentiment that while schools cannot respond to all SES related issues, they can provide resources that may allow parents to be more engaged.

In addition to family characteristics, individual child characteristics have also been shown to have an impact on family engagement. Becker and Bowen (2018) discussed influencers of diversity (Leigh, 2008) that affect service providers' perspectives about working with DMLs and their families. These characteristics help to describe and understand the strengths and needs of the whole DML, rather than simply looking at one aspect. Understanding the following may help to engage families in their child's education in meaningful ways and help to identify goals and objectives to promote student outcomes: (a) prior school experiences, (b) the language(s) used by the child and family, (c) the cultural views of the family in connection with the student's educational placement, (d) the type and degree of hearing loss, and (e) current academic achievement.

Availability of Resources

Family engagement requires families with a CLD background to have a vested interest in their child's educational experience. In order to have a true partnership, families must have access to resources, including materials in their heritage language, that allow them to fully participate. Within the Newcomer Program (described above), schools may also establish a *Family Center* to provide orientation and support to parents. These may include: (a) additional support to students in their school environment, (b) a physical location within a school for families to go to connect with school professionals and community resources, (c) access to interpreter and translator services, (d) parent liaisons, (e) English and/or sign language classes for parents and family, and (f) opportunities for families to connect with other families and to the community (Georgis et al., 2014). Furthermore, many communities have refugee centers sponsored by both private and public organizations and churches. Schools should establish partnerships with these organizations to provide a second level of support for families and youth. These organizations often have access to interpreters and cultural brokers that can help support the schools' endeavors to engage immigrant and refugee families.

Conclusion

Research has continually shown that students with involved parents do better in school, particularly when the involvement is linked to student learning. There is limited research documenting the engagement of families who have children who are d/Dhh and even less for families from diverse backgrounds with children who are DMLs. Many of the challenges that have been described in the general EL and EL special education literature (e.g., past educational experiences, home/school communication, and conflicts with time) also impact families who have children who are d/Dhh, including DMLs. There may be other obstacles for families with children who are DMLs including learning bimodal languages (i.e., spoken and sign), access to resources, and navigating the educational system.

Schools should implement traditional and non-traditional parental involvement programs and support parents to become advocates for their children. Building trust between families and education professionals lays the foundation for successful family engagement. Schools can accomplish this by: (a) establishing a welcoming environment and a climate of respect, (b) focusing on quality interactions, (c) improving communication by utilizing spoken language interpreters and cultural brokers, (d) serving as a liaison to connect families to community resources, (e) inviting parents to be engaged by defining family engagement, (f) providing meaningful opportunities for families to be involved, (g) having high expectations for parent involvement, (h) respecting cultural and linguistic diversity, and (i) making school events accessible.

Discussion Questions

1. Which components of family engagement are included in your professional practice? Which are missing or could be enhanced?
2. What does research in family engagement for DMLs in early intervention and school age populations tell us?
3. Identify challenges and possible solutions to enhance family engagement for DMLs (provide a minimum of three answers).
4. What resources exist in your school or community to support DML families?
5. What early intervention activities can parents engage in to support children's bilingual and multilingual language acquisition?

Resources

Websites

- American Society for Deaf Children (https://deafchildren.org/): The Society connects families with deaf and hard of hearing children to the Deaf community. The website has information on deaf role models, learning ASL, and a variety of resources.
- Center for Disease Control and Prevention. Parent Engagement in Schools Fact Sheets: Brochures (www.cdc.gov/healthyyouth/protective/parent_engagement.htm): for School Districts, teachers and school staff, and parents and families
- Colorín Colorado (www.colorincolorado.org/guides-toolkits): A bilingual site for educators and families of ELLs. Includes guides for teachers, administrators and families to foster engagement.
- Early Intervention Network, Laurent Clerc National Deaf Education Center (https://clerccenter.gallaudet.edu/national-resources/clerc-center-sites/early-intervention-network-supporting-linguistic-competence-for-children-who-are-deaf-or-hard-of-hearing.html.): The Center provides a review of 5 evidence-based factors to understand when developing linguistic competence in children who are deaf and hard of hearing using ASL.
- National ASL and English Bilingual Consortium for Early Childhood Education (www.bilingualece.org/): This is a membership organization of professionals who are dedicated to the development, management,

and coordination of ASL and English bilingual early childhood programs including empowering diverse families.
- National Association for Family, School and Community Engagement (https://nafsce.org): This is a membership association dedicated to the advancement of family, school and community partnerships.
- National Center for Hearing Assessment and Management (NCHAM; www.infanthearing.org/familysupport/): Family Support and Partnership, Just in Time tool (available in English and Spanish).
- Ontario Cultural Society for the Deaf (2008; https://ocsdeaf.org/): The ASL Parent-Child Mother Goose Program: ASL rhymes, rhythms & stories. Canada: Mississauga: Ontario.
- PACER Center (www.pacer.org/cultural-diversity/organizations.asp): This website provides a list of organizations involved in parent engagement for families from diverse cultures.
- US Department of Education: Family and Community Engagement (www.ed.gov/parent-and-family-engagement): This website provides many resources for families and professionals to better understand engagement. Of particular note, there is a toolkit of resources and a handbook on family and community engagement.
- US Department of Education: English Learner tool kit (2016; www.colorincolorado.org/guide/us-department-education-english-learner-tool-kit): This ten-chapter toolkit features recommendations on how to implement best practices with ELLs, including a chapter on communicating with parents and serving ELLs with disabilities.
- US Department of Education: Newcomer tool kit (2017; https://www2.ed.gov/about/offices/list/oela/newcomers-toolkit/ncomertoolkit.pdf.): This website provides an in-depth overview of the Newcomer Program, including strategies for establishing partnerships with families.

Books

- Donohue, C. (2017). *Family engagement in the digital age.* Routledge. This book explores how professionals can use technology to engage with parents and families in early childhood settings.
- Lynch, E. W., & Hanson, M. J. (Eds.). (2002). *Developing cross-cultural competence: A guide for working with children and their families* (4th ed.). Paul H. Brookes Publisher.

- Mapp, K. Carver, I., & Lander, J. (2017). *Powerful partnerships: A teacher's guide to engaging families for student success.* Scholastic. This book guides school professionals to develop respectful relationships with families and provide engagement opportunities throughout the year.

FAMILY-CENTERED BRIEF

FAMILY-CENTERED BRIEF

CHAPTER 2
Family Engagement: Developing Partnerships for d/Deaf and Hard of Hearing Multilingual Learners

by Sandy K. Bowen & Sharon Baker

PURPOSE OF THE CHAPTER
Explains how a family-centered approach leads to a child's success in school.

DEFINING KEY TERMS
Family engagement
When a student's family members (such as parents, grandparents, aunts/uncles, siblings) connect with the student's school in order to support the student's progress.

TIPS FOR FAMILIES

- Talk to the teacher (you can ask for an interpreter)
- Participate in school activities and events
- Talk to your child about school in a positive way

TIPS FOR EDUCATORS

- Communicate with families about their child's progress and needs
- Let families know they are welcome to in- and after-school activities
- Translate home materials into the home language

TAKE-HOME MESSAGE
When families engage in their child's education, the child is more likely to have...

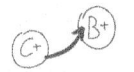

- higher grades and test scores
- better behaviour
- improved social skills

RESOURCES
National Association for Family, School and Community Engagement https://nafsce.org
National Center for Hearing Assessment and Management (NCHAM) www.infanthearing.org/familysupport/
PACER Center www.pacer.org/cultural-diversity/organizations.asp
U.S. Department of Education: Family and Community Engagement
www.ed.gov/parent-and-family-engagement ⟶ click on the "Family" tab

Deaf and Hard of Hearing Multilingual Learners: Foundations, Strategies, and Resources (2022)

References

Anderson, K. J., & Minke, K. M. (2007). Parent involvement in education: Toward an understanding of parents' decision making. *The Journal of Educational Research, 100*(5), 311–323. https://doi.org/10.3200/JOER.100.5.311-323

Andrews, J. F., & Baker, S. (2019). ASL nursery rhymes: Exploring a support for early language and emergent literacy skills for signing deaf children. *Sign Language Studies, 20*(1), 5–40. https://doi.org/10.1353/sls.2019.0007.

Arias, M. B., & Morillo-Campbell, M. (2008). *Promoting ELL parental involvement: Challenges in contested times*. Education Policy Research Unit. https://files.eric.ed.gov/fulltext/ED506652.pdf

Azevedo Brown, E., & Coleman, R. (2002). *Signing Time!* [Television series]. Hollywood: American Public Television.

Baker, S. (2010). *The importance of fingerspelling for reading*. Visual Language and Visual Learning Science of Learning Center [Research Brief No. 1]. Gallaudet University.

Baker, T. L., Wise, J., Kelley, G., & Skiba, R. J. (2016). Identifying barriers: Creating solutions to improve family engagement. *School Community Journal, 26*(2), 161.

Becker, S. J., & Bowen, S. K. (2018). Service providers' perspective on the education of students who are deaf or hard of hearing and English learners. *American Annals of the Deaf, 163*(3), 356–373.

Behl, D. D., Blaiser, K., Cook, G., Barrett, T., Callow-Heusser, C., Brooks, B. M., . . . & White, K. R. (2017). A multisite study evaluating the benefits of early intervention via telepractice. *Infants & Young Children, 30*(2), 147–161. https://doi.org/10.1097/IYC.0000000000000090

Behl, D. D., Houston, K. T., Guthrie, W. S., & Guthrie, N. K. (2010). Tele-intervention: The wave of the future fits families' lives today. *The Exceptional Parent (Online), 40*(12), 23.

Benedict, B., Crace, J., Holmes, T., Hossler, T., Oliva, G., Raimondo, B., Richmond, M. A., Sass-Lehrer, M., Swann, M., & Vincent, J. (2015). Deaf community support for families: The best of partnerships (Ch. 18). In *National Center for Hearing Assessment and Management eBook: A Resource Guide for Early Hearing Detection and Intervention (EHDI)*. National Center for Hearing Assessment and Management, Utah State University, Logan, UT.

Blaiser, K. M., Behl, D., Callow-Heusser, C., & White, K. R. (2013). Measuring costs and outcomes of tele-intervention when serving families of children who are Deaf/hard-of-hearing. *International Journal of Telerehabilitation*, *5*(2), 3–10. https://doi.org/10.5195/IJT.2013.6129

Bowen, S. K. (2016). Early intervention: A multicultural perspective on d/Deaf and hard of hearing multilingual learners. *American Annals of the Deaf*, *161*(1), 33–42.

Bower, H. A., & Griffin, D. (2011). Can the Epstein Model of parental involvement work in a high-minority, high-poverty elementary school? A case study. *Professional School Counseling*, *15*(2), 77–87.

Breiseth, L. (2011, August). *Engaging ELL families: 20 strategies for school leaders with questions for reflection and checklists*. www.colorincolorado.org/pdfs/articles/Engaging-ELL-Families_A-Checklist-for-School-Leaders.pd

Brewster, C., & Railsback, J. (2003). *Building trust with schools and diverse families: A foundation for lasting partnerships*. Northwest Regional Educational Laboratory. www.adlit.org/article/21522/

Brown, M. R., Dennis, J. P., & Matute-Chavarria, M. (2019). Cultural relevance in special education: Current status and future directions. *Intervention in School and Clinic*, *54*(5), 304–310. https://doi.org/10.1177/1053451218819252

Calderon, R. (2000). Parental involvement in deaf children's education programs as a predictor of child's language, early reading, and social-emotional development. *Journal of Deaf Studies and Deaf Education*, *5*(2), 140–155. https://doi.org/10.1093/deafed/5.2.140

Calderon, R., & Greenberg, M. T. (2012). Social and emotional development of deaf children: Family, school, and program effects. In *The Oxford handbook of deaf studies, language, and education: Second edition* (Vol. 1). Oxford University Press. https://doi.org/10.1093/oxfordhb/9780199750986.013.0014

Cawthon, S. W., Garberoglio, C. L., Caemmerer, J. M., Bond, M., & Wendel, E. (2015). Effect of parent involvement and parent expectations on postsecondary outcomes for individuals who are d/Deaf or hard of hearing. *Exceptionality*, *23*(2), 73–99. https://doi.org/10.1080/09362835.2013.865537

Centers for Disease Control and Prevention. (2015). *Parent engagement.* www.cdc.gov/healthyyouth/protective/parent_engagement.htm

Cheng, T. L., Goodman, E., & Committee on Pediatric Research. (2015). Race, ethnicity, and socioeconomic status in research on child health. *Pediatrics, 135*(1), e225-e237. https://doi.org/10.1542/peds.2014-3109

Clark, M. D., Cue, K. R., Delgado, N. J., Greene-Woods, A. N., & Wolsey, J. L. A. (2020). Early intervention protocols: Proposing a default bimodal bilingual approach for deaf children. *Maternal and Child Health Journal, 24*(11), 1339–1344.

Clerc Center. (n.d.). *Research agenda: Area of focus: Family engagement.* https://www3.gallaudet.edu/clerc-center/research/research-agenda/family-engagement.html

Cole, B., Stredler-Brown, A., Cohill, B., Blaiser, K., Behl, D., & Ringwalt, S. (2016). The development of statewide policies and procedures to implement telehealth for Part C service delivery. *International Journal of Telerehabilitation, 8*(2), 77–82.

DesJardin, J. L. (2006). Family empowerment: Supporting language development in young children who are deaf or hard of hearing. *The Volta Review, 106*(3), 275–298.

Elementary and Secondary Education Act (ESEA). (2015). *US Department of Education.* www.ed.gov/ESEA

Epstein, J. L. (2010). School/family/community partnerships: Caring for the children we share. *Phi Delta Kappan, 92*(3), 81–96. https://doi.org/10.1177/003172171009200326

Epstein, J. L., Sanders, M. G., Simon, B. S., Salinas, K. C., Jansorn, N. R., & Van Voorhis, F. L. (2002). *School, family, and community partnerships: Your handbook for action* (2nd ed.). Corwin.

Every Student Succeeds Act (ESSA). (2015). *US Department of Education.* www.ed.gov/ESSA

Georgis, R., Gokiert, R. J., Ford, D. M., & Ali, M. (2014). Creating inclusive parent engagement practices: Lessons learned from a school community collaborative supporting newcomer refugee families. *Multicultural Education, 21*(3), 23–27.

Gietz, M. R., Andrews, J. F., & Clark, M. D. (2020). ASL stories with handshape rhyme: An exploratory intervention to support English vocabulary with signing deaf readers *Archives of Psychology, 4*(2). https://doi.org/10.31296/aop.v4i2.139

Gonzales, S. M., & Gabel, S. L. (2017). Exploring involvement expectations for culturally and linguistically diverse parents: What we need to know in teacher education. *International Journal of Multicultural Education, 19*(2), 61–81. https://doi.org/10.18251/ijme.v19i2.1376

Grant, K. B., & Ray, J. (2016). *Home, school, and community collaboration: Culturally responsive family engagement* (3rd ed.). Sage.

Guiberson, M. (2014). Bilingual skills of deaf/hard of hearing children from Spain. *Cochlear Implants International, 15*(2), 87–92.

Hamilton, B., & Clark, M. (2020). The Deaf mentor program: Benefits to families. *Psychology, 11,* 713–736. https://doi.org/10.4236/psych.2020.115049

Hoover-Dempsey, K. V., & Sandler, H. M. (1995). Parental involvement in children's education: Why does it make a difference? *Teachers College Record, 97*(2), 310–331. https://doi.org/10.3102/00346543067001003

Hoover-Dempsey, K. V., & Sandler, H. M. (1997). Why do parents become involved in their children's education? *Review of Educational Research, 67*(1), 3–42. https://doi.org/10.3102/00346543067001003

Hoover-Dempsey, K. V., Walker, J. M. T., Sandler, H. M., Whetsel, D., Green, C. L., Wilkins, A. S., & Closson, K. E. (2005). Why do parents become involved? Research findings and implications. *Elementary School Journal, 106*(2), 105–130.

Hornby, G., & Lafaele, R. (2011). Barriers to parental involvement in education: An explanatory model. *Educational Review, 63*(1), 37–52. https://doi.org/10.1080/00131911.2010.488049

Humphries, T., & MacDougall, F. (1999). "Chaining" and other links: Making connections between American Sign Language and English in two types of school settings. *Visual Anthropology Review, 15*(2), 84–94.

Individuals with Disabilities Education Act (IDEA) of 2004, 20 U.S.C. §§ 1400–1482 (2015).

Individuals with Disabilities Education Act. (2012, May). *FEDC issue brief.* www.efrconline.org/myadmin/files/fedc_Parent_Participation.pdf

Jezewski, M. A., & Sotnik, P. (2001). *Culture brokering: Providing culturally competent rehabilitation services to foreign-born persons.* Center for International Rehabilitation Research Information and Exchange.

Kalyanpur, M., & Harry, B. (2012). *Cultural reciprocity in special education: Building family-professional relationships*. Brookes.

Kluwin, T. N., & Corbett, C. A. (1998). Parent characteristics and educational program involvement. *American Annals of the Deaf, 143*(5), 425–432. https://doi.org/10.1353/aad.2012.0132

Leigh, G. (2008). Changing parameters in deafness. In M. Marschark & P. C. Hauser (Eds.), *Deaf cognition: Foundations and outcomes* (pp. 24–51). Oxford University Press.

Lin, Y., & Ku, F. (2020). Reading and writing instruction for young deaf children using Taiwan Sign Language. In L. Wang & J. Andrews (Eds.), *Literacy and deaf education: Toward a global understanding* (pp. 305–327). Gallaudet University Press.

Lynch, E. W. (2011). Developing cross-cultural competence. In E. W. Lynch & M. J. Hanson (Eds.), *Developing cross-cultural competence: A guide for working with children and their families* (pp. 41–75). Brookes.

Machado-Casas, M., Sánchez, P., & Ek, L. D. (2014). The digital literacy practices of Latina/o immigrant parents in an after-school technology partnership. *Multicultural Education, 21*(3), 28–33.

Moeller, M. P. (2000). Early intervention and language development in children who are deaf and hard of hearing. *Pediatrics, 106*(3), e43–e43. https://doi.org/10.1542/peds.106.3.e43

Moeller, M. P., Carr, G., Seaver, L., Stredler-Brown, A., & Holzinger, D. (2013). Best practices in family-centered early intervention for children who are deaf or hard of hearing: An international consensus statement. *Journal of Deaf Studies and Deaf Education, 18*(4), 429–445. https://doi.org/10.1093/deafed/ent034

National Center for Cultural Competence. (2004). *Bridging the cultural divide in health care settings: The essential role of the cultural broker programs*. https://nccc.georgetown.edu/culturalbroker/acknowledge.html

National Center for English Language Acquisition. (n.d.). *Elevating English language learners (Els): Programs for newcomer students*. https://ncela.ed.gov/files/feature_topics/newcomers/ElevatingELs_ProgramsForNewcomerStudents.pdf

National Center for Hearing Assessment and Management. (2014). *A practical guide to the use of tele-intervention in providing listening and spoken-language services to infants and toddlers who are deaf or hard of hearing.* www.infanthearing.org/ti-guide/index.html

National Center for Hearing Assessment and Management. (2018). *Telehealth and EHDI systems.* www.infanthearing.org/telehealth/

National Center on Parent, Family, and Community Engagement. (2011). *The parent, family, and community engagement (PFCE) framework for early childhood systems.* https://childcareta.acf.hhs.gov/sites/default/files/public/pfce-framework_for_ec_systems_final_508.pdf

Poole, M. E., Fettig, A., McKee, R. A., & Gauvreau, A. N. (2020). Inside the virtual visit: Using tele-intervention to support families in early intervention. *Young Exceptional Children.* https://doi.org/10.1177/1096250620948061

Powers, G. W., & Saskiewicz, J. A. (1998). A comparison study of educational involvement of hearing parents of deaf and hearing children of elementary school age. *American Annals of the Deaf, 143*(1), 35–39. https://doi.org/10.1353/aad.2012.0108

Purcell-Gates, V., Lenters, K., McTavish, M., & Anderson, J. (2014). Working with different cultural patterns and beliefs: Teachers and families learning together. *Multicultural Education, 21*(3–4), 17–22.

Reed, S., Antia, S. D., & Kreimeyer, K. H. (2008). Academic status of deaf and hard-of-hearing students in public schools: Student, home, and service facilitators and detractors. *Journal of Deaf Studies and Deaf Education, 13*(4), 485–502. https://doi.org/10.1093/deafed/enn006

Rodriguez-Valls, F., & Torres, C. (2014). Partnerships and networks in migrant education: Empowering migrant families to support their children's success. *Multicultural Education, 21*(3/4), 34–38.

Roy, D. (2013, February). The birth of a word. *The Huffington Post Blog.* www.huffpost.com/entry/the-birth-of-a-word_b_2639625

Short, D. J., & Boyson, B. A. (2012). *Helping newcomer students succeed in secondary schools and beyond.* Washington, DC: Center for Applied Linguistics. www.cal.org/resource-center/ publications/helping-newcomer-students

Stredler-Brown, A. (2017). Examination of coaching behaviors used by providers when delivering early intervention via telehealth to families of children who are deaf or hard of hearing. *Perspectives of the ASHA Special Interest Groups.* 2(9), 25–42. https://doi.org/10.1044/persp2.SIG9.25.

Substance Abuse and Mental Health Services Administration (2016). Rural behavioral health: Telehealth challenges and opportunities. *In Brief, 9*(2), 1–13.

Tarasawa, B., & Waggoner, J. (2015). Increasing parental involvement of English language learner families: What the research says. *Journal of Children and Poverty, 21*(2), 129–134. https://doi.org/10.1080/10796126.2015.1058243

Tervalon, M., & Murray-Garcia, J. (1998). Cultural humility versus cultural competence: A critical distinction in defining physician training outcomes in multicultural education. *Journal of Health Care for the Poor and Undeserved, 9*, 117–125.

Thompson, B. C., Mazer, J. P., & Flood Grady, E. (2015). The changing nature of parent-teacher communication: Mode selection in the smartphone era. *Communication Education, 64*(2), 187–207. https://doi.org/10.1080/03634523.2015.1014382

Tirado, M. (2011). Role of mobile health in the care of culturally and linguistically diverse US populations. *Perspectives in Health Information Management, 8*(Winter), 1e.

Turnbull, A. A., Turnbull, H. R., Erwin, E. J., Soodak, L. C., & Shogren, K. A. (2015). *Families, professionals, and exceptionality: Positive outcomes through partnerships and trust.* Pearson.

U.S. Department of Education. Office of English Language Acquisition. (2016a). *English Learner Took Kit* (Rev. ed.). Author. https://www2.ed.gov/about/offices/list/oela/english-learner-toolkit/index.html

U.S. Department of Education. Office of English Language Acquisition. (2016b). *Newcomer Tool Kit Took Kit.* Author. www2.ed.gov/about/offices/list/oela/newcomers-toolkit/ncomertoolkit.pdf

Voss, J., & Lenihan, S. (2015, December). Fostering resilience for children living in poverty: Effective practices & resources for EHDI professionals. *Journal of Early Hearing Detection and Intervention.* Issues Briefs for early hearing detection and intervention. National Center on Hearing Assessment and Management.

Walker, J. M. T., Wilkins, A. S., Dallaire, J. P., Sandler, H. M., & Hoover-Dempsey, K. V. (2005). Parental involvement: Model revision through scale development. *Elementary School Journal, 106*, 85–104.

Wieber, W. B., & Quiñonez-Sumner, L. (2016). Promoting immigrant parents' engagement in early intervention through culturally and linguistically responsive service delivery. *The Journal of Early Hearing Detection and Intervention, 1*(1), 78–86.

Xu, K. A. (2013). *Facilitating American Sign Language learning for hearing parents of deaf children via mobile devices* [Doctoral dissertation]. Georgia Institute of Technology.

Yoshinaga-Itano, C. (2014). Principles and guidelines for early intervention after confirmation that a child is deaf or hard of hearing. *Journal of Deaf Studies and Deaf Education, 19*(2), 143–175. https://doi.org/10.1093/deafed/ent043.

Zaidman-Zait, A., & Young, R. A. (2008). Parental involvement in the habilitation process following children's cochlear implantation: An action theory perspective. *Journal of Deaf Studies and Deaf Education, 13*(2), 193–214. https://doi.org/10.1093/deafed/enm051

Zarate, M. E. (2007). *Understanding Latino parental involvement in education: Perceptions, expectations and recommendations.* Tomas Rivera Policy Institute. https://files.eric.ed.gov/fulltext/ED502065.pdf

Zhang, C., & Bennett, T. (2003). Facilitating meaningful participation of culturally and linguistically diverse families in the IFSP and IEP process. *Focus on Autism and Other Developmental Disabilities, 18*(1), 51–59.

3
Developing a Comprehensive Language Profile to Support Learning: The Assessment of d/Deaf and Hard of Hearing Multilingual Learners

Lianna Pizzo and Laurie Ford

LEARNING OBJECTIVES

Readers will:

1. Learn about the process and steps of conducting a comprehensive language profile.
2. Understand the considerations for selecting and administering assessments for d/Deaf and hard of hearing multilingual learners.
3. Learn how to include families in the assessment process of their child who is d/Deaf and hard of hearing and a multilingual learner.
4. Explore how to minimize biases when making decisions based on assessment data.

Although global statistics on bilingualism have not been firmly established, statistics show that over 50% of the world is bilingual or multilingual (Bialystok, 2013; Grosjean, 2010). From the statistics that are available, the rate of bilingualism or multilingualism is even higher for some countries or regions of the world. For example, 64.6 percent of people living in the European Union have indicated that they use more than one language (Eurostat, 2019). Furthermore, bilingualism is prevalent in a number of countries that only recognize one national language, making the country socially bilingual despite remaining institutionally monolingual (Robert, 2017). The Netherlands is one example of this pattern, as it only recognizes Dutch as a national language but reports 86.4% of individuals speaking more than one language across the country (Eurostat, 2019). Consequently, bilingualism is an important global phenomenon to recognize.

Considering the number of bilingual individuals globally, it is unsurprising that many school-aged children are growing up bilingual as well. For example, there are nearly 12 million bilingual learners[1] in US schools, an increase of 1.2 million from ten years ago (Kids Count Data Center, 2016). d/Deaf and hard of hearing (d/Dhh) learners currently educated in public schools have not been unaffected by these trends (Cannon & Guardino, 2012; Cannon et al., 2016; GRI, 2013). For instance, d/Dhh multilingual learners (DMLs), or d/Dhh children who come from homes where a language other than English or sign language is used, constitute approximately 35% of the d/Dhh population in US schools (GRI, 2013).

Although there has been an increase in the research involving topics relevant to the education of DMLs in recent years, there remain relatively few articles that address considerations relevant to assessment practices for this population (Baker & Scott, 2016; Pizzo & Chilvers, 2016). For the purposes of this book chapter, we will focus more specifically on considerations for assessing the language development of DMLs. Specifically, we will discuss how to use assessment data to compile a comprehensive language profile that can inform teaching and promote learning. This chapter will be organized to focus on three areas: (a) the process of creating a comprehensive language profile, (b) involving families in the assessment process, and (c) making meaningful decisions based on the learner's language profile.

Theoretical Framework

In this chapter, the framework of Linguistically Responsive Teaching (LRT) is used to discuss assessment practices for children who are DMLs. LRT focuses on the specialized knowledge required to provide high-quality education for children who are linguistically diverse (Lucas & Villegas, 2013; Lucas et al., 2008). One key component of this framework is that educators need to possess knowledge of multiple assessment practices that have the potential to impact program and pedagogy (Lucas et al., 2008). It is especially important to view DMLs in terms of all of their languages, as without examining skills in all areas, key information will be lost (Pizzo & Chilvers, 2019). In addition, multiple sources of data are needed for DMLs, as traditional assessment approaches may lack validity when used with DMLs, d/Dhh, or bilingual populations (Baker & Scott, 2016; Cawthon, 2007; Cawthon & Wurtz, 2008; Duarte & Gutierrez-Gomez, 2004; Espinosa & López, 2007).

Developing a Comprehensive Language Profile

A language profile is comprehensive when it captures a learner's abilities in all languages to which they are regularly exposed (Pizzo, 2016; Pizzo & Chilvers, 2016, 2019). All comprehensive assessments (for language or other areas) should include multiple measures, sources, and theoretical orientations to understanding a learner's abilities. For DMLs, however, the inclusion of *all* spoken and sign languages is the major distinguishing feature of a comprehensive language profile. Although the inclusion of all languages a child possesses has been made about spoken language bilingual learners for more than ten years (e.g. Espinosa & López, 2007), schools continue to struggle in the administration of assessments in a learner's home language if it differs from the language of the school. For example, by not including skills in all languages during a profile, it is challenging to: (a) determine a child's true levels of linguistic ability; (b) plan for instruction (it is instructionally different to teach an English language skill that a child already has in the first language, than to teach a concept to which a child has never been exposed); or (c) examine whether a child has a language difference versus an additional language disability.

There are five major areas of language that should be addressed in a comprehensive language profile for the various spoken and sign languages assessed: (a) phonological features in spoken or signed languages (as appropriate), (b) morphology, (c) semantics, (d) syntax, and (e) pragmatics. In addition, the inclusion of a learner's general communication abilities, use of home signs, or use of constructed sign systems should also be included. As the purpose of this chapter is to examine the process of conducting a comprehensive language assessment rather than assessing exact language skills, a thorough discussion of each of these areas of language will not be included. However, any assessor of language needs to be well versed in these areas to ensure that the profile is both comprehensive, as well as accurately interpreted. See Table 3.1 for brief definitions of these areas.

Each comprehensive language profile will be different. There is no single battery of assessment approaches or tools that can be used for all learners. Therefore, the components of a comprehensive language profile need to focus on findings related to language proficiency and skills, rather than an assessment tool or technique. Thus, the purpose of the assessment must be made clear and an assessment plan is needed to ensure that all questions about a child's language abilities can be answered through the methods employed. See Figure 3.1 for the process of developing a high-quality comprehensive language profile.

TABLE 3.1 Five Features of Language

Feature of Language	Definition	Selected Examples for Spoken Language	Selected Examples for Natural Sign Languages
Semantics	The meaning of language.	• Spoken language vocabulary	• Sign language vocabulary
Syntax	The structure of sentences including word order.	• Sentence length • Sentence complexity	• Sign order may vary to convey the same meaning

Feature of Language	Definition	Selected Examples for Spoken Language	Selected Examples for Natural Sign Languages
Phonology	The study of the smallest contrastive units of language. Phonology is traditionally considered to be based on sound systems; however, phonology also "includes the equivalent component of the grammar in sign languages, because it is tied to the grammatical *organization*, and not to particular content" (Brentari et al., 2018).	• Phonological awareness such as rhythm and rhyme • Understanding and use of phonemes • Phonics	• The shape of the hand • The place the hand is located • The movement attached to the hand • Sublexical elements of sign language
Morphology	The formation of individual words and how they relate to each other.	• Root words • Prefixes • Suffixes	• Handshapes • Classifiers • Classifier-vocabulary connections
Pragmatics	The social contexts and use of language.	• Turn-taking in conversation • Social conventions • Eye contact • Modifying language based on your audience	• Culturally relevant signs • Context dependent signs

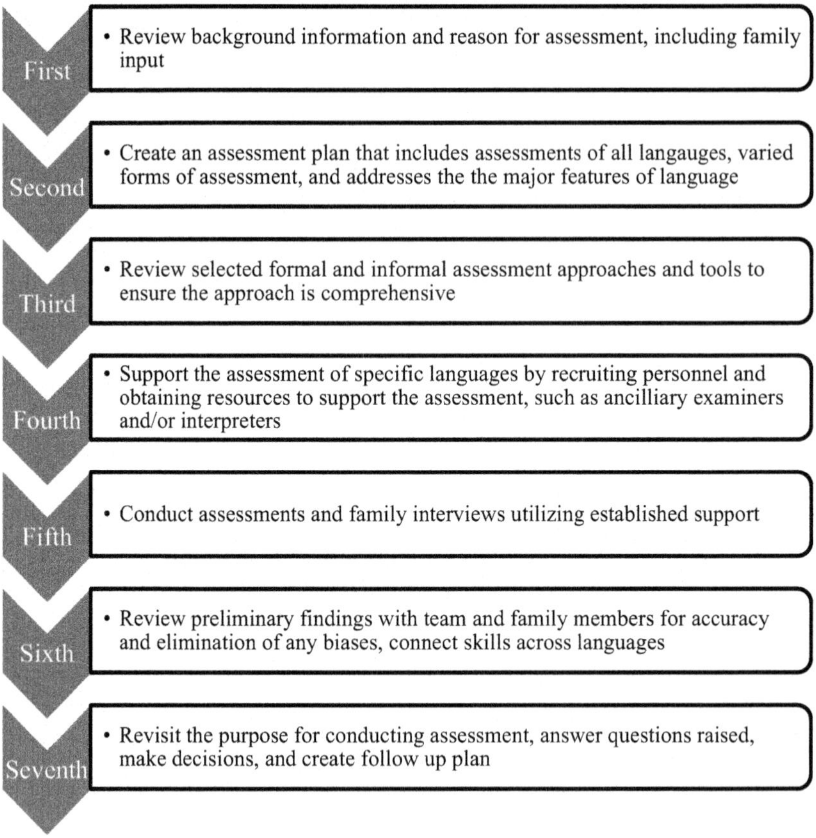

First: Review background information and reason for assessment, including family input

Second: Create an assessment plan that includes assessments of all langauges, varied forms of assessment, and addresses the the major features of language

Third: Review selected formal and informal assessment approaches and tools to ensure the approach is comprehensive

Fourth: Support the assessment of specific languages by recruiting personnel and obtaining resources to support the assessment, such as ancilliary examiners and/or interpreters

Fifth: Conduct assessments and family interviews utilizing established support

Sixth: Review preliminary findings with team and family members for accuracy and elimination of any biases, connect skills across languages

Seventh: Revisit the purpose for conducting assessment, answer questions raised, make decisions, and create follow up plan

FIGURE 3.1 Stages of Developing a High-Quality Comprehensive Language Profile

Assessor Qualifications

An assessor is the person conducting the assessment. This person can be any educator or related service provider that is trained in assessment (e.g., teacher, school psychologist, early interventionist, etc.). In a linguistically responsive framework, the assessor needs to possess specific knowledge and beliefs in order to conduct an appropriate assessment that provides valid and useful data for instructional decision making. Throughout all aspects of the assessment, the assessor must also take care to consider the ways that bias may be impacting the assessment and attempt to reduce that bias when possible. For linguistically responsive assessment practices, assessors need to develop three orientations essential toward realizing this goal: (a) sociolinguistic consciousness, (b) value for linguistic diversity, and (c) inclination to advocate for bilingual learners (Lucas & Villegas, 2013). Sociolinguistic consciousness includes understanding the sociopolitical nature of language and its relation to culture, identity, and society. By valuing linguistic diversity, educators adopt a stance that bilingualism and multilingualism are beneficial, while actively behaving in ways that demonstrate this belief. Finally, assessors need to be willing to act to ensure access to educational opportunities, and social and political capital.

In addition to developing orientations that support the assessment process, an assessor must possess specific knowledge and skills. Lucas and Villegas (2013) outline four categories of knowledge and skills they deem necessary for engaging in linguistically responsive instruction: (a) gathering information about the specific learner at hand, (b) understanding of languages and bilingual language learning, (c) identifying the language demands inherent in a task, and (d) employing instructional strategies to scaffold learning. The knowledge and skills an assessor needs are related to these categories, but they are not directly aligned. Therefore, we are proposing knowledge of three specific areas of assessment that are essential for the assessor to complete a high-quality assessment in a linguistically responsive framework (Lucas & Villegas, 2013): (a) knowledge of the types of assessment being used, (b) knowledge of the language that is being assessed, and (c) knowledge of how to work with families to gather high-quality data.

Determine the Purpose of the Comprehensive Language Profile

A comprehensive language profile is useful to understand a learner's current levels of language skills as well as overall language proficiency. This profile may be used to inform a DML about an individual learning plan or objectives, measure growth over time, or determine eligibility for services. Each comprehensive language profile will have an outlined purpose for the assessment based on the child's language background, referral/inquiry question, and family input. For example, a profile may be used to develop a learning plan, consider how to use language skills in one language to support the development of others, or address any cultural strengths that can support language learning.

A comprehensive language profile can also collect data that can be compared over time to determine if a child is progressing in language skills. These assessments can either provide an overall language proficiency level or be diagnostic in nature to examine individual skill development; a comprehensive language profile can contribute key knowledge towards aims such as these.

Finally, assessment data is essential for determining services for DMLs. Not all countries have laws or mechanisms for determining how or if a child should receive additional language services based on their language diversity. Some countries have tried to establish parameters to provide bilingual and multilingual learners with additional language support as they develop their language skills. In the United States, for example, the identification of students for English language services is one of the primary aspects of laws governing bilingual education. English learners (ELs), or children who have been determined eligible to receive these services under the law, currently comprise 9.5 percent, or 4.8 million, of students in US public schools (NCES, 2018). As mentioned previously, there are nearly 12 million bilingual learners in US schools, indicating that not all children who are bilingual are designated as ELs.

In the United States, the major distinction between a child who is bilingual and an English learner is the language proficiency of the child in the English language. An EL is a bilingual child who also experiences challenges in the English language requiring additional services to meet their language learning needs. As a result, the numbers of ELs in the schools are typically lower than the number of children who are actually learning more than one language in the home and school. In addition, the number of ELs tends to decrease in the older grades, as more children gain language proficiency and exit services as they get older (National Center for Education Statistics, 2018).

For children who are DMLs, there is very little research about: (a) how they are identified for EL services (if at all), (b) how they are served, (c) who delivers additional language services, or (d) how they are formally monitored for language growth. The distinction between the nature of additional language services to support children who are navigating multiple languages, versus language services required to address language development related to hearing loss, remains unclear. Even so, a comprehensive language profile can contribute to all aspects of these complex educational decisions, including eligibility, services, and progress monitoring.

Creating and Reviewing an Assessment Plan: Selecting Assessments for DMLs

In order to develop a comprehensive language profile of a DML, it is important to "consider which of the available tools have the power, validity, and rigor to evaluate specified language skills and provide an accurate picture of a child's language capacities" (Henner et al., 2018, p. 2). There is no one test that can provide a complete picture of a learner's language abilities that also meets the professional standards for assessment. Therefore, multiple measures, sources, and approaches to assessment are required to capture the information necessary to create a comprehensive language profile that can inform the development of an appropriate educational programming (Pizzo & Chilvers, 2016). For learners who have typical hearing levels and are bilingual, standardized tests are frequently used to assess and monitor English language development (Espinosa & López, 2007). For DMLs, the use of standardized tests has significant limitations that affect the validity of the data being collected and the overall ecological utility of the assessment information provided.

Standardized Assessment of Language Proficiency

A fundamental component of standardized assessment is that the administration of the test should be standardized, or consistent across administrations (AERA et al., 2014). These tests are created and vetted to ensure that if a test is administered properly, stakeholders can have confidence in the scores produced. Psychometrics is used to demonstrate whether a test has validity. Validity includes whether an assessment tool measures what it is supposed to measure, as well as reliability, or the extent to which the assessment produces stable and consistent scores (AERA et al., 2014).

When a test is used for a population for which it is not intended, the validity of the assessment is impacted. There are no standardized tests specifically designed for DMLs. Subsequently, the tests used may have threats to their validity when used with DMLs. Fortunately, there are strategies to reduce these threats when assessing DMLs, including translation or interpretation of test content, and the intentional use of assessment accommodations.

Translation. Despite the international growing linguistic diversity, very few formal assessments are available in languages other than English, which is viewed as a major limitation in the field of assessment (Barrueco et al., 2012; Espinosa & López, 2007). Beyond English, Spanish-language assessments are the most widely available in the United States, due to the demographic trends in some public schools (Barrueco et al., 2012). Many of the assessments available in Spanish are translated versions of popular English-based assessments that were not designed with the Spanish language in mind (Pizzo & Chilvers, 2016). For languages other than Spanish, official translations are limited, and more attention to language diversity in assessment is needed.

When a test is translated, it introduces a level of bias before the assessment even begins, as the psychometric properties that establish a test's validity do not necessarily transfer to the new assessment (Barrueco et al., 2012). In addition, when a test is standardized across different cultural groups, the content of the test may be inconsistent with the cultural characteristics with which a child or family are familiar (Barrueco et al., 2012). There are many examples in the United States in which the test expects a learner to perform a skill to which they may not have been exposed. For example, a common skill assessed in early childhood is whether the child can independently feed oneself at an early age. There are cultures in which the adults in the family feed their children for much longer before teaching them mealtime independence. If the test contains a question about the age the child was able to eat small bites of food using their hands, a child might be judged on a skill that they have never had the opportunity to learn. In this instance, a translated question does not eliminate the hidden cultural bias the test might contain.

Cultural bias may also inadvertently influence the answers a family member may give the assessor during an interview or assessment. If a specific question violates the cultural norms to which the family adheres, the family member may feel uncomfortable answering the question. In this case, the family could even give an answer that is more socially acceptable in their culture than what is actually occurring, which could affect the child's overall assessment scores.

When a test is formally translated, the similarity across the original and translated version of the test needs to be equivalent, a concept aptly named equivalence (Barrueco et al., 2012). There are three key types of equivalence necessary for the translation to be considered high-quality (Barrueco et al., 2012): (a) content equivalence, (b) semantic equivalence, and (c) structural equivalence. Content equivalence requires the test questions and domains be vetted to ensure relevance to the cultural group of the population being assessed. Semantic equivalence ensures that each version of the test is actually assessing the same constructs and difficulty level in both languages. For example, a common word in one language may translate into a more complicated word in the new language or the reverse may be true. Finally, structural equivalence requires that the structure of the test needs to remain the same, including test item formats and response options. For example, a test that uses multiple choice for one language should use multiple choice for the translated items and not change the test items to an open-ended response.

Given that there are a small number of tests developed to assess sign languages, or are translated into sign language, translations of tests are frequently used when administering a test. In these cases, the examiner might administer the test in another language directly (if they use the language), collaborate with an ancillary examiner, or use an interpreter to translate test content. These types of test administration also pose threats to validity, while at the same time adding an additional layer of complexity to the test administration and procedures. For example, even if an assessor frequently administers a specific test in another language, interpreting it the exact same way each time is challenging. Although many research projects are able to address this issue through the use of videotaping to ensure consistency across administrations, the use of video in an assessment is more challenging in school-based practices. In order to use video of an assessment to determine consistency, two conditions must be met: (a) a photo release signed by the parent, and (b) time allotted for the assessor to re-watch previous assessments and reflect on whether their administration is consistent across learners. With these conditions, an assessor has the ability to increase the standardization of their administration in another language. However, meeting these conditions is challenging when the assessor is relying on additional staff to assist with the translations, such an ancillary examiner or interpreter.

A consideration with the interpretation of English assessments for d/Dhh children includes interpretation from an oral to a sign language. Crossing language modalities impacts the semantic equivalence of the assessment, as the use of a visual language may modify the content or difficulty of the test (Miller, 2008; Qi & Mitchell, 2011). When the sign is visually similar to the object being referenced, a concept known as iconicity, it may inadvertently give a child the cues to the correct answers (Ansell & Pagliaro, 2001, 2006; Miller, 2008; Thurlow et al., 2008). In addition, sign languages may have linguistic structures that do not exist in English, which can either increase the level of difficulty of the item or provide additional strategies to help solve the item (Ansel & Pagliaro, 2001, 2006; Kritzer et al., 2004). For example, in an expressive vocabulary assessment a learner may be asked to define the word clock, but the sign for clock is "time on the wall", which provides the learner with the answer. Although translation can provide an avenue for assessment when limited options are available, "because the disadvantages of translating or developing remain severe, researchers and practitioners should select from existing signed language assessments when possible" (Henner et al., 2018). An example of how a learner's language can be assessed across four languages and two modalities, with collaboration among an international team of educators, can be seen in Box 3.1.

Accommodations. The assessment of d/Dhh learners using standardized tests often includes the use of accommodations in order to access test directions and content (Qi & Mitchell, 2011). Accommodations typically employed with a d/Dhh learner include: (a) extended time, (b) use of a sign language interpreter for test directions, (c) separate locations for testing, and (d) computer administration (Cawthon, 2007; Cawthon &

Box 3.1 Bram

Bram is a sixteen-year-old immigrant from the Netherlands. His father passed away a few years ago and his mother's job moved them to the midwestern United States last year. He has a bilateral severe-to-profound hearing loss and uses both spoken language and sign language. He has a cochlear implant and consistently uses it. Bram's family speaks Dutch and his mother's second language is English. He used a combination of spoken Dutch and the Sign Language of the Netherlands (SLN) in school prior to moving to the United States. He is currently in a separate classroom for d/Dhh children learning ASL and English for the majority of the school day, and was recently mainstreamed for math in a general education classroom with an ASL interpreter.

Bram was assessed through a combination of standardized assessments and performance-based assessments. Even though Bram has only been learning ASL for approximately a year, standardized tests were administered by a school psychologist through an ASL interpreter. The interpreter has had some basic training on assessment, but does not know the intricacies of the specific tests used. No tests designed specifically to examine ASL proficiency were used. There was no one available to assess Bram's SLN abilities, but the district paid for the translation of key school records pertaining to his sign language development. A family interview was also conducted with a spoken language interpreter.

In order to get a better portrait of Bram's SLN skills, the assessment team was able to connect with professionals in the Netherlands to assist with the assessment. An hour-long informal language proficiency interview was conducted via video conference and the findings were shared with the US assessment team to be included in the final report. His oral Dutch proficiency was also included in the report by asking his parents to complete a formal language survey about his skills in the home and community.

Bram's English reading and writing skills were significantly below age range, as expected for a new language learner of English. However, he has quickly acquired ASL over the past year. Parent report indicates that he rarely has an opportunity to practice spoken Dutch outside of the home, but he remains in contact with friends from the Netherlands via social media and email in written Dutch.

Online Research Laboratory, 2008). Similar accommodations are often employed with students who are bilingual, as the use of simplified English is also a common strategy to provide access to the test content for this population (Abedi et al., 2000, 2005). Although the above accommodations have been deemed potentially useful with d/Dhh learners and bilingual children, they should only be used when it is determined that a specific child will benefit from them (Qi & Mitchell, 2011). When selected accommodations are not appropriate for the specific learner or employed erroneously, they may be a threat to validity by altering the skills or constructs being assessed (Cawthon, 2007).

Informal Assessments of Language Proficiency

Informal approaches to assessments are also valuable tools to examine language learning and growth over time and add to the comprehensive language profile. Common informal assessment approaches include: (a) Naturalistic Assessment, (b) Play Based Assessment and Performance Based Assessment, (c) Curriculum Based Assessment, (d) Standards Based Assessment, (e) Portfolio Assessment, and (f) Dynamic Assessment. Each has its own theoretical frameworks and approaches to gathering assessment data. All of the common informal assessment approaches fall within one of the three models of informal assessment: (a) embedded models, (b) authentic models, and (c) mediated models (Losardo & Syverson, 2011). Embedded models examine learners' abilities across their natural contexts. Authentic models examine learners' abilities in authentic, or real-world, tasks. Mediated models examine the relationship between teaching and learning, as well as the potential for new learning. See Table 3.2 for an outline of these models and the informal assessment approaches that fall within them.

Data collected through these assessment approaches are typically documented in the form of rubrics, checklists, rating scales, observational notes, student work samples, and portfolios (Helm et al., 2007). The strategies of documentation have strong roots in early childhood education and care as a part of monitoring learning over time (e.g., Reggio Emilia Curriculum Philosophy or Montessori Education). Strong documentation strategies are necessary to capture and preserve high-quality assessment

TABLE 3.2 Informal Assessment Approaches for a Comprehensive Language Profile

Assessment Model	Assessment Approach	Theoretical Framework	Definition	Example(s)
Embedded Model (Losardo & Syverson, 2011)	Naturalistic Assessment	Ecological Theory (Bronfenbrenner, 1979)	Naturalistic assessment includes observations of the child in their natural environments while engaged in authentic situations with familiar people.	A DML is observed by their teacher during a typical classroom lesson for language use and understanding. The teacher has proficiency in the child's instructional and home languages. An observation form that records the learner's language skills (in all languages used) and context of the observation is used to document the information.
	Play-based Assessment	Ecological Theory (Bronfenbrenner, 1979)	Play-based Assessment is a form of naturalistic assessment where a child's abilities are observed and recorded during play.	A DML's home language is observed while playing at a local playground with their family during an Early Intervention home visit. Documentation occurs through the use of a traditional running record that captures each language and social interaction that occurs.

(*Continued*)

TABLE 3.2 (Continued)

Assessment Model	Assessment Approach	Theoretical Framework	Definition	Example(s)
Authentic Model (Losardo & Syverson, 2011)	Performance-Based Assessment	Social-Constructivist Theory (New, 1998) & Ecological Theory (Bronfenbrenner, 1979)	Performance based assessment requires children to demonstrate their knowledge by performing a task that is typical to their daily activities.	A DML's performance in reading and writing is observed during a group project. The learning is documented through the use of a language checklist of age appropriate language skills that the teacher updates routinely over the course of the year.
	Curriculum-Based assessment*	Social-Constructivist Theory (New, 1998) & Ecological Theory (Bronfenbrenner, 1979)	Curriculum-based assessment examines a child's learning of the curriculum being taught, typically by requiring a child to perform a specific skill or activity based on the lesson.	During an ASL lesson the teacher deconstructs an ASL poem to the class for the use of spatial relationships. Using the poem as a model, the students are asked to: (a) identify the major components of ASL in the poem and (b) create their own ASL poem. Documentation occurs through: (a) an anecdotal record of the number of questions the DML got correct and (b) a rubric evaluating the newly created poem.

Developing Comprehensive Language Profile 83

Assessment Model	Assessment Approach	Theoretical Framework	Definition	Example(s)
	Portfolio Assessment (Arter & Spandel, 1992; Lynch & Struewing, 2001)	Social-Constructivist Theory (New, 1998) & Ecological Theory (Bronfenbrenner, 1979)	Portfolio assessment is a purposive collection of a learner's work and other relevant assessment data. There are four types of portfolios that can be employed in a classroom: Showcase, Evaluative, Working, and Archival.	A set of work samples from class are included in a DML's portfolio to demonstrate their best examples of writing ability (Showcase Portfolio). A compilation of video sign language samples is collected and integrated into a video portfolio at the end of the year that is designed to demonstrate growth over time (Evaluative). Virtually all of a DML's formal and informal language outcomes during lessons are kept and stored for later use in a more targeted portfolio (Working). Selected information from a school year is included in a portfolio that will follow the DML across multiple grades and teachers (Archival).

(*Continued*)

TABLE 3.2 (Continued)

Assessment Model	Assessment Approach	Theoretical Framework	Definition	Example(s)
	Standards-Based Assessment*	Bloom (1956)	In Standards-Based assessment, performance-based tasks are used to determine if a learner has mastered the state or local standards addressed by the instructional content.	A DML is given a set of tasks to evaluate their skills in relation to the *Gallaudet K-12 ASL Content Standards* (Gallaudet University Laurent Clerc National Deaf Education Center & California School for the Deaf-Fremont, 2018). Each set of standards are developmentally more advanced than the previous one, allowing educators to track progress over time as learners acquire new skills in ASL.
Mediated Model (Losardo & Syverson, 2011)	Dynamic Assessment (Poehner & Lantolf, 2005)	Vygotsky's Social-Interactionist Theory (1962)	Dynamic assessment is a way of evaluating which instructional strategies are effective in supporting learning for a child through a test, teach, and test again approach.	A DML is assessed on a set of vocabulary words. Those words are then taught to them. The words are reassessed for acquisition. This process is repeated with new words until successful teaching strategies are identified.

* There are also traditional tests used for summative assessment that are considered as curriculum-based or standards-based assessment.

and observation data (Helm et al., 2007) to be utilized within the comprehensive language profile.

Informal approaches to assessment are commonly used in the classroom setting, or in the home environment for younger children, as informal assessments are able to capture smaller increments of learning and can provide information to inform instructional content or strategy use more frequently. Informal approaches also often occur in natural environments that can address functional communication skills in addition to formal language development. A strength of informal approaches to assessment is that they can be administered more frequently than standardized measures. In Box 3.2, we can see how Xiao Yan's educational team conducted informal assessments (observations, language samples, and family interviews) to gain a profile of her language skills.

Informal assessment approaches are considered better able to meet the developmental, cultural, and linguistic needs of learners, especially young children (Barrueco et al., 2012; Espinosa & López, 2007). While informal assessments have the potential to reduce the inherent biases of the assessment tools themselves, they remain vulnerable to the cultural and linguistic biases of the assessors, as not all educators will understand the culture or language(s) of the child or the assessors may have their own cultural influences or preconceptions about language learning (Espinosa & López, 2007). Therefore, educators need to engage in careful reflection about their own potential biases about children and their cultural and linguistic contexts, in order to reduce assumptions about the child's performance and the data collected, while keeping cultural overgeneralizations to a minimum (Pizzo & Chilvers, 2016). For more information on informal assessment approaches see Table 3.2.

Supporting the Assessment of Specific Languages

An understanding of the major considerations unique to assessing a specific language is important, as each language has particular features important to developing proficiency. For example, sign language is a visual language that includes constructs such as the use of space and facial expressions. Without knowledge of these important dimensions of the language, major

> **BOX 3.2 XIAO YAN**
>
> Xiao Yan is a ten-year-old girl, who was born in Canada, moved to Hong Kong at age one, and returned to Canada at age four. She has a severe-to-profound sensorineural hearing loss. She has been wearing bilateral hearing aids since she was approximately five years old and was diagnosed with Down syndrome shortly after birth. There are multiple languages present in the home. Her father is from the Philippines and speaks Filipino and English. Her mother is from China and speaks Mandarin, Cantonese, and English. With English as their common language, her parents use it as the primary language in the home, even when they lived in Hong Kong. Since returning to Canada, Xiao Yan has attended Mandarin school on Saturdays in addition to her schooling during the week in English.
>
> Xiao Yan's language, sensory, and cognitive abilities made assessment more challenging. Naturalistic observations were conducted in the classroom and the playground. Language samples were conducted in English by the classroom teacher. A teacher of the d/Deaf and hard of hearing who is also fluent in Mandarin conducted an interview with the family to document her Mandarin skills.
>
> Currently Xiao Yan has limited expressive language skills. She used mostly one-to-two-word sentences that were functional in nature (e.g., "bathroom please" or "more crackers"). She also used gestures and pointing to supplement her spoken language skills. When she was upset, she would scream or hit the table to convey her emotions. Her receptive abilities were unclear, as she answered questions or responded to teacher prompts inconsistently. She often walked away from people who were actively speaking to her. While she was able to identify a short number of sight words (mostly names of her classmates), she is unable to engage in reading tasks.
>
> Xiao Yan's level of English was more developed than her Mandarin skills. Although she could repeat some basic Mandarin words, she could not produce them independently to meet her needs. She appeared to enjoy approximating Chinese characters; however, she was unable to generate a complete Mandarin sentence in writing.

assessment findings may be overlooked or misinterpreted. As previously noted, finding an assessor that is proficient in all of a learner's languages is challenging and may impact the results of an assessment (Espinosa & López, 2007). As such, collaboration among professionals, use of video technology, and additional resources may be needed to accurately select and conduct assessments.

Assessing Natural Sign Language(s)

There are a limited number of formal assessments designed to capture sign language proficiency when compared to those of spoken language (see Singleton & Suppella, 2011 and Henner et al., 2018 for more information about specific assessments available). Any tests of sign language should be conducted by someone qualified in both the testing methods and the language itself (Singleton & Suppella, 2011). Learners who are d/Dhh often modify their sign language for the person with whom they are interacting; therefore, if the examiner has less advanced sign language skills, the learner might not demonstrate their full range of abilities in the test session.

In the United States and Canada, for example, there are a small number of assessments designed to measure ASL proficiency. The best practice includes the use of established ASL assessments for learners who use ASL (Henner et al., 2018). Even when using high-quality ASL assessments, there may be limitations when assessing a child who uses a constructed sign system in self-contained and mainstream classrooms, as the child's signs may not be represented on the test (Henner et al., 2018). When examining ASL abilities, the assessor should also have knowledge of regional and local signs used in the school context (Jamieson & Simmons, 2011), as the child may be using local signs that are not represented on formal ASL tests, and the majority of learners who have a home language other than English will be first generation and likely learning ASL (Pizzo, 2016). Consulting a sign language specialist can assist an assessor in selecting and implementing sign language assessments. The use of informal assessment approaches when assessing sign languages is also a necessary component of a comprehensive language profile.

Additional Natural Sign Language(s) in the Home

When creating a comprehensive language profile, it is important to include the extent and nature of sign language use in the home. For DMLs, the sign language of the home may be different from the sign language of the school. For example, parents who are d/Dhh and move from Mexico to the United States may use Mexican Sign Language at home while the child is learning ASL in school. The assessment of any other sign languages that the learner may have learned is crucial for DMLs. For example, an adolescent learner may have moved to Australia from the UK. In this case, the learner was using British Sign Language (BSL) and is now learning Australian Sign Language, or Auslan. While assessing the learner's use of Auslan is typical, examining the learner's use of BSL is also important when considering a comprehensive language profile, especially for d/Dhh immigrants.

Assessing multiple sign languages is challenging, as it requires the ability to engage the learner in both languages. If the learner was using that language in their previous school setting, a review of their school records may be able to provide some insight into those abilities despite the inability to compile new assessment data on this language. In addition, video conferencing may be a way to include an ancillary examiner, interpreter, or language proficient assessor who is capable of collecting new data on the learner's sign skills in a sign language from a different country.

Assessing Spoken Language

When deemed appropriate for an individual learner, spoken language assessment should be included in the comprehensive language profile. A review of the learner's language background and audiogram are necessary in planning a spoken language assessment. For DMLs that use spoken language, assessment by someone who is familiar with their personal speech characteristics might be necessary to fully document their abilities (Jamieson & Simmons, 2011). For assessments of the learner's home spoken language skills, finding an assessor familiar with their speech may be challenging, as the school personnel are not guaranteed to know or use the learner's home language. Even if it is not possible to find an assessor that knows the learner's speech characteristics, the school personnel should do their best to capture the learner's language abilities while documenting the potential limitations of the assessment context. By recognizing the limitations of the assessment, the assessor is able to better interpret scores gained by the assessment tool or observation strategy used.

In addition, spoken language assessments should be selected in collaboration with speech and language specialists, and should consider issues of auditory accessibility in the assessment (Pizzo & Chilvers, 2019). For example, an old cassette, a scratched CD, or poor speaker quality on a computer in an assessment that requires the use of audio will not create optimal conditions when assessing spoken language. As such, any technology used in an assessment should be vetted prior to administration. Assessors should also select an appropriate acoustical environment for the spoken language assessment. Finally, the test session should be discontinued immediately if at any point the content is inaccessible to the learner or they become frustrated by the task.

Assessing General Communication Skills

Regardless of whether a direct assessment of their spoken language in the home is administered, it is essential for the learner's varied communication abilities in the home to be addressed. Communication abilities include all of the ways in which a learner engages and conveys information to others in the home above and beyond what conventional language can convey (Bruce & Borders, 2015). If direct assessment cannot be performed, formal or informal family interviews are important in understanding the day-to-day language and communicative life of the learner in the home.

Assessing Home Signs

When discussing a learner's communication patterns, it is also important to document their use of home signs, or gestural communication systems used to communicate in the home (Goldin-Meadow, 2003). Their sign systems may include many properties, but not all, of conventional language (Goldin-Meadow et al., 2014). The characteristics of a learner's sign system used in the home can provide a window into the linguistic features a learner commands, as well as the functional communication of the learner. Therefore, it is important to understand a learner's use of home signs when going through the process of completing a high-quality language profile.

Assessing Written Language

For many DMLs, their only access to the spoken language of the school or broader community may be through reading and writing. While assessing a language through the use of print complicates the assessment due to the addition of reading skills in addition to the language skills for this area, it may be the only way to capture what a learner knows about the language. In addition to academic literacy, functional literacy tasks may also be necessary to determine what skills a learner possesses and how they functionally use the language in their broader environment and community. To see an example of how academic ASL skills were assessed and assisted a team in determining recommendations, goals, and objectives for Mariana, see Box 3.3.

Box 3.3 Mariana

Mariana is a six-year-old girl of Mexican descent born in the United States. Her parents are monolingual Spanish speakers. She has two older male siblings and a younger sister. Mariana was delivered after a full-term pregnancy. Her newborn hearing screening indicated a potential hearing loss; however, lack of access to quality healthcare resulted in her not being formally identified for services until 18 months of age, when her parents grew concerned about her slowly progressing spoken language skills. At that time, Mariana was diagnosed with a bilateral severe-to-profound hearing loss and received a cochlear implant. She also began receiving Early Intervention services, once a week in the home and twice a week in a center-based play group. Mariana was the most successful using American Sign Language (ASL) in her Early Intervention setting, and appears to understand some Spanish at home. At age three, Mariana transitioned into a preschool class at a school for the d/Deaf.

When Mariana turned six years old, she received her triennial psychoeducational evaluation to examine her progress in learning. The assessor was trained in the assessment of d/Dhh children and administered individualized, standardized assessments using ASL. This battery of tests targeted cognitive ability, developmental skills, and content area knowledge. The school's ASL specialist and speech and language therapist also provided language assessment information for the evaluation. Classroom observations were also completed and data was collected from the teacher using performance-based measures of classroom learning.

Findings from the assessments included cognitive development for non-verbal tasks in the above-average range, social-emotional development on par for children her age, and grade-level math skills. Her language skills in ASL were stronger in regards to her functional and social communication; however, her academic ASL skills were identified as an area of need. Her spoken English was minimal, and her spoken Spanish was unable to be assessed at that time due to the lack of access to qualified assessors. Testing indicated early first-grade reading skills. In her classroom, she has demonstrated the ability to identify over a hundred words in English print, but remains challenged in answering comprehension questions about grade-level text when read independently.

Involving Families in the Assessment Process

Families must be involved in the assessment process, as they are important to both the collection and interpretation of data. Families should be consulted when creating the assessment plan. Including assessment goals that are family-driven increases the applicability and relevance of the assessment data collected. Assessment information about how the child communicates at home is also important. Information from families is key to demonstrating a complete portrait of a learner's linguistic abilities across contexts. Finally, families should be asked for input and opinions on the preliminary findings before the profile is completed. Asking for feedback reduces data collection errors, provides context for interpretation of information, and allows for examination of language skills across varied settings.

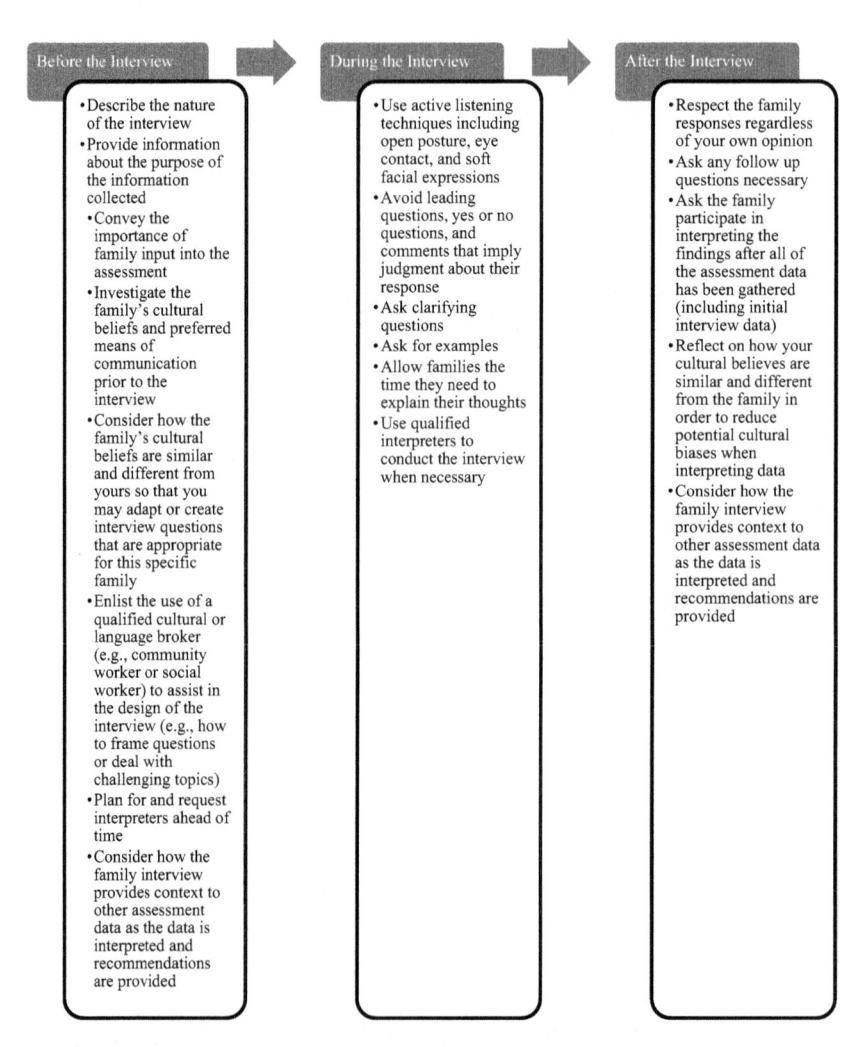

Before the Interview	During the Interview	After the Interview
• Describe the nature of the interview
• Provide information about the purpose of the information collected
• Convey the importance of family input into the assessment
• Investigate the family's cultural beliefs and preferred means of communication prior to the interview
• Consider how the family's cultural beliefs are similar and different from yours so that you may adapt or create interview questions that are appropriate for this specific family
• Enlist the use of a qualified cultural or language broker (e.g., community worker or social worker) to assist in the design of the interview (e.g., how to frame questions or deal with challenging topics)
• Plan for and request interpreters ahead of time
• Consider how the family interview provides context to other assessment data as the data is interpreted and recommendations are provided	• Use active listening techniques including open posture, eye contact, and soft facial expressions
• Avoid leading questions, yes or no questions, and comments that imply judgment about their response
• Ask clarifying questions
• Ask for examples
• Allow families the time they need to explain their thoughts
• Use qualified interpreters to conduct the interview when necessary	• Respect the family responses regardless of your own opinion
• Ask any follow up questions necessary
• Ask the family participate in interpreting the findings after all of the assessment data has been gathered (including initial interview data)
• Reflect on how your cultural believes are similar and different from the family in order to reduce potential cultural biases when interpreting data
• Consider how the family interview provides context to other assessment data as the data is interpreted and recommendations are provided

FIGURE 3.2 High-quality Interview Techniques

Family-centered practices have been widely used in special education, especially early intervention, as a framework for working with families in various aspects of program and service delivery (see chapter 2, Bowen & Baker, 2022; Woods et al., 2011). Family-centered practices include (a) affording families respect, (b) responding to families' concerns about their child, and (c) supporting families' decision-making by providing unbiased information and clear explanations (Division for Early Childhood of the Council for Exceptional Children, National Association for the Education of Young Children, & National Head Start Association, 2014; Woods et al., 2011). With limited assessments in languages other than English, families are key informants that share information about their DMLs' home language and/or communication skills.

Family-centered assessment practices may look different from other family-centered practices in action (Stone-MacDonald et al., 2018). Specifically, interviewing families to gather information requires a specific skill set that supports the rapport between the interviewer and the family, while working to obtain valid information about a learner's language abilities. It is important that we value families as the informants and experts about their child. Although families know their child best, they may not feel as confident in an interview, as they may feel intimidated or nervous by the assessment process. High-quality interview techniques are presented in Figure 3.2, and in Box 3.4, we see this in action with Kaia's family, as well as in other vignettes provided in this chapter.

Interpreting Assessment Data

Upon completion of a learner's comprehensive language profile, a report or document is used to capture the information gathered. During the writing process, the assessor must interpret and reflect on the data. In addition, care must be taken to use strengths-based language while minimizing the influence of bias in the final document. References to the child's appearance, terms such as "cute" or "pretty", and subjective evaluations of a child's abilities without supporting data should be avoided. In addition, as the assessor is interpreting data from a variety of assessments (e.g., standardized or informal assessments), a thorough discussion of how

Box 3.4 Kaia

Kaia is a thirteen-year-old girl born in Massachusetts, USA. Her parents are Cape Verdean and speak Creole, Portuguese, and English. She has one sibling, a younger sister. Kaia has a bilateral moderate sensorineural hearing loss that was diagnosed shortly after birth. She has had consistent access to high-quality health care and hearing aids, which she uses regularly. Kaia is educated in a general education classroom in a public school, with itinerant services provided by a teacher of the d/Deaf and hard of hearing (d/Dhh), a speech and language specialist, and a reading specialist. Her language skills include a combination of American Sign Language (ASL), spoken English, and Creole.

Data was collected to examine her current level of language skills. Classroom assessments including curriculum-based and performance-based tests of language and reading skills were conducted by her general education teacher and itinerant teacher of the d/Dhh. Checklists were collected from the teacher of the d/Dhh regarding Kaia's current levels of ASL. The speech and language specialist provided information gathered through naturalistic assessment about Kaia's use of spoken English skills. A family interview was conducted with Kaia's parents to examine her use of language in the home and community.

Classroom assessments indicated that Kaia is able to engage with academic content appropriately with the support of her ASL interpreter. Without the interpreter, she can engage peers in social conversation and play, but will frequently misunderstand questions posed to her, especially those about academic content. She has developed some strategies to address misunderstandings, such as summarizing what was said and asking for confirmation. Her reading and writing skills are approximately a year below grade level, yet she has been making steady progress in these areas. Parent interviews indicated that, with her hearing aids, Kaia is able to engage her family in Creole, but has similar misunderstandings in the home as she does at school. She rarely interacts with the Portuguese language in

> the home or community. Her mom attends bimonthly ASL classes offered at the school for the d/Deaf, but her father is unable to go to the classes because he works in the evenings. Kaia's younger sister and mother are progressing in their ASL developments; whereas, her father only knows a few isolated signs. Her sister has taken on the role of interpreter for Kaia within the family when necessary, translating ASL directly to Creole or vice versa.

the data relate to each other is needed. For example, a child may perform well on a standardized test in an individualized setting, but struggle with demonstrating the same knowledge on a performance-based assessment in the classroom. One assessor may interpret this finding as the standardized test overestimated the child's abilities. Another assessor may focus on the role of the environment, including the potential barriers to language input in a busy classroom, in allowing the child to demonstrate their true abilities. These differences are key in the types of educational goals needed for this child.

For DMLs, these kinds of contextual situations are important to consider as language can be context-dependent. For example, a DML may use their home language more frequently in a classroom that has a number of other students who also use that language. Another example may be that a DML may modify their language abilities to be aimed at the person with whom they are conversing (e.g., using more or less advanced language). Therefore, it is necessary to consider all possible explanations for a learner's performance, including: (a) the type of assessment used, (b) who is administering it, (c) where it is being administered, and (d) the learner's conversational partners, in order to fully explain what the learner can do and how they do it.

As such, the role of the assessor's orientations (Lucas & Villegas, 2013) is particularly important during the meaning-making stage of a comprehensive language profile. For instance, institutional and individual biases based on race, language, and/or culture may influence the interpretation of the findings. One strategy for reducing bias in assessment is to involve families in the interpretation process. Asking for a family's thoughts and perspectives on the data before writing the report can help to resolve discrepancies and clarify any information as necessary. By working with families at every stage of the assessment process, the clarity and validity of the findings are improved.

Conclusion

DMLs have varied exposure and use of languages in the home, community, and school. While each DML is unique in their language experiences, there are some broad recommendations that can help in the development of a comprehensive language profile:

- Evaluate all of the languages in a DML's life.
- Use multiple sources of assessment data (e.g., performance-based assessment, standardized assessment, and curriculum-based assessment) to adequately capture a learner's abilities across languages and within various settings (e.g., home, community, and school).
- Use standardized test results with caution as significant threats to their validity are likely when used with DMLs.
- Consider the availability of assessments in languages other than English, including access to standardized assessments of sign language (see Barrueco et al., 2012 for a comprehensive review of Spanish language assessments available for purchase) for those children who use sign as a primary mode of communication.
- Work with families to collect information about a learner's skills and interpret assessment data to reduce bias in the language profile and contribute to the quality of the final assessment summary.

Developing a comprehensive language profile is important to the design, implementation, and evaluation of a DML's educational program and services. Using a linguistically responsive framework that values the families as key participants in gathering information about their children will improve the assessment process for both children and their families. By systematically examining the entirety of a learner's linguistic and communication repertoire, educators can improve the quality of the educational program and strive to promote language learning across the years.

Discussion Questions

1. Describe the process of developing a comprehensive language profile.
2. What are the qualifications an assessor needs to have in order to conduct valid assessments and reduce bias?
3. Brainstorm ways to engage families more actively in the assessment process.
4. Reflect on your own biases regarding the use of various assessment approaches to measure language proficiency for DMLs.

Resources

Organizations

- Early Childhood Technical Assistance Center (http://ectacenter.org): ECTA helps build state and local system capacity to improve outcomes for children with disabilities and their families. Their website includes information about working with families to get high-quality assessment data. While they focus specifically on the Child Outcomes Summary process—a national OSEP project to gather information about how children are progressing in special education—the videos and resources can be beneficial to promote assessment practices.
- National Research Center for Hispanic Children and Families (www.hispanicresearchcenter.org): Since 2013, this organization has been working to "advance understanding of early care and education (ECE) issues for low income Hispanic families." It regularly publishes research, webinars, and blog posts on topics relevant to that mission.
- TESOL (www.tesol.org): The largest organization in the world focused exclusively on English language teaching for speakers of other languages. Publishes TESOL Quarterly, a scholarly journal publishing high-quality peer-reviewed conceptual and research articles.

Websites

- ¡Colorín Colorado! (www.colorincolorado.org/node/36865/research): ¡Colorín Colorado! is a national multimedia project that offers bilingual, research-based documents, activities, and advice for educators and families of English language learners (ELLs). It includes a list of current research and reports on assessment of ELLs.
- WIDA Can Do Descriptors (https://wida.wisc.edu/teach/can-do/descriptors): The Can Do Descriptors highlight what language learners can do at various stages of language development. The current edition is organized around four overarching communicative purposes: Recount, Explain, Argue, and Discuss. Also see the WIDA assessment list for a variety of tools for various learners: https://wida.wisc.edu/assess/choosing-assessment

Reports and Position Statements

- National Association of the Deaf Position Statement on High Stakes Assessment and Accountability (www.nad.org/about-us/position-statements/position-statement-on-high-stakes-assessments-and-accountability/): This position statement outlines best practices and principles on the use of standardized assessment with d/Dhh populations, specifically those used for high-stakes decision-making.
- The National Center on Parent, Family, and Community Engagement (https://eclkc.ohs.acf.hhs.gov/sites/default/files/pdf/family-engagement-ongoing-child-assessment-eng.pdf): This report addresses strategies to share child assessment data with families of young children.

Journal Articles

- Acar, S., & Blasco, P. (2018). Guidelines for collaborating with interpreters in early intervention and/or early childhood special education. *Young Exceptional Children, 21*(3), 170–184. This article addresses "how to's" for educators looking to use interpreters when talking with families of children in early intervention or early childhood special education.

Family-Centered Brief

FAMILY-CENTERED BRIEF

CHAPTER 3
Understanding Language Skills Using Assessments

by Lianna Pizzo & Laurie Ford

PURPOSE OF CHAPTER
Presents information regarding the assessment of children who are d/Deaf and hard of hearing (d/Dhh) and how families should be involved in the process.

DEFINING KEY TERMS
Comprehensive language profile
A summary of your child's spoken and/or sign language skills that uses assessment results to describe your child's strengths as a multilingual learner

Standardized assessments
- taken by all children in school
- the test may be translated the test or make some changes to help your child participate

Informal assessments
- give information about a child's progress
- observations, checklists, interviews with family members, and/or portfolios that include samples of a child's work

THE FAMILY'S ROLE IN ASSESSMENTS

Share information about your child in an **interview** or a **report form**

Ask if you have any questions or need more information

Your parenting skills will not be judged

THE FAMILY'S ROLE IN RESULTS
You will be involved in reviewing assessment results and making decisions about your child's educational goals and program. You may be encouraged to:

provide more information about results & request an interpreter if needed

ask questions about results & request them in your home language

correct information from results that you think is not true

RESOURCES
¡Colorín Colorado! www.colorincolorado.org/families

The National Center on Parent, Family, and Community Engagement
eclkc.ohs.acf.hhs.gov/sites/default/files/pdf/family-engagement-ongoing-child-assessment-eng.pdf

Deaf and Hard of Hearing Multilingual Learners: Foundations, Strategies, and Resources (2022)

Note

1 Bilingual learner is defined as a child who has a home language other than English.

References

Abedi, J., Courtney, M., Mirocha, J., Leon, S., & Goldberg, J. (2005). Language accommodations for English Language Learners in large-scale assessments: Bilingual dictionaries and linguistic modification. CSE Report 666. *National Center for Research on Evaluation, Standards, and Student Testing (CRESST)*.

Abedi, J., Lord, C., Hofstetter, C., & Baker, E. (2000). Impact of accommodation strategies on English language learners' test performance. *Educational Measurement: Issues and Practice, 19*(3), 16–26.

AERA, APA, & NCME. (2014). *Standards for educational and psychological testing*. Washington, DC: Joint Committee on the Standards for Educational and Psychological Testing of the American Educational Research Association, the American Psychological Association, and the National Council on Measurement in Education.

Ansell, E., & Pagliaro, C. M. (2001). Effects of a signed translation on the types and difficulties of arithmetic story problems. *Focus on Learning Problems in Mathematics, 23*(2-3), 41–69.

Ansell, E., & Pagliaro, C. M. (2006). The relative difficulty of signed arithmetic story problems for primary-level deaf and hard of hearing students. *Journal of Deaf Studies and Deaf Education, 11*(2), 153–170. https://doi.org/10.1093/deafed/enj030

Arter, J. A., & Spandel, V. (1992). Using portfolios of student work in instruction and assessment. *Educational Measurement: Issues and Practice*, 11 (1), 36–44.

Baker, S., & Scott, J. (2016). Sociocultural and academic considerations for school-age d/Deaf and hard of hearing multilingual learners: A case study of a Deaf Latina. *American Annals of the Deaf, 161*(1), 43–55. https://doi.org/10.1353/aad.2016.0010

Barrueco, S., López, M., Ong, C., & Lozano, P. (2012). *Assessing Spanish-English bilingual preschoolers: A guide to best approaches and measures*. Brookes.

Bialystok, E. (2013). The impact of bilingualism on language and literacy development. In T. K. Bahatia & W. C. Ritchie (Eds.), *The handbook of bilingualism and multilingualism* (2nd ed., pp. 624–648). Blackwell.

Bloom, B. S. (1956). *Taxonomy of educational objectives, handbook: The cognitive domain.* David McKay.

Bowen, S. K., & Baker, S. (2022). Family engagement: Developing partnerships for d/Deaf and hard of hearing multilingual learners. In J. E. Cannon, C. Guardino, & P. V. Paul (Eds.), *Deaf and hard of hearing multilingual learners: Foundations, strategies, and resources* (pp. 30–66). Routledge.

Brentari, D., Fenlon, J., & Cormier, K. A. (2018). *Sign language phonology.* Oxford University Press.

Bronfenbrenner, U. (1979). *The ecology of human development.* Harvard University Press.

Bruce, S. M., & Borders, C. (2015). Communication and language in learners who are deaf and hard of hearing with disabilities: Theories, research, and practice. *American Annals of the Deaf, 160*(4), 368–384.

Cannon, J. E., & Guardino, C. (2012). Literacy strategies for deaf/hard of hearing English language learners: Where do we begin? *Deafness and Education International, 14*(2), 78–99. https://doi.org/10.1179/1557069X12Y.0000000006

Cannon, J. E., Guardino, C., & Gallimore, E. (2016). A new kind of heterogeneity: What we can learn from d/Deaf and hard of hearing multilingual learners. *American Annals of the Deaf, 161*(1), pp. 8–16. https://doi.org/10.1353/aad.2016.0015.

Cawthon, S. W. (2007). Hidden benefits and unintended consequences of No Child Left Behind polices for students who are deaf or hard of hearing. *American Educational Research Journal, 44*(3), 460–492. https://doi.org/10.3102/0002831207306760

Cawthon, S. W., & Online Research Laboratory. (2008). Accommodations use for statewide standardized assessments: Prevalence and recommendations for student who are deaf or hard of hearing. *Journal of Deaf Studies and Deaf Education, 13*(1), 55–96. https://doi.org/10.1093/deafed/enm029

Cawthon, S. W., & Wurtz, K. A. (2008). Alternate assessment use with students who are deaf or hard of hearing: An exploratory mixed-methods analysis of portfolio, checklists, and out-of-level test formats. *Journal of Deaf Studies and Deaf Education, 14*(2), 155–177. https://doi.org/10.1093/deafed/enn027

Division for Early Childhood of the Council for Exceptional Children, National Association for the Education of Young Children, & National Head Start Association. (2014). Frameworks for response to intervention in early childhood: Description and implications. *Communication Disorders Quarterly, 35*(2), 108–119.

Duarte, G., & Gutierrez-Gomez, C. (2004, June/July). Early childhood assessment: Best practices and concerns. *NABE News*, p. 5.

Espinosa, L., & López, M. (2007). *Assessment considerations for young English language learners across different levels of accountability*. www.first5la.org/files/AssessmentConsiderationsEnglishLearners.pdf

Eurostat. (2019). Foreign language skills statistics. *Education and Training in the EU—Facts and Figures*. Retrieved August 21, 2019, from https://ec.europa.eu/eurostat/statistics-explained/index.php/Foreign_language_skills_statistics

Gallaudet Research Institute. (2013). *Regional and national summary report of data from the 2011–12 annual survey of deaf and hard of hearing children and youth*. Gallaudet University.

Gallaudet University Laurent Clerc National Deaf Education Center & California School for the Deaf-Fremont. (2018). *ASL content standards: Kindergarten-grade 12*. Gallaudet University Laurent Clerc National Deaf Education Center and California School for the Deaf-Riverside.

Goldin-Meadow, S. (2003). *The resilience of language: What gesture creation in deaf children can tell us about how all children learn language*. Psychology Press.

Goldin-Meadow, S. Namboodiripad, S., Mylander, C., Özyürek, A., & Sancar, B. (2014). The resilience of structure built around the predicate: Homesign gesture systems in Turkish and American deaf children. *Journal of Cognition and Development, 16*(0), 1–26. https://doi.org/10.1080/15248372.2013.803970

Grosjean, F. (2010). Bilingualism, biculturalism, and deafness. *International Journal of Bilingual Education and Bilingualism, 13*(2), 133–145.

Helm, J. H., Beneke, S., & Steinheimer, K. (2007). *Windows on learning: Documenting young children's work* (2nd ed.). Teachers College Press.

Henner, J., Novogrodsky, R., Reis, J., & Hoffmeister, R. (2018). Recent issues in the use of signed language assessments for diagnosis of language disorders in signing deaf and hard of hearing children. *The Journal of Deaf Studies and Deaf Education, 23*(4), 307–316. https://doi.org/10.1093/deafed/eny014

Jamieson, J. R., & Simmons, N. R. (2011). Children and youth who are hard of hearing: Hearing accessibility, acoustical context, and development. In M. Marschark & P. E. Spencer (Eds.), *The oxford handbook of deaf studies, language, and education* (Vol. 2, pp. 290–305). Oxford University Press.

Kids Count Data Center. (2016). *Children who speak a language other than English at home.* https://datacenter.kidscount.org/data/tables/81-children-who-speak-a-language-other-than-english-at-home?loc=1&loct=2#detailed/2/2-52/true/870,573,869,36,868/any/396,397

Kritzer, K., Pagliaro, C., & Ansell, E. (2004). Deaf/hard of hearing students' use of language cues to solve signed story problems. *EdPitt, 1*(1). www.pitt.edu/~edpitt/currentissueKRITZER.html

Losardo, A., & Syverson, A. (2011). *Alternative approaches to assessing young children* (2nd ed.). Brookes.

Lucas, T., & Villegas, A. (2013). Preparing linguistically responsive teachers: Laying the foundation in preservice teacher education. *Theory Into Practice, 52*(2), 98–109. https://doi.org/10.1080/00405841.2013.770327

Lucas, T., Villegas, A., & Freedson-Gonzalez, M. (2008). Linguistically responsive teacher education: Preparing classroom teachers to teach English language learners. *Journal of Teacher Education, 59*(4), 361–373. https://doi.org/10.1177/0022487108322110

Lynch, E. M., & Struewing, N. A. (2001). Children in context: Portfolio assessment in the inclusive early childhood classroom. *Young Exceptional Children, 5*(1), 2–10.

Miller, M. (2008). Sign iconicity and receptive vocabulary testing. *American Annals of the Deaf, 152*(5), 441–449. https://doi.org/10.1353/aad.2008.0008

National Center for Education Statistics. (2018). *The condition of education 2018: English language learners in public schools.* Washington, DC: US Department of Education. Institute of Education Sciences, National Center for Education Statistics. https://nces.ed.gov/programs/coe/pdf/coe_cgf.pdf

New, R. (1998). Theory and praxis in Reggio Emilia. In C. Edwards, L. Gandini, & G. Forman (Eds.), *The hundred languages of children: The Reggio Emilia approach-advanced reflections* (2nd ed., pp. 261–284). Ablex.

Pizzo, L. (2016). d/Deaf and hard of hearing multilingual learners (DMLs): The development of communication and language. *American Annals of the Deaf, 161*(1), 17–32.

Pizzo, L., & Chilvers, A. (2016). Assessment and d/Deaf multilingual learners: Considerations and promising practice. *American Annals of the Deaf, 161*(1), 56–66.

Pizzo, L., & Chilvers, A. (2019). Assessment of language and literacy in children who are d/Deaf and hard of hearing. *Education Sciences, 9*(3), 223.

Poehner, M. E., & Lantolf, J. P. (2005). Dynamic assessment in the language classroom. *Language Teaching Research, 9*(3), 233–265.

Qi, S., & Mitchell, R. E. (2011). Large-scale academic achievement testing of deaf and hard-of-hearing students: Past, present, and future. *Journal of Deaf Studies and Deaf Education, 17*(1), 1–18. https://doi.org/10.1093/deafed/enr028

Robert, M. (2017). *The Bilingual world: a study on bilingualism and its cognitive effects.* https://repositori.upf.edu/bitstream/handle/10230/33988/Serras_Robert_2017.pdf?isAllowed=y&sequence=1

Singleton, S., & Suppella, S. (2011). Assessing children's proficiency in natural signed languages. In M. Marschark & P. E. Spencer (Eds.), *The oxford handbook of deaf studies, language, and education* (Vol. 2, pp. 306–322). Oxford University Press. https://doi.org/10.1093/oxfordhb/9780199750986.013.0022

Stone-MacDonald, A., Pizzo, L., & Feldman, N. (2018). *Fidelity of implementation in assessment of infants and toddlers.* Springer International Press.

Thurlow, M., Johnstone, C., Thompson, S., & Case, B. (2008). Using universal design research and perspectives to increase the validity of scores on large-scale assessments. In R. C. Johnstone & R. E. Mitchell (Eds.), *Testing deaf students in an age of accountability* (pp. 63–75). Gallaudet University Press.

Vygotsky, L. (1962). *Thought and language* (E. Hanfmann & G. Vakar, Eds. & Trans.). The MIT Press.

Woods, J. J., Wilcox, M. J., Friedman, M., & Murch, T. (2011). Collaborative consultation in natural environments: Strategies to enhance family-centered supports and services. *Language, Speech, and Hearing Services in Schools, 42*(3), 379–392. https://doi.org/10.1044/0161-1461(2011/10-0016)

4
Language Development, Assessment, and Intervention for d/Deaf and Hard of Hearing Multilingual Learners

Kathryn Crowe and Mark Guiberson

LEARNING OBJECTIVES

Readers will:

1. Appreciate the complexity of defining multilingual language acquisition and how this can impact d/Deaf and hard of hearing multilingual learners' (DMLs) language skills.
2. Describe features of typical language acquisition for learners who are multilingual.
3. Learn about the state of research on the speech, spoken language, and sign language outcomes of DMLs and the evidence for and against multilingualism.
4. Understand the importance of family language policy in supporting language development and language maintenance for DMLs.
5. Describe strategies, considerations, and resources for assessing the speech and language skills of DMLs.
6. Understand how evidence-based practice relates to intervention and educational support when working with DMLs.

DOI: 10.4324/9781003259176-4

d/Deaf and hard of hearing multilingual learners (DMLs) are a growing population across many countries (Cannon et al., 2016; Crowe & Guiberson, 2019) and an estimated 7,117 spoken languages and 144 sign languages are used around the world (Eberhard et al., 2020). Increased access to language through early detection of hearing loss, earlier fitting of hearing aids and cochlear implants, the availability of advanced hearing devices, and greater awareness of and access to sign languages means that more learners with hearing loss are growing up in environments where access to two or more languages is possible. Raising and educating DMLs to become competent users of more than one language requires the caregivers, educators, and clinicians working with these learners to have an extensive range of skills and knowledge in addition to those necessary for working with monolingual learners. Specific knowledge is needed in the areas of: (a) multilingual language acquisition; and (b) assessment, intervention, and education practices suitable for supporting multilingual learners. This is all in addition to holding current knowledge of best practices for raising and educating d/Deaf and hard of hearing (d/Dhh) learners. Within this chapter we focus on what needs to be considered by caregivers and families, educators, and clinicians when supporting DMLs in gaining the best language competence possible.

Understanding Multilingualism

Defining Multilingualism

Learners vary greatly in their proficiency across languages due to a multitude of factors including: (a) exposure to each language, (b) age of acquisition of each language, (c) opportunities to use each language, (d) domains in which each language is used, (e) the linguistic competence of the language models, and (f) the combination of languages being acquired (Paradis et al., 2011). Reflecting these differences between learners, multilingualism has been defined in many different ways, and many different terms are used to describe children who are acquiring more than one language, such as dual language learners, English learners, English language learners, bilingual, multilingual, linguistically diverse, and polyglot. Definitions of multilingualism vary along dimensions that reflect meaningful differences in the ways that learners acquire their languages, such as the age of acquisition, the broader linguistic context of the community that the child lives in, and whether the multilingualism is additive or subtractive. While definitions of these terms typically only consider spoken languages, the dimensions that they describe are equally applicable to learners acquiring signed languages, or learners acquiring spoken and signed languages.

Learners may become multilingual in either a simultaneous or sequential manner. That is, they may receive frequent exposure to two or more languages regularly from birth, or soon after birth, and simultaneously acquire competence in more than one language (Paradis et al., 2011). After having already acquired a strong foundational basis of phonology, morphology, semantics, and syntax in a first language, learners may acquire additional languages in a sequential manner (Tabors, 2008). The broader linguistic context that the child is acquiring languages in, and developing in, is also important. In some situations, children are acquiring the majority language(s) of their ethnolinguistic community. This is the official language(s) with high status or usage within the community, such as English in the United States or Mandarin in China. In other situations, children are acquiring minority languages of their ethnolinguistic community— languages used less frequently and by a minority group in the larger community, such as Arabic in the United States or Hokkien in China. Finally, looking at the pattern of language gain and language loss over time, multilingualism can also be described as additive or subtractive. Additive multilingualism means that the child is gaining linguistic competence in the languages that they use over time (Paradis et al., 2011), which is the situation that most would assume when thinking of multilingual language acquisition. However, subtractive multilingualism also occurs, where competence in one or more languages is lost as the child grows older (Guiberson et al., 2006; Paradis et al., 2011).

Two examples demonstrating how these three different dimensions of multilingualism may operate for a DML are shown in Box 4.1 and 4.2. Box 4.1 illustrates how Ewa acquired languages sequentially (Polish and then Icelandic and Íslenskt táknmál [Icelandic Sign Language]), used two minority languages (Polish and Íslenskt táknmál), and is showing signs of subtractive multilingualism (loss of Polish language skills). Box 4.2

Box 4.1 Ewa

Ewa is a five-year-old girl with severe-to-profound hearing loss born to Polish parents. Ewa's family moved to Iceland when Ewa was three years old. Ewa has had a cochlear implant since she was 18 months old and was learning to listen and speak in Polish before her move to Iceland. In Iceland, Ewa receives speech-language pathology and education services in Icelandic and Íslenskt táknmál (Icelandic Sign Language), and her parents speak to her in Polish. Like all five-year-old children in Iceland, Ewa has attended preschool five days a week since she was three years old. Ewa is acquiring the new languages well and able to communicate with her peers and teachers in both Icelandic and Icelandic Sign Language. Her parents speak Polish with her at home as they do not speak Icelandic or sign. Ewa's parents are concerned that her Polish language skills seem to be diminishing and that Ewa prefers to speak Icelandic to them, even when she knows that they can't understand her.

Box 4.2 Arjun

Arjun is a nine-year-old boy who lives with his parents and extended family in New Delhi. He has a moderate bilateral hearing loss and has used hearing aids since he was six months old. Members of his family have spoken to him in both Hindi and English since he was born and he is proficient in both languages, showing similar skills to his peers in reading and writing both languages. He attends a mainstream school where he receives his education in Hindi and English. Arjun also learns Punjabi at school as an additional language and is doing well in this class.

exemplifies how Arjun acquired Hindi and English simultaneously, and is now sequentially acquiring Punjabi. He uses three languages which are all majority languages in the community that he lives in and his multilingualism is additive.

Differences in children's language learning environments and experiences can manifest as differences in the speed, sequence, and success of acquisition of each language. Due to this, multilingual learners exhibit more diverse and complex variations than monolingual learners in their language acquisition (Paradis, 2011). When applied to DMLs, many definitions of multilingualism do not capture these diverse and complex variations of this population. Further, such definitions are not helpful to professionals faced with the full scope of multilingual learners in their classrooms and clinics every day. In acknowledging this complexity, this book utilizes a definition of multilingualism that is broad and inclusive (Cannon & Guardino, 2022; see Chapter 1).

Multilingual Advantages, Disadvantages, and Outcomes

Cognitive Advantages and Disadvantages

For a long time, multilingualism was believed by many to be a cause of delays and difficulties in children's development. Children acquiring more than one language were viewed as experiencing delays in their language and cognitive skills, and were often misdiagnosed as having language disorders (Cruz-Ferreira, 2011; Peal & Lambert, 1962). However, there is a growing body of evidence that indicates that multilingualism may have advantages for children (Giovannoli et al., 2020; Gunnerud et al., 2020) and adults (Celik et al., in press) with typical hearing, although this is not unanimously supported in the literature.

Briefly, advantages for hearing multilinguals have been reported in three domains: (a) cognition, (b) neurological protection, and (c) language. The basis of cognitive and neurological advantages is believed to lie in multilinguals having to use the same cognitive processes as monolinguals but at a much higher level, due to the cognitive competition of knowing two languages. Choosing the correct word from the correct language is an example. Consider being shown a picture of a car and being asked, "What is this?" To a monolingual English user, it is simply *car*, but to a multilingual language user who knows three languages it may equally be *car* (English), *auto* (German), or *bil* (Danish). The cognitive consequences of this constant competition within the cognitive-linguistic system may cause executive functions (working memory, switching, and inhibition) and other cognitive functions (selective attention, attention splitting, sustained attention, and metacognition) to become stronger and more efficient than typically seen in monolingual language users (Bialystok & Barac, 2012; Crowe & Cupples, 2020; Miyake et al., 2000).

The hyper-functioning of these systems is considered by some researchers to create a cognitive reserve for multilinguals. Cognitive reserve is "the idea that engagement in stimulating physical or mental activity can act to maintain cognitive functioning in healthy aging and postpone the onset of symptoms in those suffering from dementia" (Bialystok et al., 2012, p. 246). Some studies have found that multilinguals maintain better levels of cognitive functioning as they age, and show less or delayed onset of symptoms associated with dementia than monolinguals (Bialystok et al., 2012; Clare et al., 2016; Perquin et al., 2013).

In contrast to the large body of research investigating the possible cognitive advantages and disadvantages of multilingualism for hearing multilinguals, there has been no research about its effects on DMLs. A small number of studies have investigated cognitive advantages for bimodal multilinguals, both hearing and d/Dhh. Theoretically, the same cognitive advantages may not exist for bimodal bilinguals as the competition required to select and inhibit words in a single modality (e.g., the *car, auto, bil,* example above) does not exist when words can be simultaneously produced across two modalities (e.g., saying *sorry* in English and signing SORRY in Australian Sign Language [Auslan]). Indeed, there are many instances where simultaneous production of words and signs exists, as in simultaneous communication, thus reducing language competition and inhibition. Six studies were identified that investigated cognitive advantages of multilingualism in bimodal bilinguals in a review by Crowe and Cupples (2020). No studies examining DMLs who used more than one spoken or signed language were identified.

Linguistic Advantages, Disadvantages, and Outcomes

In terms of linguistic advantages, in addition to being able to use more than one language, multilinguals have been shown to have advantages in word learning (Bialystok et al., 2009) and metalinguistic tasks associated with phonology, morphology, and syntax (Bialystok & Barac, 2012; Bialystok et al., 2003; Sun et al., 2018). These advantages are hypothesized to arise from the ability of multilingual people to transfer understanding or knowledge about how languages work between the languages they know. At present there is little research evidence to support such a transfer of linguistic knowledge directly between signed languages and spoken and written languages in d/Dhh children (Holzinger & Fellinger, 2014; Tang, 2017), although this may be occurring through processes such as translanguaging. The transfer that occurs has been considered to be a component of a more general *cultural transfer* (Hermans et al., 2008a, 2008b, 2010), which relates to content rather than linguistic and metalinguistic knowledge.

Some researchers have also reported linguistic disadvantages of multilingualism for multilingual children with typical hearing, such as smaller vocabulary size. These differences may diminish as multilingual children get older and their competences in all of their languages increase (Bialystok et al., 2010; Paradis & Jia, 2017). However, studies examining the outcomes of large numbers of multilingual children have not shown long-term negative impacts of multilingualism (Hambly et al., 2013; McLeod et al., 2016). A systematic review of studies that included multilingual children with communication disorders such as specific language impairment, phonological disorders, autism spectrum disorder, and intellectual disability reported that multilingualism is rarely a disadvantage (Uljarević et al., 2016).

Research examining speech, language, and literacy outcomes of DMLs compared to those of their monolingual peers (i.e. d/Dhh and with typical hearing) and multilingual peers (i.e. with typical hearing) is scant. Where evidence does exist, studies examine the spoken language outcomes of DMLs using two or more spoken languages, with or without the use of signed languages, but do not consider the signed language outcomes of DMLs (see Crowe, 2018). Crowe (2018) provides a detailed examination of the literature concerning the outcomes of DMLs, concluding that there is not strong evidence to suggest that DMLs have either better or worse outcomes than their peers. However, it should be noted that existing studies examine only small groups of DMLs, meaning that the currently available evidence does not examine the full range of DMLs. Therefore, it is not yet possible to understand the characteristics of most DMLs, their experiences, or their outcomes.

Multilingual Language Acquisition

The variability of second language acquisition is influenced by learner characteristics and external factors (Guiberson & Banerjee, 2012). Learner characteristics include: (a) age of exposure to a second language; (b) language usage patterns; and (c) language, social, and cognitive skills. External factors include: (a) family level of education and acculturation, (b) family language usage patterns, (c) languages used in classroom instruction or learning, and (d) the quantity and quality of exposure to both languages. Despite this variability, multilingual learners who are developing competence in a second language progress through a series of predictable stages (Echevarria & Graves, 2014; Tabors, 2008; Wong Fillmore, 1979). Although researchers have used a range of terms to describe these stages, the general progression and description of stages is consistent, as shown in Figure 4.1. It must be remembered that, like first language development,

Silent Receptive	Early language - Language emergence	Intermediate fluency	Advanced fluency
• Children "gather data" about the new language through spectating, listening, and watching. • Children may use non-verbal strategies (e.g., gesture, eye gaze, showing, vocalizing). • Children do not yet produce the new language, but they begin to learn and understand new words.	• Children develop basic interpersonal communication skills (BICS) or social language (e.g., routine greetings or expressions). • Children rely on contextual cues to understand language. • Children may mispronounce words and often repeat or recite memorable language. • Children begin to use individual words and combine words. They use telegraphic and formulaic language as they begin to use phrases.	• Children have strong BICS or social language. • Children begin to build their own sentences and use sentences that are more complex. • Increased grammatical errors are common as more sophisticated language is attempted - "speak now learn later" phase (Wong Fillmore, 1979). • Children are developing Cognitive Academic Language (CALP), but need extensive support to learn and use this language. • Children have strengths in comprehension, but still may misunderstand others, and may miss classroom content especially with advanced content or when highly decontextualized (e.g., reading with no visual supports).	• Children learn to use language fluently for social and academic purposes, and require continued rich exposure to language. • CALP or advanced academic language continues to develop. • Children have near native user-levels of comprehension, but still are learning advanced language, especially in topic areas (e.g., science, social studies, health). • While considered fluent users, these multilingual children are at risk for academic challenges if not supported through sheltered language instruction or other explicit supports, especially in relation to advanced literacy skills expected in middle-school and secondary school.

FIGURE 4.1 Stages of Multilingual Language Acquisition

there is a great deal of variability in terms of rate and patterns observed in the acquisition of additional languages.

Another important consideration is the type of language that is required of children in instructional settings. When considering development in a second language, it is important to distinguish conversational language from academic language, or basic interpersonal communicative skills (BICS) from cognitive academic language proficiency (CALP) Cummins (1981, 1999). BICS includes everyday social language, from greetings to "small talk", while CALP is the language of learning used to understand the world and advanced academic topics. In the beginning stages of second language development, children's acquisition occurs mostly in the domain of BICS, with some development of CALP. In intermediate and advanced stages, children have strong BICS and are working to acquire CALP. BICS can be acquired in as little as two years, whereas CALP may take five-to seven years or more to develop (Thomas & Collier, 1997). This distinction is important when casually observing the language skills of a multilingual learner. For example, the language competence observed by a child engaging with peers in a play situation (BICS) requires a different level of competence than participating fully in curricular learning (CALP). It should be noted that, while BICS and CALP have been the cornerstones of discussion about bilingual language pedagogy for many decades, recent literature is pointing to the interconnectedness of these concepts in approaches such as translanguaging (Aukerman, 2007).

Certain *typical multilingual behaviors* can be seen in multilingual children which are not observed in monolingual children and often interpreted as signs of a language disorder. "*Code-mixing*" is the alternate usage of languages at the utterance or phrase level. This may involve the alternate use of phonological, lexical, morphosyntactic, or pragmatic patterns from each language within the same utterance or discourse. Code-mixing is often a source of concern and misunderstanding; however, there is a body of research showing that code-mixing is a normal multilingual behavior seen at all levels of proficiency and unrelated to language ability or disability (Guiberson, 2013). Specific to signed language, these natural language behaviors have also been defined as "cross-signing", "sign-speaking", and "sign-switching" (see Zeshan & Webster, 2020; Chen Pichler et al., 2019). An example of typical switching and mixing behaviors in signed languages is given by Anesuishe in Box 4.3. Anesuishe lost her hearing

> **BOX 4.3 ANESUISHE**
>
> Anesuishe is a 12-year-old girl who experienced a sudden hearing loss when she was eight years old. She now has a profound bilateral loss. Anesuishe grew up in Zimbabwe speaking Shona at home with her family and using Shona and English at school. After she lost her hearing, her parents moved her to a school for the deaf where she learned Zimbabwe Sign Language (ZSL) and continued to learn English through lip-reading, reading, and writing. When Anesuishe was 11 years old her parents moved to Canada where she began attending a school for the deaf and uses American Sign Language (ASL) and spoken and written English. She continued to use spoken Shona with her family at home. Anesuishe's teachers noticed that Anesuishe often code-switches between ZSL and ASL. They have observed that she will often start a sentence in ASL but soon start using signs that are not part of ASL. She will also use signs they do not recognize as belonging to ASL in the middle of fluent ASL sentences. In addition, she will sometimes combine phonological features of a sign from ASL and a sign from ZSL to create a new sign, such as using the handshape, orientation, and location from an ASL sign, but with the movement of a ZSL sign.

after acquiring skills in Shona and English, then acquired Zimbabwe Sign Language (ZSL) and is now acquiring American Sign Language (ASL). Anesuishe's signing shows influences of both ZSL and ASL in different ways. Changes and shifts in a child's language dominance or usage, as well as language loss (i.e., the loss of skills in the child's first language), are also frequently observed features of multilingual language acquisition. Again, these behaviors are influenced by learner and external variables, and are not signs of a language disorder.

Multilingual children are disproportionately identified as having speech and/or language disorders and disabilities (Guiberson, 2009). For example, Developmental Language Disorder is over-diagnosed in 50–60% of multilingual children (Barragan et al., 2018; Morgan et al., 2013) compared to the established prevalence rate of 7–10% (Kohnert, 2010; Nayeb et al., 2021). The inaccurate placement of multilingual children in special education programs can take various forms including overrepresentation, underrepresentation, and misidentification. Overrepresentation occurs when the percentage of multilingual children identified as having speech and language disorders and/or placed in special education programs is greater than that in the school population as a whole. Overrepresentation is often due to children having lower skills than their peers in the language used in academic settings being erroneously attributed to a disability. Learners who are multilingual are commonly misdiagnosed with a learning disability, a speech and language disorder, or a cognitive disability. Conversely, underrepresentation occurs when students with disabilities are not identified and therefore do not receive appropriate services. In these instances, educators or others may attribute language or learning difficulties to multilingualism when there actually is an organic disability (e.g. learning disability, speech language disability, or cognitive disability) that is constraining development. Finally, misidentification occurs when students with disabilities are identified as having a disability different from the one they actually have. For example, a multilingual child may be identified with a speech language disability when they actually have a learning disability. All forms of inaccurate identification are problematic, because learners will not receive the appropriate placement, instruction, and opportunities to address their learning needs.

Generally, speech and language disorders are present when *all* the languages that a child uses are affected, not just one language. For example, if a DML has word-finding difficulties in her second language, but not in her first, it is likely that this is a product of her lower level of proficiency in her second language compared to her first. Conversely, if word-finding difficulties occur in all the languages that a DML uses, then a language disorder may be present.

Supporting Deaf and Hard of Hearing Multilingual Learners

One of the difficulties in precisely describing DMLs as a population and distilling best intervention and educational practices is that these learners are at the nexus of two incredibly heterogeneous populations: learners who are d/Dhh and learners who are multilingual. The diversity of learners who are d/Dhh has frequently been described in context with their linguistic, cultural, social, cognitive, and developmental differences (Leigh & Crowe, 2020). Learners who are multilingual have also been frequently described as varying in many ways that are relevant to developing language competence, including (a) age and amount of exposure to each language, (b) the combination of languages used, (c) the language and literacy skills in each language of family members, (d) educators and others in the learner's environment, and (e) the language(s) used in formal education. The idea that "everything works for somebody, but nothing works for everybody" (Marschark, 2018, p. 222) is even more pertinent for DMLs. Three important areas to consider in supporting the language development of DMLs are: (a) language policy; (b) spoken, signed, and written language assessment; and (c) intervention and educational support.

Language Policy

Bowen and Baker (2022; see Chapter 2) described family engagement with DMLs who are acquiring multiple languages, including engaging the family in creating a Family Language Policy (FLP; Spolsky, 2004). A FLP allows the learner, family, and professionals to work together to create a realistic roadmap of how language(s) will be used in the learner's environment to achieve the desired language outcomes. Understanding any implicit FLP that a family may have and working with the family to develop the FLP into a plan that will support their desired outcomes requires understanding the perspectives of stakeholders. Three aspects of language should be considered in a FLP: (a) ideologies, (b) practices, and (c) management (Sherman et al., 2016). Adapted from Schwartz (2012), these three components refer to: (a) *language ideologies*—DMLs', families', and professionals' beliefs about language and how language is, and should be, used; (b) *language practices*—how, when, how often, and with whom the languages are currently used; and (c) *language management*—the planning and execution of special efforts or interventions to change language practices. Schwartz and Verschik (2013) provide comprehensive information about a FLP and how it relates to learners, families, and educators.

A FLP is important for DMLs because raising a child to be a successful multilingual language learner may be difficult for many caregivers, even under ideal conditions. Data from a longitudinal Australian study examining children with typical hearing from birth to five years revealed that the number of children who used the language of their home (i.e., their caregiver's language) decreased over the first five years of life (Verdon et al., 2014). Data from the United States illustrates that for children with typical hearing, three of every four children who grow up in multilingual environments will become multilingual (Pearson, 2007). Five factors were proposed to differentiate children who would and would not become multilingual: (a) language input, (b) the status of the languages, (c) access to literacy, (d) family use of language(s), and (e) community support for language(s) (Pearson, 2007). Most of these factors can be addressed through a FLP. There is little information available about how the multilingual status of children who are d/Dhh changes over time. However, data from a population-based study of three-year-old Australian d/Dhh children showed decreases in the rate of spoken language multilingualism between caregivers and their children. Only 13% of children used two or more spoken languages compared to 20% of caregivers, and only 2% of children used a spoken language other than English in their early intervention program (Crowe et al., 2012). Conversely, when examining the rates of use of Auslan and other forms of signed communication (e.g., simultaneous communication), 25% of the children were reported to use sign language at home, compared to only around 8% of caregivers. Given the difficulties faced in successful multilingual language acquisition in children without challenges accessing communication, the need for FLP planning for DMLs is clear. For children who are d/Dhh, such as Saya (see Box 4.4) FLP is a critical element of valuing and supporting language development. At just six years of age, Saya is exposed to three spoken languages (English, Spanish, and Q'anjob'al) and two signed languages (ASL and K'iche' language [Mayan Sign Language]). Managing exposure to all of these languages and ensuring that Saya receives enough quality input in each language is a crucial goal of FLP.

> **Box 4.4 Saya**
>
> Saya is from the Tz'uluma' area of Guatemala, and his mother and grandmother speak Q'anjob'al, a Mayan language. His father speaks both Spanish and Q'anjob'al. When Saya was two-to-three years old his family noticed that he was not talking, so they began using some home sign and some basic Mayan Sign Language (locally known as K'iche' language). His uncle and others in his community are deaf and use K'iche', and in Guatemala there is a large community of K'iche' signers. Saya was identified with a severe-to-profound bilateral hearing loss at age six, when his family moved to Los Angeles. Saya then received hearing aids and he wears them for about nine hours a day. His father thinks that Saya will catch up and speak well. In the area of Los Angeles that Saya's family lives, there is a large community of Q'anjob'al speakers, and several individuals who use K'iche' sign, but no children use who use K'iche' sign. Saya attends an early intervention program five days a week, where Spanish, English, and American Sign Language are used. Saya's family is soon to have a meeting with the school district staff to create a family language policy. Saya's parents want him to achieve at school and have a good life in America, but they also want him to be able to use the same languages as his family and his community.

Assessment of Speech, Spoken Language, and Signed Language

Approaches to Assessment

There are many different ways to approach the assessment of spoken and signed languages for DMLs. Which approaches are appropriate and possible will vary depending on factors such as (a) the needs of the learners, (b) the skills of the assessor, (c) the assessment resources available, and (d) the information that is available about the languages being assessed. In most cases, multiple means of assessment will be required to fully describe a DML's linguistic functioning. De Lamo White and Jin (2011) described five types of assessment approaches: (a) norm-referenced standardized measures, (b) criterion-referenced measures, (c) language-processing measures, (d) dynamic assessment, and (e) sociocultural approaches. An example of how these different assessment approaches could be used with a DML is given in Box 4.5 with the case of Emma, who is acquiring Auslan, Cantonese, and English.

> ### Box 4.5 Emma
>
> Emma is a six-year-old child who lives with her parents and grandparents in Australia. Emma received bilateral cochlear implants when she was seven months old. Her parents are fluent users of Cantonese, Mandarin, and English, and have recently started learning Australian Sign Language (Auslan). Emma's grandparents use Cantonese and Mandarin, and do not understand any English or Auslan. At home her parents speak to Emma in English and use basic Auslan, and her grandparents speak to her in Cantonese, although the family uses English, Cantonese, and Mandarin with each other. Emma has shown slow progress in developing spoken language. At five years of age she had a vocabulary of approximately 80 words with some known only in Auslan, some known only in English, some only known in Cantonese, and some known in more than one language. She is using some two-word utterances. For the past six months Emma has been enrolled in a sign-bilingual school where Auslan and spoken and written English are used. The speech-language pathologist at the school is about to conduct an assessment of Emma's skills and will need to use a variety of assessment approaches to gain an understanding of Emma's language environment and her speech and language skills in all of the languages that she uses. The speech-language pathologist could assess Emma's speech in English using a norm-referenced standardized assessment and assess Emma's speech in Cantonese informally

by asking Emma's parents and grandparents to record the words that she uses in Cantonese and comparing how Emma's and her parents say these words. The English and Cantonese forms of the MacArthur-Bates Communicative Development Inventories could be used to examine vocabulary and word combinations in both languages using the parents' reports; Auslan signs could be recorded on these forms as well. Use of conceptual scoring would allow for Emma's full competence in all of her languages to be considered. The Student Oral Language Observation Matrix (SOLOM) could be administered in all three languages to track their developments over time. The speech-language pathologist could conduct dynamic assessment in a test-teach-retest paradigm to examine Emma's ability to learn new words and signs and observe which intervention strategies are most effective in supporting Emma's acquisition of vocabulary. Interviews with Emma's family about her home language environment and experiences, and with her teacher about Emma's use of language at school, would also add to the picture of Emma's global language functioning.

Norm-Referenced Standardized Measures

Norm referenced standardized measures are instruments most commonly used for conducting formal assessments of spoken, signed, and written language skills. These are considered by many to be key to comprehensively monitoring development and diagnosing disorders. Standardized assessments, such as the Clinical Evaluation of Language Fundamentals (CELF 5; Wiig et al., 2013) provide a means of assessing one child's language skills and comparing their performance on the test to the performance of a large group of children with similar characteristics, usually typically developing native users of the language. While there is often a choice of norm-referenced standardized tests available to assess widely used languages, such as English, Spanish, Cantonese, and Arabic, there are no standardized assessments available for the majority of the languages used globally, and very few that assess signed languages. Standardized assessments are usually inadequate and inappropriate for the assessment of children who are multilingual, as standardized assessments consider performance in one language used by a child only, not their general language competence, meaning that comparing multilingual children's performance to that of their monolingual peers does not account for the different development trajectories or language experiences of these groups (Bedore & Peña, 2008). Despite this, there are a small number of measures that have been specifically designed and normed for multilingual children with typical hearing (see Guzman-Orth et al., 2017 for more information).

Criterion-Referenced Measures

Criterion-referenced measures examine a child's performance on a skill, but rather than comparing their performance to that of their peers, their performance is measured against a criterion that states whether their performance was appropriate or not (De Lamo White & Jin, 2011). Criterion-referenced assessments include checklists and analysis of language samples. Such methods have often been used in assessing multilingual learners, and in some cases DMLs. For example, the Student Oral Language Observation Matrix (SOLOM; Montebello Unified School District Instructional Division, 1978) has been used in a number of studies of DMLs (Guiberson, 2014). Criterion-referenced measures have more flexibility than norm-referenced standardized assessments, and for multilingual children, conceptual scoring is often possible. Conceptual scoring allows for responses with the correct meaning to be scored as correct, regardless of the language or modality in which the response is, making results more representative of the total language competence of a child (Bedore et al., 2005).

Language-Processing Measures

Language-processing measures approach spoken, signed, and written language assessment from a different perspective, examining children's ability to process language as well as the systems and processes that underlie language acquisition (De Lamo White & Jin, 2011). As such, language-processing measures are not designed to give information about a child's skills in any particular language, but information about how well the child is able to acquire, process, and utilize these skills in spoken, signed, and written languages. Two common language-processing measures that can be used with DMLs are (a) non-word repetition and/or non-sign repetition, and (b) verbal fluency. Non-word and non-sign repetition are process-based measures that have been shown to be sensitive to differentiating multilingual children with typical and atypical language developments (e.g., Boerma & Blom, 2017). They have been used with children who are d/Dhh and monolingual spoken language users (e.g., Hansson et al., 2007) and bimodal users of spoken and signed languages (e.g., Marshall et al., 2006).

Verbal fluency tasks are quick and informal means of qualitatively assessing lexico-semantic skills related to lexical organization and retrieval. Studies of semantic and phonological fluency (i.e. using handshapes) have been conducted with children and adults who use spoken and/or signed languages (e.g., Beal-Alvarez & Figueroa, 2017) and d/Dhh children who use spoken English and Sign Supported English (e.g., Marshall et al., 2018). While research describing the use of these processing measures for DMLs is currently lacking, these means of assessment show great potential for examining the underlying linguistic skills of these learners.

Dynamic Measures

Dynamic assessment is an approach that considers the language learning potential of a child (De Lamo White & Jin, 2011). Dynamic assessment commonly occurs in test-teach-retest paradigms. This provides information about the learner's current use of a language structure or strategy and the effect that an intervention strategy has on supporting the learner's use of that structure or strategy in a more advanced way (De Lamo White & Jin, 2011). Dynamic assessment is often recommended as being appropriate for use with multilingual children, but in reality, this assessment approach is currently still used more often in research than in practice (Arias & Friberg, 2017). Some research exists describing dynamic assessment with d/Dhh children using spoken language (Asad et al., 2013; Lederberg & Spencer, 2009) and signed language (Mann et al, 2014, 2015). This is a very promising assessment approach for use with DMLs, as it can be adapted to any of the languages used by these learners and can target a range of skills that may be of interest to clinicians and educators.

Sociocultural Approaches

Sociocultural approaches to assessment provide a holistic evaluation of a child's linguistic and communicative abilities in relation to their social and cultural environments (De Lamo White & Jin, 2011). Collecting information from the child, their parents, caregivers, and teachers through observation, conversation, and interview techniques provides a well-rounded understanding of the learner's real-world functioning. Examples of procedures for sociocultural assessment approaches are outlined in Cheng (1990, 1997) and Westby (1990). Examples of parent interview questionnaires that could be used with DMLs are provided in the Resource List.

Assessing Multilingual Learners

The assessment of multilingual children, including DMLs, must come from an understanding of two fundamental concepts. First, for DMLs, each language a learner knows is not a separate entity. The combination and interaction of the languages a learner knows creates a linguistic profile which may be unique to each individual and shapes all aspects of their language, speech, and/or signing. The linguistic system of a DML is not the same as that of a monolingual user. Therefore, an assessment that does not consider all the language known by a DML, and that only compares performance to monolingual language users, will misrepresent a DML's language competence and knowledge. Typically, this results in an underestimation of the learner's skills. This assessment approach with multilingual children with typical hearing is also not a reliable indicator of language competence or disorder (Cruz-Ferreira, 2018). Second, the commonly held notion that multilingual people have, or should have, equal skills in all of the languages is a misconception. In reality, balanced bilinguals are rare (Grosjean, 1989). For the assessment of DMLs, this means that comparing performances between a learner's languages or comparing their performance to those of their peers' is far less meaningful than identifying the relative strengths and weaknesses, examining the underlying language processes, and understanding the learner's linguistic environment.

Together, these fundamental concepts mean that the use of norm-referenced standardized assessments alone is neither best nor good practice for DMLs. Best practice requires the use of a range of assessment approaches to gain a robust understanding of a DML's complete language system, taking into consideration all of the languages that they use, whether in spoken, signed, or written form. In relation to these concepts, recommendations were developed to describe the current knowledge about best practices in the assessment of multilingual learners' speech perception (Hapsburg & Peña, 2002), speech production (e.g., International Expert Panel on Multilingual Children's Speech, 2012), and language (e.g., Guzman-Orth et al., 2017).

While a range of assessments is necessary, this can be somewhat hampered by: (a) the limited availability of measures and assessment tools for examining the spoken, signed, and written language skills in all of the languages used by DMLs; (b) the limited information on the linguistic features of the languages used by DMLs and the patterns of typical spoken, signed, and written language acquisition in these languages; and (c) professionals lacking the linguistic and metalinguistic knowledge in the languages used by DMLs to assess these learners' skills. The magnitude that these difficulties present for assessing the spoken, signed, and written language skills of DMLs is significant. It is impossible to provide comprehensive information about every spoken and signed language and language combination that DMLs may use. However, knowledge and resources are available to assist professionals in assessment of DMLs. The Multilingual Children's Speech website (see Resource section) provides information on the assessments of speech production in over 40 languages. It also provides free access to assessments, such as the Intelligibility in Context Scale (ICS; McLeod et al., 2012), which has been translated into over 60 languages. The ICS can be used to assess speech intelligibility in all the languages a child speaks, and a companion sign language version has also been developed to examine sign intelligibility (Crowe et al., 2019). A measure of language skill that can be used across languages and has been used with DMLs is the SOLOM (Montebello Unified School District Instructional Division, 1978). The SOLOM is a free rubric that defines skills in comprehension, fluency, vocabulary, production, and grammar. A signed language version of the SOLOM has also recently been developed (Crowe et al., 2019). Information about assessments of signed language skills in a range of signed languages is available through the Sign Language Assessment Instruments website (see Resources). Henner et al. (2018) provide an overview of signed language assessments as well as their pitfalls and possibilities. There are also resources available to guide assessment practices when the assessor does not use the same language(s) as the child (e.g., Lockart & McLeod, 2013; McLeod et al., 2017).

Awareness of the similarities and differences between the phonetic and phonemic inventories, phonological and phonotactic structures, morphology, syntax, semantic boundaries, and pragmatic norms of the languages a DML uses is important for planning assessments, interpreting assessment results, and planning and delivering intervention and support. If a DML is using a language in which their educator or speech-language pathologist is not fluent, these professionals will need to learn about the linguistic features and structures of the language. The Multicultural Topics in Communications Sciences and Disorders website (see *Resources*) considers phonetic, phonological, semantic, and syntactic aspects of a range of spoken languages and American Sign Language. In addition to this, searching the internet for the name of a language, followed by *language* (e.g., "Faroese language") yields information about the structure of the language in question. There is often information for languages with a small number of users (e.g., "Inuit Sign Language"), as well as links to other sources.

Knowledge of the typical patterns and progress of acquisition of languages is also important. Useful resources that relate to typical speech acquisition and phonological development are present within the Multilingual Children's Speech website (*see Resources*). The International Guide to Speech Acquisition (McLeod, 2007) provides information about the phonetic inventories, consonant clusters, tones, syllable shapes, stress, and dialects of a wide range of languages. McLeod and Crowe (2018) also provide information about the typical age of consonant acquisition across 27 different languages.

Educational Support

The shortage of evidence for effective interventions used with DMLs requires professionals to read more broadly and draw on evidence outside of their immediate discipline. General language approaches supporting DMLs should be considered as an important part of professional expertise. These include approaches such as *translanguaging, linguistically responsive teaching, and culturally responsive leadership and pedagogy*. Translanguaging grew out of the knowledge of how multilingual people utilize two or more languages, often in different modalities, in their daily lives (see Kusters, 2017). When applied to educational contexts, translanguaging describes a multilingual learner's use of all their linguistic resources, pooled between all of their languages, to make and share meaning (Swanwick, 2017). This approach seeks to recognize the overall linguistic competence of DMLs, rather than their competence or incompetence within a specific language. Swanwick (2017) provides an excellent guide to translanguaging in the context of d/Dhh education. However, it should be noted that critics suggest that translanguaging in a classroom setting may result in students with more significant hearing loss being marginalized from linguistic interactions (see De Meulder et al., 2019). Care should always be taken to ensure that the individual needs of all children within the classroom are being met. *Linguistically responsive teaching* is an approach to classroom pedagogy that suggests educators working with learners who are multilingual require "familiarity with the students' linguistic and academic backgrounds; an understanding of the language demands inherent in the learning tasks that students are expected to carry out in class; and skills for using appropriate scaffolding so that English Language Learners can participate successfully in those tasks" (Lucas et al., 2008, p. 366). Linguistically responsive teaching is an approach widely used with multilingual children with typical hearing across a broad range of curriculum areas and education levels, and has also been discussed with regards to DMLs (Pizzo, 2016; see Cannon & Guardino, 2022, Chapter 1).

Culturally responsive leadership and pedagogy applies this idea much more broadly to look both within and beyond the classroom, considering "how the school leaders' identities, values, practices, actions, policies, and everyday discourses influence a school's climate, culture, and teacher efficacy" (O'Brien, 2019, p. 121).

Conclusion

DMLs vary greatly in their spoken, signed, and written language acquisition, profiles, and outcomes, which is not adequately captured by the various definitions of multilingualism. DMLs are a heterogenous population with diverse language experiences and a range of patterns and progress when acquiring language. However, there is a typical broad pattern of acquisition from which children move: from a silent period of language to an advanced fluency stage (see Figure 4.1). In relation to hearing loss, audiological, linguistic, cultural, social, cognitive, and developmental differences add to the variability observed in DMLs' development and outcomes.

For multilingual learners with typical hearing, the cognitive and linguistic advantages and disadvantages of multilingualism have been widely researched and the findings disseminated. In comparison, research examining the cognitive aspects of language for DMLs is sparse. Within the past five years, research with DMLs has grown, and the prospect of better understanding the spoken, signed, and written language outcomes of these learners is high.

Supporting DMLs and their families to achieve their language and educational goals requires a collaborative effort, with an emphasis on developing a comprehensive FLP. In addition, professionals must work together to understand the learner's skill, functioning level, and language learning potential (e.g., through appropriate assessment). Overall, the acquisition of multiple languages by d/Dhh learners does not seem to adversely affect these learner's outcomes (Crowe, 2018), and DMLs should be supported in acquiring language(s) to the best of their abilities.

Discussion Questions

1. What are three dimensions along which the language acquisition of multilingual children can vary?
2. What advantages does multilingualism have?
3. Describe what is meant by the terms BICS and CALP.
4. Name the three elements of a family language policy.
5. How can the skills of DMLs be assessed when no norm-referenced, standardized assessments are available in the language(s) that they use?
6. If caregivers and professionals cannot find research evidence of interventions that may support the language learning of DMLs directly, which other sources of information may be informative?

Resources

Articles, Books, and Chapters

- Genesee, F. (2007). A short guide to raising children bilingually. *Multilingual Living Magazine, Jan/Feb*, 1–9. Available at www.psych.mcgill.ca/perpg/fac/genesee/A%20Short%20Guide%20to%20Raising%20Children%20Bilingually.pdf
- Snoddon, K. & Weber, J. C. (Eds) (2021). *Critical perspectives on plurilingualism in deaf education.* Multilingual Matters. This book provides an international perspective on acquiring multiple languages.
- Marian, V., Blumenfeld, H. K., & Kaushanskaya, M. (2007). The Language Experience and Proficiency Questionnaire (LEAP-Q): Assessing language profiles in bilinguals and multilinguals. *Journal of Speech, Language, and Hearing Research, 50*(4), 940–967. https://doi.org/10.1044/1092-4388(2007/067). This is a questionnaire designed to help educators and clinicians understand a multilingual learner's language environment, experiences, and skills.
- Paradis, J., Emmerzael, K., & Duncan, T. S. (2010). Assessment of English language learners: Using parent report on first language development. *Journal of Communication Disorders, 43*(6), 474–497. https://doi.org/10.1016/j.jcomdis.2010.01.002. This describes the Alberta Language and Development Questionnaire, a questionnaire designed

to help educators and clinicians understand a multilingual learner's language environment, experiences, and skills.
- Tuller, L. (2015). Clinical use of parental questionnaires in multilingual contexts. In S. Armon-Lotem, J. de Jong, & N. Meir (Eds.), *Methods for assessing multilingual children: Disentangling bilingualism from language impairment* (pp. 301–330). Multilingual Matters. This chapter describes the COST IS0804 Questionnaire, designed to help educators and clinicians understand a multilingual learner's language environment, experiences, and skills.
- Verdon, S., Wong, S., & McLeod, S. (2016). Shared knowledge and mutual respect: Enhancing culturally competent practice through collaboration with families and communities. *Child Language Teaching and Therapy, 32*(2), 205–221. https://doi.org/10.1177/0265659015 620254. A parent-friendly introduction to bilingualism and the practicalities of raising a bilingual child.

Websites

- CHESL Centre (www.ualberta.ca/linguistics/cheslcentre): This website provides information about working with children acquiring English as a second language, focused on language development.
- Colorín Colorado (www.colorincolorado.org): This website provides information on education for teachers and families of English language learners, particularly focused on Spanish speakers.
- Creative Multilingualism (www.creativeml.ox.ac.uk/resources): This website includes information, resources, and research about multilingualism and cultural diversity.
- Multilingual Children's Speech (www.csu.edu.au/research/multilingual-speech): This website provides information on assessing the speech production skills of children who speak a range of languages.
- The Sign Language Assessment Instruments (www.signlang-assessment. info/index.php/home-en.html): provides information about assessments of signed language skills in a range of signed languages.
- The Student Oral Language Observation Matrix (SOLOM; www.cal. org/twi/EvalToolkit/appendix/solom.pdf): a matrix of language skills that can be used to examine all languages that a DML uses.

Development, Assessment, Intervention

Family-Centered Brief

FAMILY-CENTERED BRIEF

CHAPTER 4
Language Development, Assessment, and Intervention for d/Deaf and Hard-of-Hearing Multilingual Learners

by Kathryn Crowe & Mark Guiberson

PURPOSE OF CHAPTER
This chapter discusses language learning, assessment, and ways to support multilingual learning in children who are d/Deaf and hard of hearing multilingual learners (DMLs).

FACTS ABOUT LEARNING MULTIPLE LANGUAGES
A child's ability to learn multiple languages depends on a variety of **Child Factors** and **External Factors** in relation to **each language being learned**

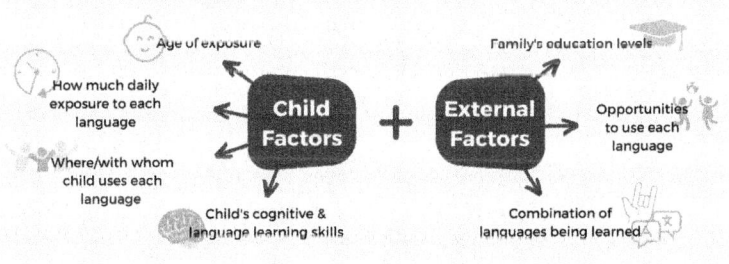

Child Factors:
- Age of exposure
- How much daily exposure to each language
- Where/with whom child uses each language
- Child's cognitive & language learning skills

External Factors:
- Family's education levels
- Opportunities to use each language
- Combination of languages being learned

Did You Know? Learning multiple languages is linked to better cognitive functioning, improved ability to learn languages, and protection against dementia later in life

TIPS FOR SUPPORTING CHILDREN LEARNING MULTIPLE LANGUAGES

Step 1 Identify the **Child's Language Profile**
- What are the child's language abilities for each language relative to each other?
- What are the child's language learning processes?
- What is the child's language environment?

Step 2 Make a **Family Language Policy**
- Which languages will the child learn?
- Who will use each language and in which contexts?

RESOURCES
Genesee, F. (Jan/Feb. 2007). A Short Guide to Raising Children Bilingually. Multilingual Living Magazine, 1-9. www.psych.mcgill.ca/perpg/fac/genesee/A%20Short%20Guide%20to%20Raising%20Children%20Bilingually.pdf

Colorín Colorado! www.colorincolorado.org/bilingual-information-families

Deaf and Hard of Hearing Multilingual Learners: Foundations, Strategies, and Resources (2022)

References

Arias, G., & Friberg, J. (2017). Bilingual language assessment: Contemporary versus recommended practice in American schools. *Language, Speech, and Hearing Services in Schools, 48*(1), 1–15. https://doi.org/10.1044/2016_LSHSS-15-0090

Asad, A. N., Hand, L., Fairgray, L., & Purdy, S. C. (2013). The use of dynamic assessment to evaluate narrative language learning in children with hearing loss: Three case studies. *Child Language Teaching and Therapy, 29*(3), 319–342. https://doi.org/10.1177/0265659012467994

Aukerman, M. (2007). A culpable CALP: Rethinking the conversational/academic language proficiency distinction in early literacy instruction. *The Reading Teacher, 60*(7), 626–635. https://doi.org/10.1598/RT.60.7.3

Barragan, B., Castilla-Earls, A., Martinez-Nieto, L., Restrepo, M. A., & Gray, S. (2018). Performance of low-income dual language learners attending English-only schools on the Clinical Evaluation of Language Fundamentals-Fourth Edition, Spanish. *Language, Speech, and Hearing Services in Schools, 49*(2), 292–305. https://doi.org/10.1044/2017_LSHSS-17-0013

Beal-Alvarez, J. S., & Figueroa, D. M. (2017). Generation of signs within semantic and phonological categories: Data from deaf adults and children who use American Sign Language. *Journal of Deaf Studies and Deaf Education, 22*(2), 219–232. https://doi.org/10.1093/deafed/enw075

Bedore, L. M., & Peña, E. D. (2008). Assessment of bilingual children for identification of language impairment: Current findings and implications for practice. *International Journal of Bilingual Education and Bilingualism, 11*(1), 1–29. https://doi.org/10.2167/beb392.0

Bedore, L. M., Peña, E. D., Garcia, M., & Cortez, C. (2005). Conceptual versus monolingual scoring: When does it make a difference? *Language, Speech, and Hearing Services in Schools, 36*(3), 188–200. https://doi.org/10.1044/0161-1461(2005/020)

Bialystok, E., & Barac, R. (2012). Emerging bilingualism: Dissociating advantages for metalinguistic awareness and executive control. *Cognition, 122*(1), 67–73. https://doi.org/10.1016/j.cognition.2011.08.003

Bialystok, E., Craik, F. I. M., Green, D. W., & Gollan, T. H. (2009). Bilingual minds. *Psychological Science in the Public Interest, 10*(3), 89–129. https://doi.org/10.1177/1529100610387084

Bialystok, E., Craik, F. I. M., & Luk, G. (2012). Bilingualism: Consequences for mind and brain. *Trends in Cognitive Sciences, 16*(4), 240–250. https://doi.org/10.1016/j.tics.2012.03.001

Bialystok, E., Luk, G., Peets, K. F., & Yang, S. (2010). Receptive vocabulary differences in monolingual and bilingual children. *Bilingualism, 13*(4), 525–531. https://doi.org/10.1017/S1366728909990423

Bialystok, E., Majumder, S., & Martin, M. M. (2003). Developing phonological awareness: Is there a bilingual advantage? *Applied Psycholinguistics, 24*(1), 27–44. https://doi.org/10.1017/S014271640300002X

Boerma, T., & Blom, E. (2017). Assessment of bilingual children: What if testing both languages is not possible? *Journal of Communication Disorders, 66*, 65–76. https://doi.org/10.1016/j.jcomdis.2017.04.001

Bowen, S. K., & Baker, S. (2022). Family engagement: Developing partnerships for d/Deaf and hard of hearing multilingual learners. In J. E. Cannon, C. Guardino, & P. V. Paul (Eds.), *Deaf and hard of hearing multilingual learners: Foundations, strategies, and resources* (pp. 30–66). Routledge.

Cannon, J. E., & Guardino, C. (2022). Learners who are d/Deaf or hard of hearing and multilingual: Perspectives, approaches and considerations. In J. E. Cannon, C. Guardino, & P. V. Paul (Eds.), *Deaf and hard of hearing multilingual learners: Foundations, strategies, and resources* (pp. 1–29). Routledge.

Cannon, J. E., Guardino, C., & Gallimore, E. (2016). A new kind of heterogeneity: What we can learn from d/Deaf and hard of hearing multilingual learners. *American Annals of the Deaf, 161*(1), 8–16. https://doi.org/10.1353/aad.2016.0015

Celik, S., Kokje, E., Meyer, P., Frölich, L., & Teichmann, B. (in press). Does bilingualism influence neuropsychological test performance in older adults? A systematic review. *Applied Neuropsychology: Adult.* https://doi.org/10.1080/23279095.2020.1788032

Chen Pichler, D., Reynolds, W., & Palmer, J. L. (2019). Multilingualism in signing communities. In S. Montanari & S. Quay (Eds.), *Multidisciplinary perspectives on multilingualism: The fundamentals* (pp. 175–204). Walter De Gruyter.

Cheng, L.-R. L. (1990). The identification of communicative disorders in Asian-Pacific students. *Journal of Childhood Communication Disorders, 13*(1), 113–119.

Cheng, L.-R. L. (1997). Diversity: Challenges and implications for assessment. *Journal of Children's Communication Development, 19*(1), 55–62. https://doi.org/10.1177/152574019001300112

Clare, L., Whitaker, C. J., Craik, F. I., Bialystok, E., Martyr, A., Martin-Forbes, P. A., Bastable, A. J., Pye, K. L., Quinn, C., Thomas, E. M., Gathercole, V. C., & Hindle, J. V. (2016). Bilingualism, executive control, and age at diagnosis among people with early-stage Alzheimer's disease in Wales. *Journal of Neuropsychology, 10*(2), 163–185. https://doi.org/10.1111/jnp.12061

Crowe, K. (2018). DHH multilingual learners: Language acquisition in a multilingual world. In H. Knoors & M. Marschark (Eds.), *Evidence-based practice in deaf education* (pp. 59–79). Oxford University Press.

Crowe, K., & Cupples, L. (2020). Bilingual cognitive advantages in multilingual and multimodal deaf and hard-of-hearing children and adults. In M. Marschark & H. Knoors (Eds.), *Oxford handbook of deaf studies in cognition and learning* (pp. 150–166). Oxford University Press.

Crowe, K., & Guiberson, M. (2019). Evidence-based interventions for learners who are deaf and/or multilingual: A systematic quality review. *American Journal of Speech-Language Pathology, 28*, 964–983. https://doi.org/10.1044/2019_AJSLP-IDLL-19-0003

Crowe, K., Marschark, M., & McLeod, S. (2019). More than a matter of skill: Exploring the concept of sign intelligibility. *Clinical Linguistics and Phonetics, 33*(10–11), 991–1008. https://doi.org/10.1080/02699206.2019.1600169

Crowe, K., McLeod, S., & Ching, T. Y. C. (2012). The cultural and linguistic diversity of 3-year-old children with hearing loss. *Journal of Deaf Studies and Deaf Education, 17*(4), 421–438. https://doi.org/10.1093/deafed/ens028

Cruz-Ferreira, M. (2011). *Recommending monolingualism to multilinguals—Why, and why not.* http://blog.asha.org/2011/08/02/recommending-monolingualism-to-multilinguals-why-and-why-not/

Cruz-Ferreira, M. (2018). Assessment of communication abilities in multilingual children: Language rights or human rights? *International Journal of Speech-Language Pathology, 20*(1), 166–169. https://doi.org/10.1080/17549507.2018.1392607

Cummins, J. (1981). The role of primary language development in promoting educational success for language minority students. In California State Department of Education (Ed.), *Schooling and language minority students: A theoretical framework*. National Dissemination and Assessment Center.

Cummins, J. (1999). *BICS and CALP: Clarifying the distinction.* ERIC Clearinghouse on Languages and Linguistics.

De Lamo White, C., & Jin, L. (2011). Evaluation of speech and language assessment approaches with bilingual children. *International Journal of Language and Communication Disorders, 46*(6), 613–627. https://doi.org/10.1111/j.1460-6984.2011.00049.x

De Meulder, M., Kusters, A., Moriarty, E., & Murray, J. J. (2019). Describe, don't prescribe. The practice and politics of translanguaging in the context of deaf signers. *Journal of Multilingual and Multicultural Development, 40*(10), 892–906. https://doi.org/10.1080/01434632.2019.1592181

Eberhard, D. M., Simons, G. F., & Fennig, C. D. (Eds.). (2020). *Ethnologue: Languages of the world* (23rd ed.). SIL International. www.ethnologue.com.

Echevarria, J., & Graves, A. (2014). *Sheltered content instruction: Teaching English language learners with diverse abilities* (5th ed.). Pearson Allyn and Bacon.

Giovannoli, J., Martella, D., Federico, F., Pirchio, S., & Casagrande, M. (2020). The impact of bilingualism on executive functions in children and adolescents: A systematic review based on the PRISMA method. *Frontiers in Psychology, 11*(2398). https://doi.org/10.3389/fpsyg.2020.574789

Grosjean, F. (1989). Neurolinguists, beware! The bilingual is not two monolinguals in one person. *Brain and Language, 36*(1), 3–15. https://doi.org/10.1016/0093-934X(89)90048-5

Guiberson, M. (2009). Hispanic representation in special education: Patterns and implications. *Preventing School Failure: Alternative Education for Children and Youth, 53*(3), 167–176. https://doi.org/10.3200/PSFL.53.3.167-176

Guiberson, M. (2013). Bilingual myth-busters series: Language confusion in bilingual children. *Perspectives on Communication Disorders and*

Sciences in Culturally and Linguistically Diverse Populations, *20*(1), 5–14. https://doi.org/10.1044/cds20.1.5

Guiberson, M. (2014). Bilingual skills of deaf/hard of hearing children from Spain. *Cochlear Implants International*, *15*(2), 87–92. https://doi.org/10.1179/1754762813Y.0000000058

Guiberson, M., & Banerjee, R. (2012). Using questionnaires to screen young dual language learners for language disorders. *14th young exceptional children, monograph: Supporting young children who are dual language learners with or at-risk for disabilities*. Council for Exceptional Children Division for Early Childhood.

Guiberson, M., Barrett, K. C., Jancosek, E. G., & Yoshinaga-Itano, C. (2006). Language maintenance and loss in preschool-age children of Mexican immigrants: Longitudinal study. *Communication Disorders Quarterly*, *28*(1), 4–17. https://doi.org/10.1177/15257401060280010601

Gunnerud, H. L., ten Braak, D., Reikerås, E. K. L., Donolato, E., & Melby-Lervåg, M. (2020). Is bilingualism related to a cognitive advantage in children? A systematic review and meta-analysis. *Psychological Bulletin*, *146*(12), 1059–1083. https://doi.org/10.1037/bul0000301

Guzman-Orth, D., Lopez, A. A., & Tolentino, F. (2017). *A framework for the dual language assessment of young dual language learners in the United States* [Research Report No. RR-17-37]. Educational Testing Service.

Hambly, H., Wren, Y., McLeod, S., & Roulstone, S. (2013). The influence of bilingualism on speech production: A systematic review. *International Journal of Language and Communication Disorders*, *48*(1), 1–24. https://doi.org/10.1111/j.1460-6984.2012.00178.x

Hansson, K., Sahlén, B., & Mäki-Torkko, E. (2007). Can a 'single hit' cause limitations in language development? A comparative study of Swedish children with hearing impairment and children with specific language impairment. *International Journal of Language and Communication Disorders*, *42*(3), 307–323. https://doi.org/10.1080/13682820600933526

Hapsburg, D. v., & Peña, E. D. (2002). Understanding bilingualism and its impact on speech audiometry. *Journal of Speech Language and Hearing Research*, *45*(1), 202–213. https://doi.org/10.1044/1092-4388(2002/015)

Henner, J., Novogrodsky, R., Reis, J., & Hoffmeister, R. (2018). Recent issues in the use of signed language assessments for diagnosis of language disorders in signing deaf and hard of hearing children. *Journal of Deaf Studies and Deaf Education, 23*(4), 307–316. https://doi.org/10.1093/deafed/eny014

Hermans, D., Knoors, H., Ormel, E., & Verhoeven, L. (2008a). Modeling reading vocabulary learning in deaf children in bilingual education programs. *Journal of Deaf Studies and Deaf Education, 13*(2), 155–174. Education, 13(2), 155–174. https://doi.org/10.1093/deafed/enm057

Hermans, D., Knoors, H., Ormel, E., & Verhoeven, L. (2008b). The relationship between the reading and signing skills of deaf children in bilingual education programs. *Journal of Deaf Studies and Deaf Education, 13*(4), 518–530. https://doi.org/10.1093/deafed/enn009

Hermans, D., Ormel, E., & Knoors, H. (2010). On the relation between the signing and reading skills of Deaf bilinguals. *International Journal of Bilingual Education and Bilingualism, 13*(2), 187–199. https://doi.org/10.1080/13670050903474093

Holzinger, D., & Fellinger, J. (2014). Sign language and reading comprehension: No automatic transfer. In M. Marschark, G. Tang, & H. Knoors (Eds.), *Bilingualism and bilingual deaf education* (pp. 102–133). Oxford University Press.

International Expert Panel on Multilingual Children's Speech. (2012). *Multilingual children with speech sound disorders: Position paper.* Bathurst, Australia: Research Institute for Professional Practice, Learning & Education (RIPPLE), Charles Sturt University.

Kohnert, K. (2010). Bilingual children with primary language impairment: Issues, evidence and implications for clinical actions. *Journal of Communication Disorders, 43*(6), 456–473. https://doi.org/10.1016/j.jcomdis.2010.02.002

Kusters, A. (2017). Special issue: Deaf and hearing signers' multimodal and translingual practices. *Applied Linguistics Review.* https://doi.org/10.1515/applirev-2017-0086.

Lederberg, A. R., & Spencer, P. E. (2009). Word-learning abilities in deaf and hard-of-hearing preschoolers: Effect of lexicon size and language modality. *Journal of Deaf Studies and Deaf Education, 14*(1), 44–62. https://doi.org/10.1093/deafed/enn021

Leigh, G., & Crowe, K. (2020). Evidence-based practices for teaching learners who are deaf or hard-of-hearing in regular classrooms. In U. Sharma (Ed.), *Oxford research encyclopedia of education: Inclusive and special education*. Oxford University Press. https://doi.org/10.1093/acrefore/9780190264093.013.ORE_EDU-01258.R2

Lockart, R., & McLeod, S. (2013). Factors that enhance English-speaking speech-language pathologists' transcription of Cantonese-speaking children's consonants. *American Journal of Speech-Language Pathology*, *22*(3), 523–539. https://doi.org/10.1044/1058-0360(2012/12-0009)

Lucas, T., Villegas, A. M., & Freedson-Gonzalez, M. (2008). Linguistically responsive teacher education: Preparing classroom teachers to teach English language learners. *Journal of Teacher Education*, *59*(4), 361–373. https://doi.org/10.1177/0022487108322110

Mann, W., Peña, E. D., & Morgan, G. (2014). Exploring the use of dynamic language assessment with deaf children, who use American Sign Language: Two case studies. *Journal of Communication Disorders*, *52*, 16–30. https://doi.org/10.1016/j.jcomdis.2014.05.002

Mann, W., Peña, E. D., & Morgan, G. (2015). Child modifiability as a predictor of language abilities in deaf children who use American Sign Language. *American Journal of Speech-Language Pathology*, *24*(3), 374–385. https://doi.org/10.1044/2015_AJSLP-14-0072

Marschark, M. (2018). *Raising and educating a deaf child* (3rd ed.). Oxford University Press.

Marshall, C. R., Denmark, T., & Morgan, G. (2006). Investigating the underlying causes of SLI: A non-sign repetition test in British Sign Language. *Advances in Speech-Language Pathology*, *8*(4), 347–355. https://doi.org/10.1080/14417040600970630

Marshall, C. R., Jones, A., Fastelli, A., Atkinson, J., Botting, N., & Morgan, G. (2018). Semantic fluency in deaf children who use spoken and signed language in comparison with hearing peers. *International Journal of Language and Communication Disorders*, *53*(1), 157–170. https://doi.org/10.1111/1460-6984.12333

McLeod, S. (2007). *The international guide to speech acquisition*. Thomson Delmar Learning.

McLeod, S., & Crowe, K. (2018). Children's consonant acquisition in 27 languages: A cross-linguistic review. *American Journal of Speech-Language*

Pathology, 27(4), 1546–1571. https://doi.org/10.1044/2018_AJSLP-17-0100

McLeod, S., Harrison, L. J., & McCormack, J. (2012). *Intelligibility in context scale*. Charles Sturt University.

McLeod, S., Harrison, L. J., Whiteford, C., & Walker, S. (2016). Multilingualism and speech-language competence in early childhood: Impact on academic and social-emotional outcomes at school. *Early Childhood Research Quarterly, 34,* 53–66. https://doi.org/10.1016/j.ecresq.2015.08.005

McLeod, S., Verdon, S., & International Expert Panel on Multilingual Children's Speech. (2017). Tutorial: Speech assessment for multilingual children who do not speak the same language(s) as the speech-language pathologist. *American Journal of Speech-Language Pathology, 26,* 691–708. https://doi.org/10.1044/2017_AJSLP-15-0161

Miyake, A., Friedman, N. P., Emerson, M. J., Witzki, A. H., Howerter, A., & Wager, T. D. (2000). The unity and diversity of executive functions and their contributions to complex "frontal lobe" tasks: A latent variable analysis. *Cognitive Psychology, 41*(1), 49–100. https://doi.org/10.1006/cogp.1999.0734

Montebello Unified School District Instructional Division. (1978). *Student Oral Language Observation Matrix (SOLOM)*. Author.

Morgan, G. P., Restrepo, M. A., & Auza, A. (2013). Comparison of Spanish morphology in monolingual and Spanish–English bilingual children with and without language impairment. *Bilingualism: Language and Cognition, 16*(3), 578–596. https://doi.org/10.1017/S1366728912000697

Nayeb, L., Lagerberg, D., Sarkadi, A., Salameh, E.-K., & Eriksson, M. (2021). Identifying language disorder in bilingual children aged 2.5 years requires screening in both languages. *Acta Paediatrica, 110*(1), 265–272. https://doi.org/10.1111/apa.15343

O'Brien, C. A. (2019). The impact of identity and culturally responsive school leadership: Leaders of schools and programs for the Deaf. In I. W. Leigh & C. A. O'Brien (Eds.), *Deaf Identities: Exploring new frontiers* (pp. 120–144). Oxford University Press.

Paradis, J. (2011). Individual differences in child English second language acquisition: Comparing child-internal and child-external factors.

Linguistic Approaches to Bilingualism, 1(3), 213–237. https://doi.org/10.1075/lab.1.3.01par

Paradis, J., & Jia, R. (2017). Bilingual children's long-term outcomes in English as a second language: Language environment factors shape individual differences in catching up with monolinguals. *Developmental Science, 20*(1), e12433. https://doi.org/10.1111/desc.12433

Paradis, J., Genesee, F., & Crago, M. B. (2011). *Dual language development and disorders: A handbook on bilingualism and second language learning* (2nd ed.). Brookes.

Peal, E., & Lambert, W. E. (1962). The relation of bilingualism to intelligence. *Psychological Monographs: General and Applied, 76*(27), 1–23. https://doi.org/10.1037/h0093840

Pearson, B. Z. (2007). Social factors in childhood bilingualism in the United States. *Applied Psycholinguistics, 28*(3), 399–410. https://doi.org/10.1017/S014271640707021X

Perquin, M., Vaillant, M., Schuller, A.-M., Pastore, J., Jean-François, D., Marie-Lise, L., Diederich, N., & MemoVie Group. (2013). Lifelong exposure to multilingualism: New evidence to support cognitive reserve hypothesis. *PLoS One, 8*(4), e62030. https://doi.org/10.1371/journal.pone.0062030

Pizzo, L. (2016). d/Deaf and hard of hearing multilingual learners: The development of communication and language. *American Annals of the Deaf, 161*(1), 17–32. https://doi.org/10.1353/aad.2016.0017

Schwartz, M. (2012). Second generation immigrants: A socio-linguistic approach to linguistic development within the framework of family language policy. In M. Leikin, M. Schwartz, & Y. Tobin (Eds.), *Current issues in bilingualism: Cognitive and socio-linguistic perspectives* (pp. 119–135). Springer.

Schwartz, M., & Verschik, A. (Eds.). (2013). *Successful family language policy: Parents, children and educators in interaction.* Springer.

Sherman, T., Hromadová, M. A., Özörencik, H., Zaepernicková, E., & Nekvapil, J. (2016). Two sociolinguistic perspectives on multilingual families. *Slovo a slovesnost, 77*(3), 202–218.

Spolsky, B. (2004). *Language policy.* Cambridge University Press.

Sun, B., Hu, G., & Curdt-Christiansen, X. L. (2018). Metalinguistic contribution to writing competence: A study of monolingual children in China and bilingual children in Singapore. *Reading and*

Writing, 31(7), 1499–1523. https://doi.org/10.1007/s11145-018-9846-5

Swanwick, R. (2017). *Languages and languaging in deaf education: A framework for pedagogy*. Oxford University Press.

Tabors, P. O. (2008). *One child, two languages: A guide for early childhood educators of children learning English as a second language* (2nd ed.). Brookes.

Tang, G. (2017). Sign bilingualism in deaf education. In O. García, A. Lin, & S. May (Eds.), *Bilingual and multilingual education* (pp. 191–203). Springer International Publishing.

Thomas, W. P., & Collier, V. (1997). *School effectiveness for language minority students*. National Clearinghouse for Bilingual Education.

Uljarević, M., Katsos, N., Hudry, K., & Gibson, J. L. (2016). Practitioner review: Multilingualism and neurodevelopmental disorders: An overview of recent research and discussion of clinical implications. *Journal of Child Psychology and Psychiatry, 57*(11), 1205–1217. https://doi.org/10.1111/jcpp.12596

Verdon, S., McLeod, S., & Winsler, A. (2014). Language maintenance and loss in a population study of young Australian children. *Early Childhood Research Quarterly, 29*(2), 168–181. https://doi.org/10.1016/j.ecresq.2013.12.003

Westby, C. E. (1990). Ethnographic interviewing: Asking the right questions to the right people in the right ways. *Journal of Childhood Communication Disorders, 13*(1), 101–111. https://doi.org/10.1177/152574019001300111

Wiig, E. H., Semel, E., & Secord, W. (2013). *Clinical Evaluation of Language Fundamentals—Fifth edition (CELF-5)*. Pearson.

Wong Fillmore, L. (1979). Individual differences in second language acquisition. In C. J. Fillmore, D. Kempler, & W. S.-Y. Wang (Eds.), *Individual differences in language ability and language behavior* (pp. 203–228). Academic Press.

Zeshan, U., & Webster, J. (Eds.). (2020). *Sign multilingualism*. Walter De Gruyter.

5
d/Deaf and Hard of Hearing Multilingual Learners and Literacy Instruction

Jessica Scott, Chidinma Amadi, and Terynce Butts

LEARNING OBJECTIVES

Readers will:

- Learn about literacy practices used with d/Dhh students such as explicit instruction, activation of background knowledge, and metacognitive strategy instruction, and how these practices may support the reading and writing development of d/Deaf and hard of hearing multilingual learners (DMLs).
- Learn about literacy practices used with English learners (with and without disabilities) such as explicit instruction, experiential learning, peer learning, using decodable texts, and word study, and how these practices may support the reading and writing development of DMLs.
- Identify how a literacy intervention to pre-teach vocabulary was adapted to use books read in American Sign Language (ASL) with elementary and high school DMLs.
- Identify instructional literacy practices for DMLs that require further research.

d/Deaf or hard of hearing multilingual learners (DMLs) are a rapidly growing subpopulation of students who are d/Deaf or hard of hearing (d/Dhh). DMLs are those who are exposed to English and/or American

DOI: 10.4324/9781003259176-5

Sign Language (ASL) at school and in the community, and may be exposed to one or more other languages in the home (Cannon et al., 2016). Evidence suggests that DMLs may not receive instructional supports that are specific to their language backgrounds in deaf education settings (Baker & Scott, 2016). However, there is research with English learners (ELs) suggesting that bilingualism may be an asset for reading (e.g., see Carlisle et al., 1999). In addition, the unique linguistic experiences among DMLs, who may or may not use multiple sign languages and/or spoken languages, require professionals to carefully consider DML language and cultural profiles in planning for instruction. These profiles should take into consideration both the unique multilingual and multicultural needs of these students and consider their linguistic *strengths* when scaffolding learning opportunities to increase literacy skills. For instance, many DMLs have been exposed to print or are able to read fluently in their heritage language (e.g., Spanish), which teachers can use as a foundation for understanding English print. Recognizing and valuing DMLs linguistic strengths as well as their cultural backgrounds is important for creating a positive and safe classroom environment (Gay, 2010).

In the United States, hearing ELs made up 9.2% of students receiving special education services in the 2013–2014 school year (Office of English Language Acquisition, 2017) and 6.6% (37,717) of students classified under the "Other Disabilities" category of the Individuals with Disabilities Education Act (IDEA), which includes students who are d/Dhh (US Department of Education, 2014–15). DMLs are a quickly expanding subpopulation of d/Dhh learners, with approximately 19.4–35% of d/Dhh students in K-12 settings classified as ELs (Cannon et al., 2016; Gallaudet Research Institute, 2013). This is a significant proportion of d/Dhh students, and their presence in classrooms is an important call for teachers and researchers to reexamine existing knowledge and practices in order to ensure that the educational needs of DMLs are addressed.

Before instruction can begin, an interdisciplinary team (see Recommendations below for a description) must first assess the DML's strengths and needs. This includes both collecting background information (e.g., what language(s) does the child already know? What was their educational experience in their home country? What is their reading and writing fluency in their native language and/or the national language of their country of origin?) and conducting formal and informal assessments (e.g., observing the student interacting with print, using an informal reading inventory assessment, and reviewing official assessment results that are available) to determine where to begin. This careful approach both avoids providing instruction that is too difficult for the child based on their literacy backgrounds, as well as instruction that is too simple and does not challenge those who have strong foundational or even advanced literacy skills (Please see Chapter 4 of this volume for a more in-depth discussion on issues of assessment with DML).

Despite the significant number of DMLs in the educational system, there has been limited research on teaching practices that may best support these learners. Cannon and Guardino (2012) completed a systematic review of the literature to identify literacy practices that were promising for use with DMLs, based on their success both with DMLs and with ELs who have disabilities. The authors recommended instructional strategies within four main skill areas: (a) conversation and fluency, (b) alphabetic principle, (c) vocabulary, and (d) comprehension.

To promote *conversation and fluency*, the authors recommended the use of guided reading, a commonly used instructional practice with children with typical hearing that shows evidence of some success with d/Dhh students (Schirmer & Schaffer, 2010). For teaching the *alphabetic principle* to DML students learning to read via auditory phonology, Cannon and Guardino (2012) recommended the use of visual phonics. Visual phonics is a "strategy that pairs abstract letters and sounds with 46 hand cues and symbols that creates more meaning for young students when learning sound-letter correspondence" (Dewes, 2017, p. 4; International Communication Learning Institute, 1996). One case study of a DML from a Spanish-speaking home, who had cochlear implants but also used sign language, found improvement from pre- to post-test for both identifying sounds within words as well as matching consonant letters to their corresponding sounds when using visual phonics (Smith & Wang, 2010).

For *vocabulary* instruction, the use of pre-teaching important terms and multimedia tools was recommended, along with peer tutoring and metacognitive instruction to support *comprehension* (Cannon & Guardino, 2012). These are all promising practices, which require specific research to determine their level of effectiveness with DMLs. In the sections that follow, additional practices that have the potential to be effective with DMLs are drawn from the literacy research with ELs, d/Dhh learners, and DMLs.

Comprehension and Decoding

Reading and writing are complex activities for all learners that require the simultaneous engagement of an array of sub-skills, even for individuals who are learning to read and write in their heritage language (the language they use for face-to-face communication in daily life). For instance, research with hearing readers indicates that they must be able to read words using phonological or morphological decoding, connect the decoded word to a concept, employ knowledge of grammar and structure to understand that word in the context of a sentence, and use comprehension strategies to make both literal and inferential meaning from the text (Perfetti et al., 2005). Writing requires many of the same skills as reading, with the additional charge of generating ideas, spelling, editing, and revising one's own work (Graves, 1975).

According to the Simple View of Reading, linguistic comprehension (e.g., vocabulary and syntactic knowledge of English) and decoding are necessary for comprehension (Gough & Tunmer, 1986). A test of the Simple View of Reading with hearing Spanish users found that both elements were necessary, and that decoding plays a stronger role in word reading for those who have less proficiency with English (Proctor et al., 2015). Like all multilingual learners, DMLs have complex linguistic backgrounds that intersect and interact with their development of literacy skills in English. For DMLs the linguistic knowledge noted in the Simple View of Reading includes all the languages they are exposed to (i.e., heritage language, spoken and printed English, and ASL or other sign languages in their educational and home environments).

Literacy and ELs

Research with ELs on successful instructional approaches to teach reading and writing includes four approaches that may be promising for use with DMLs: (a) explicit vocabulary instruction, (b) experiential learning opportunities, (c) peer learning, and (d) scaffolding.

Explicit Vocabulary Instruction

Explicit instruction consists of direct, structured instruction that is modeled for the learners, who are then provided repeated practice of the skill(s) (Goeke, 2008). Learners are active participants in the lesson, which is scaffolded to meet their skill levels. Information is presented to the learner in meaningful chunks that culminate in comprehension of concepts through learner-directed projects that are iteratively monitored by the learner and teacher. One commonly used instructional strategy found to be successful with ELs is explicit vocabulary instruction (Fishkin, 2010; Kieffer & Lesaux, 2010; Leacox & Jackson, 2014). Explicit vocabulary instruction includes direct, structured lessons where the teacher models the process of understanding meaning and use, then provides sufficient practice using the vocabulary in context (Beck et al., 2002). Explicit instruction is beneficial for transferring content and language from the first language to the second language (Musti-Rao et al., 2018). For instance, Kieffer and Lesaux (2010) describe the importance of rich vocabulary instruction that includes high utility words (e.g., hypothesize, strategy, and words that appear frequently within and across disciplines [Palumbo et al., 2015]) being taught directly and explicitly.

Leacox and Jackson (2014) studied incidental and explicit vocabulary instruction for Spanish-speaking ELs. In this study, one group of students was exposed to new English vocabulary via incidental exposure through a teacher read-aloud. The second group was exposed to new English vocabulary via explicit instruction using a multilingual e-book that made clear links between the English word and the definition of the same vocabulary word in Spanish. The authors found that although learning occurred in both conditions, students learned more words in an explicit instruction condition (Leacox & Jackson, 2014). This demonstrates the importance of explicit instruction in English vocabulary acquisition, which has been found to be effective with DMLs (Cannon et al., 2010; Guardino et al., 2014). These findings also indicate that instruction should draw upon the linguistic *strengths* and *resources* of students (e.g., making connections with their heritage language in any modality) in order to have the greatest impact.

The teaching of vocabulary with diverse students can and should be made culturally responsive by considering cultural communication styles and language usage (Gay, 2002). In Box 5.1, we see an example of a

Box 5.1 Maria

Maria has been in Mr. Stephen's eleventh grade resource classroom for students who are d/Deaf and hard of hearing (d/Dhh) since the beginning of the semester. Her family immigrated to the United States three months prior to her joining Mr. Stephen's class. When enrolling in her new school, her parents (via a Spanish Interpreter) stated that she used Lengua de Señas Mexicana (Mexican Sign Language, LSM) as her primary mode of communication at her previous school. Her classmates are all Deaf and users of American Sign Language (ASL), but they attend a general education school with predominantly hearing students. Mr. Stephen is a teacher of d/Dhh students and teaches in a small group classroom within the school. Maria is learning ASL in school through immersion because her teacher and her peers use ASL to communicate. Maria's family speaks Spanish at home and Maria learned to read and write in Spanish before she moved to the United States. Maria is adjusting to her new school, has made friends quickly, and is attentive in class. One afternoon during independent reading time, she hurried to grab a graphic novel. Mr. Stephen asked Maria in ASL about what she was reading. She responded using the ASL that she knew and then continued her description using LSM. Since Mr. Stephen does not know LSM, Maria described the pictures by using gestures and body language. However, she ignored the text entirely during her description. When Mr. Stephen pointed to some vocabulary in print, Maria shook her head or identified something from the pictures. Mr. Stephen decided to perform a vocabulary assessment and was surprised by the results. Mr. Stephen noticed that many of the words Maria didn't recognize in print were words that she used regularly in ASL while signing with her classmates.

Mr. Stephen wants to use Maria's linguistic strengths (i.e., her ability to read and write in Spanish and her quickly developing ASL skills) to support her development of English print vocabulary. He selected important English print vocabulary from an upcoming lesson and found the equivalent words in Spanish by conferring with an

> EL specialist at his school that is fluent in Spanish. Then he explicitly taught her the vocabulary by showing flashcards with a picture equivalent to the word and the printed English and Spanish words. He explained the vocabulary concept using ASL, explicitly teaching the sign equivalent and moving among all three languages to ensure comprehension. Explicit instruction allowed Mr. Stephen to make connections between the three languages in Maria's life to increase her literacy skills.

teacher making connections between languages to support a DML in her acquisition of English vocabulary. By focusing on and leveraging student knowledge and strength, Maria's teacher was able to support her English vocabulary development through connecting her existing knowledge of Spanish and Lengua de Señas Mexicana with her growing knowledge of English and ASL. This action not only focused on Maria's strengths but also demonstrated value in her language and culture.

Experiential Learning Opportunities

Fishkin (2010) argued that hands-on instruction is a necessary component of educational experiences for EL students, stating: "ELL students learn best when they can engage in hands-on activities which allow them to gain additional experiences in using new skills and work cooperatively with other students" (p. 16). In a case study of an EL in a history class, Jaffee (2010) describes the importance of experiential learning to connect new language and vocabulary in English with hands-on experiences. In a study examining the learning preferences of ELs, researchers found a general preference for tactile, kinesthetic modes of learning through experiences and interactions with peers and the environment (Park, 2002). Together, these findings suggest that providing DMLs with opportunities for hands-on, experiential instruction may be more effective and even preferred by the students themselves compared to other types of teaching strategies.

Peer Learning

Peer learning is a promising practice for supporting the literacy development of ELs (Cole, 2013). Peer learning is a practice that emphasizes opportunities for students to teach and learn from one another. Peer learning can range from peer tutoring (i.e., with one child in the role of teacher and the other in the role of student) to collaborative and cooperative learning (i.e., the children are teamed together to learn or problem-solve; Cole, 2013). Peer learning has been found to be effective for EL students in the development of language and literacy skills (Cole, 2013; Silverman et al., 2017; Thorius & Graff, 2018), and some have argued its potential use with students with disabilities (Thorius & Graff, 2018) and DMLs (Cannon & Guardino, 2012). Teaching with a culturally responsive lens considers multiple dimensions of instruction, including relationships with peers and adults in the classroom environment (Gay, 2010). If implemented appropriately, peer learning may contribute to a culturally responsive classroom environment by building relationships between DMLs and other d/Dhh learners.

Scaffolding

Scaffolding is an educational practice that provides learners with the support they need to be successful in completing tasks that would be too difficult for them to complete on their own (August et al., 2015). Scaffolding is associated with Vygotsky's (1978) concept of the zone of proximal development (i.e., the difference between what a learner can complete independently and what the learner can do with support). Research shows that scaffolding is an important element of literacy instruction for ELs (August et al., 2015). Peercy (2011) conducted a case study to explore strategies used by teachers of ELs. The researcher found scaffolding was an important instructional practice for allowing students to read and understand texts in English. Similar findings resulted from another case study of a child that uses Arabic and attended school in the United States (Palmer et al., 2007). These studies suggest that scaffolding is an effective practice with ELs and a promising practice with d/Dhh students (Borgna et al., 2011). Box 5.2 shows an example of how scaffolding can be put to use in a classroom to support a DML's development. Mr. Luke used his knowledge of Gabriel's

> Box 5.2 Gabriel
>
> Gabriel is fourteen years old with a bilateral severe-to-profound hearing loss. He recently moved to the United States with his family from Cameroon where his parents primarily spoke French at home. In Cameroon, he was enrolled in a school that used spoken French and he was performing similar to his classroom peers across all academic subjects. Upon settling in their new neighborhood his family enrolled him in the local high school where he will receive support from a teacher of the deaf and hard of hearing (TDHH).
>
> Partway through his first semester, Gabriel found that his favorite class was Mr. Luke's Environmental Science class where his TDHH, Mr. McEwan, co-taught. Mr. Luke and Mr. McEwan provided an outline of the day's content to the class ahead of time and scaffolded versions of the expected lab report, with sentence stems and a vocabulary reference to make the activity more accessible. Gabriel used the outline to follow instructions and recognize new English vocabulary that Mr. McEwan pre-taught him the day before during one-on-one instruction. For lab work, the students were divided into groups and worked together to perform experiments to solve scientific problems. Gabriel enjoyed all the hands-on activities and learning with the group. Both teachers circulated throughout the class to provide language and literacy support to Gabriel as he was still acquiring English. One peer in Gabriel's group, Andrew, also provided support to help Gabriel if he misunderstood anything or omitted some crucial information from his lab report. The scaffolded support in an inclusive environment has increased Gabriel's English literacy skills in his favorite academic subject.

background and needs to ensure that he had scaffolded opportunities to participate in classroom instruction. Teachers should consider their DML's specific language profiles, strengths, and needs to ensure that additional scaffolding (e.g., Mr. Luke's use of sentence stems) is appropriately supportive of student learning.

Literacy and ELs With Disabilities

Literacy instruction for DMLs may be informed by successful instructional strategies used with ELs with disabilities, because these strategies address unique language and learning needs of these students. Musti-Rao and colleagues (2018) identified strategies and practices in their comprehensive chapter on special education and EL students, including (a) use of decodable texts, and (b) opportunities to engage in word study. These practices and the research supporting them are explored in detail below.

Decodable Texts

Decodable texts focus on morphological and phonological patterns to provide students with explicit information about how words are constructed. Research completed on the use of decodable texts with ELs who have disabilities includes two studies that examined the effectiveness of a supplemental reading program with ELs in kindergarten through third grade. The authors found that regular instruction using decodable texts led to improvement in decoding skills, which in turn predicted improvement in reading fluency (Gunn et al., 2000), reading comprehension, and vocabulary (Gunn et al., 2002). Two years after instruction, there was a discernible effect on oral reading fluency among students who participated in the intervention (Gunn et al., 2005). These findings suggest a benefit to using decodable texts for ELs with disabilities. As demonstrated in Box 5.3, for those students who are learning and using spoken language, experiences with text that help them "break the code" of English can be stepping stones toward reading more authentic literature. In Ye-jun's case, her transition from a logographic or non-alphabetic language to an alphabetic language may highlight the need for decodable texts that use vocabulary following predictable spelling patterns. These texts support the process of learning to use phonology to sound out English words. Others have noted the complexities of learning to read an alphabetic script after having learned a non-alphabetic script, specifically among d/Dhh learners (Wang et al., 2016). Decodable texts may be an appropriate intervention for some DMLs depending on whether the student uses a spoken language; however, these types of texts may be less useful for DMLs who primarily use a signed language.

> **Box 5.3 Ye-jun**
>
> Ye-jun is a Korean female in 2nd grade who emigrated to Canada six months ago. Her parents enrolled her in a listening and spoken language resource classroom in a general education school where English is used for instruction. Ye-jun has a moderate-to-severe hearing loss and is developing receptive and expressive English skills. Her parents speak English, but use Korean at home with Ye-jun, who has near age-appropriate language and literacy skills. At school she is learning to decode words in English. Moving from a non-alphabetic language to an alphabetic one is challenging, but Ye-jun is working hard to develop her phonics and fluency skills. Her teacher, Mrs. Rhodes, collaborated with the school's reading specialist who suggested using decodable texts—designed to incorporate words that are consistent with letter-sound relationships that are explicitly being taught to a novice reader—to help Ye-jun improve her phonics knowledge, reading fluency, and English vocabulary.
>
> Ye-jun began to show growth in her ability to make connections between letters and sounds. Because of Ye-jun's progress, Mrs. Rhodes implemented the use of decodable text into her instruction right away. Ye-jun showed consistent excitement and motivation in acquiring and practicing her decoding skills. Mrs. Rhodes spent some time every day sitting with Ye-jun as she read the decodable texts. Mrs. Rhodes used scaffolding during their daily reading time to explicitly point out and describe the meaning of new vocabulary. Mrs. Rhodes encouraged Ye-jun to take the books home to practice reading with her parents. Soon, Mrs. Rhodes noticed that Ye-jun's ability to decode unknown words and her fluency of English sight-word vocabulary were improved. Through their daily interactions, Mrs. Rhodes learned that Ye-jun enjoyed reading and learning about sports and animals. In an effort to continue improving her decoding skills, Mrs. Rhodes began choosing texts for Ye-jun that were related to her interests. This opened the door for Mrs. Rhodes to assess Ye-jun's reading comprehension skills.

Word Study

Word study, or word work, is an instructional practice that systematically teaches students patterns in spelling and orthography and how these patterns may be related to word meanings (Williams et al., 2009). One study that included ELs with reading difficulties found that word study instruction was effective for improving reading comprehension (Wanzek & Roberts, 2012). Other interventions that included a word study element, along with instruction on phonemic awareness and sentence reading, were also found to be effective for improving reading skills (Baker et al., 2016; Linan-Thompson & Hickman-Davis, 2002). Most studies examining the use of word study with ELs who have disabilities have incorporated this type of instruction into a comprehensive literacy intervention. More evidence is needed to understand the precise role word study instruction can have on literacy development.

Literacy and d/Dhh Learners

In addition to research with ELs and ELs with disabilities, there are educational practices researched with d/Dhh learners that may support the literacy development of DMLs. The existing literature encourages the use of (a) explicit instruction, (b) activation of background knowledge, and (c) use of metacognitive strategy instruction to support literacy development. Of all literacy practices researched for use with d/Dhh students, these specific practices were chosen because elements of each are also recommended for use with ELs (Musti-Rao et al., 2018; Rivera et al., 2008) and are approaches that can be used across multiple languages.

Explicit Instruction

As was found with ELs above, explicit instruction is an effective strategy for use with d/Dhh students in many facets of literacy. For example, explicit phonological awareness instruction for d/Dhh students who used spoken English resulted in improved phonological awareness skills (Gilliver et al., 2016). Similarly, explicit instruction in the alphabetic principle resulted in improved understanding and application to word reading

(Trezek & Hancock, 2013). Other researchers used explicit instruction to teach morphology and found that the student use of morphological awareness improved after intervention (Richels et al., 2016; Trussell & Easterbrooks, 2015). The wide array of skills that have been found to be improved after explicit instruction makes this a promising practice for teaching DMLs.

Activation of Background Knowledge

Activation of background knowledge may occur through explicit instruction, direct experiences, or accessible opportunities to read and learn (e.g., field trips, videos, and books presented with accessibility options on a digital reader [e.g., magnification, text-to-voice, and links to videos of ASL signs connected to English words]; Elbro & Buch-Iversen, 2013; Fisher et al., 2012). Prior research has identified a lack of background knowledge as a potential source of reading difficulties for some d/Dhh children (Andrews & Mason, 1991). This is perhaps related to limited communication opportunities due to restricted language accessibility (Hall et al., 2017). Understanding the interplay of language and culture that may contribute to students' background knowledge is essential for effective instruction. A literature review found that in some reading tasks (e.g., cloze assessments), d/Dhh students may rely a great deal on their background knowledge in order to understand text (Strassman, 1997). One case study of a deaf reader found that with sufficient background knowledge, the learner was able to connect concepts and more easily comprehend English texts (Yurkowski & Ewoldt, 1986). Although much of the available research in this area is dated, this strategy remains promising. DMLs have complex linguistic lives and receive exposure to experiences, concepts, and ideas across multiple languages. This means that building background knowledge to connect concepts during literacy experiences is likely to support textual understanding.

Metacognitive Strategy Instruction

Finally, research points to the importance of metacognitive strategy instruction for literacy development of students from a variety of backgrounds. Metacognitive literacy strategies are approaches to text that proficient readers use to construct meaning during the reading process, such as (a) comprehension monitoring, (b) making connections, (c) inferencing (including predictions), and (d) determining importance (see Table 5.1; Harvey & Goudvis, 2007). Although not all of these strategies have been tested for use with d/Dhh students, there is evidence for the potential effectiveness of two strategies. First, Benedict et al. (2015) conducted a single case design study of the use of one metacognitive comprehension strategy with three elementary school students in a general education classroom. All three participants

TABLE 5.1 Definitions of Metacognitive Reading Comprehension Strategies (Harvey & Goudvis, 2007)

Metacognitive Strategy	Definition
Comprehension Monitoring	When a reader actively attends to what they understand during reading. Comprehension monitoring can help a reader identify when they have lost focus on the text, lack the background knowledge to understand it, or have stopped comprehending the text for any other reason.
Making Connections	When a reader connects what they are reading in a text to something that they already know about because of prior knowledge or personal experience.
Making Inferences	When a reader derives meaning from a subtext or an indirect implication of a statement in a text. Making inferences asks the reader to "read between the lines" to make meaning and includes other skills such as visualization.
Determining Importance	When a reader sorts through information presented to them in a text to determine what is essential for their comprehension of the information or story, and what might be less important for understanding.

used listening and spoken language and various types of amplification. The researchers studied the use of a specific comprehension strategy called comprehension monitoring. This strategy involves teaching children to be aware of their own reading comprehension and employ repair strategies (e.g., rereading, using context clues, and looking up unknown words in the case of comprehension difficulties). The authors concluded that this strategy is a potentially effective tool for literacy learning with these three students (Benedict et al., 2015). Similarly, a qualitative study of one classroom using a total communication approach at a state school for the deaf found that the specific strategy of making predictions (a form of inferencing) seemed to support the reading abilities of participating middle-school-age d/Dhh students (Brigham & Hartman, 2010).

Luckner and Handley (2008) conducted a literature review on reading comprehension research with d/Dhh children. They found that skilled readers tended to use more metacognitive comprehension strategies than less skilled readers. They concluded that explicit comprehension strategy instruction, including metacognitive strategies, was a promising tool for supporting the literacy of d/Dhh students. Box 5.4 gives an example of how teaching a student to utilize a metacognitive strategy, in Kwame's case the strategy of making predictions, can not only improve comprehension but also the student's ability to monitor their own comprehension. In some cases, this might be an important instructional experience that helps students link their abilities to read and identify individual English words with how these words can be combined to communicate. Incorporating multiple languages—Kwame, for instance, uses four different languages with varying degrees of proficiency—will foster connections between language, knowledge, and culture during the learning process. As with both explicit instruction and activation of background knowledge, there has been no specific research on the use of metacognitive strategy instruction with DMLs. However, given the volume of research identifying the success of reading comprehension strategies for d/Dhh students, practitioners may consider the metacognitive comprehension strategy as a promising practice with this sub-population of learners.

Box 5.4 Kwame

Kwame is a ten-year-old male student in the 5th grade who has a moderate, bilateral sensorineural hearing loss and uses listening and spoken language to communicate. His family immigrated from Ghana to the United Kingdom for a job opportunity at a university when Kwame was eight years old. His first home language is Twi, a dialect of Akan (a language spoken in Ghana), although his parents are also fluent in and use English at home. In school, Kwame began learning English and British Sign Language (BSL) in a small group resource classroom with other d/Dhh students. His teacher, Mr. Johnson, uses a total communication approach for instruction (i.e., BSL signs, gestures, fingerspelling, and speech to communicate with his class). Kwame enjoys school. After being provided a reading assessment, Mr. Johnson noted that one of Kwame's strengths was his word recognition in English, while he needed to work on his ability to understand key details in a story. Mr. Johnson decides to use explicit instruction using metacognitive strategies to improve Kwame's reading comprehension. He decides to teach prediction in an effort to highlight the importance of details in a text. Mr. Johnson, who is a veteran teacher, has found that increasing prediction skills can increase attention to key details for other d/Dhh students in his classroom.

Mr. Johnson picks a story for Kwame. The story has familiar characters, but is one that Kwame has not read previously. Mr. Johnson and Kwame begin to read together, and periodically, Mr. Johnson will pause and ask Kwame what he thinks will happen next. At first, Kwame simply responds that he doesn't know. Mr. Johnson encourages Kwame to guess based upon what has previously happened in the story, what he knows about the characters, and what would help the story move forward. These predictions, Mr. Johnson explains, don't have to match the story exactly. It is important that Kwame *thinks* as he's reading and understands how context clues in the story can help him make predictions. Mr. Johnson and Kwame read short stories daily. In addition, Mr. Johnson uses graphic organizers that provide a visual cue for making predictions to scaffold Kwame's learning. Kwame quickly begins to make predictions with Mr. Johnson's support. Mr. Johnson continues to monitor his ability to comprehend by reading with him one-on-one.

Literacy and DMLs

Although the evidence is still growing, there is some research available that suggests potentially effective practices for the literacy development of DMLs. The existing literature falls broadly into two categories: (a) experiences of DMLs in the US education system, and (b) vocabulary instruction for DMLs.

Experiences of DMLs in the US Education System

Two studies explored the experiences of DMLs who were partially educated in the US educational system (Baker & Scott, 2016; Wang et al., 2016). Two of the participants were Asian (Wang et al., 2016), and one was Latina (Baker & Scott, 2016). In Wang and colleagues' (2016) case study of two DMLs who are Asian and entered postsecondary education in the United States, the researchers found that a number of factors were important for their later academic success, such as (a) home literacy environment, (b) family support, (c) Deaf identity, and (d) access to visual language and Deaf culture. The authors posited that these factors coalesced around two broader areas that were supportive of literacy development: (a) early language and family involvement, and (b) visual learning and bilingualism. Having families that were involved in the earliest stages of language development and continued to be active in their child's education provided a foundation for later success. Having accessible environments that utilized a visual language, included deaf role models, and provided opportunities to learn a written language was another factor that both participants had in common that may have influenced their later success. In his theoretical framework, Cummins (1979, 1981) argued that first language knowledge can support second language acquisition, which may be related to these findings.

In contrast, the case study of a Latina who is a DML described her trajectory through public schooling in the United States. The researchers found that her teachers reported a lack of resources that could inform their abilities to modify instruction to meet her specific literacy needs (Baker & Scott, 2016). Because an aspect of culturally relevant instruction includes specific consideration of minority students and how the learning environment might oppress or hinder their growth (Kieran & Anderson, 2019), it appears that more attention needs to be paid to effective ways of modifying instruction to meet a DML's needs. Combining the lack of available resources with reduced access to spoken English had a measurable effect on literacy development. This suggests a need for more classroom-based research on easy-to-implement instructional strategies to support the literacy development of DMLs.

Vocabulary Instruction

Two studies examined the effectiveness of a vocabulary intervention with DMLs. The intervention included pre-teaching functional English math vocabulary to DMLs before reading a book on DVD in ASL (Cannon et al., 2010; Guardino et al., 2014). There were four DML participants in Cannon and colleagues' (2010) study, ages ten to twelve, enrolled in a school for the deaf that used ASL. The researchers found that a combination of pre-teaching targeted ASL vocabulary followed by viewing of books on DVDs presented in ASL was more effective than watching the DVDs alone to increase receptive print vocabulary acquisition. Guardino and colleagues' (2014) replicated the study with high-school-age participants and found the intervention increased targeted vocabulary for older participants as well. The effectiveness of this intervention across two studies makes it a promising practice in need of further research with students who are DMLs.

FUTURE DIRECTIONS

Recommendations for the DML Population

While the knowledge-base is still growing, there are teachers working with a diverse range of DMLs that need tools and resources to support their students' growth and development. Recommendations for supporting the literacy needs of DMLs include providing opportunities for experiential and kinesthetic learning (Jaffee, 2010; Park, 2002) that activate and build background knowledge. These instructional practices may also connect classroom experiences with opportunities to build linguistic knowledge. This linguistic competence has the potential to connect new knowledge in English to the DMLs' known language(s). These connections both support language development and demonstrate to the DMLs the inherent value of their linguistic abilities and how these can be leveraged to support new knowledge. Please see Table 5.2 for a comprehensive list of the practices reviewed in this article, the literature they are taken from (e.g., hearing EL,

TABLE 5.2 Comprehensive List of the Practices

Skill	Strategy	Origin	Modifications for DML students*
Alphabetic principle and decoding	Visual phonics	DML research (Cannon & Guardino, 2012)	Visual phonics could be used to teach letter-sound pairings in a heritage, home, or first language as well as English.
	Decodable texts	Hearing EL with disabilities research (Gunn et al., 2000; Gunn et al., 2002)	Dual language decodable texts could be used when available.
Vocabulary	Explicit instruction of new words prior to reading	DML research (Cannon et al., 2010; Guardino et al., 2014). Hearing EL research (e.g., Beck et al., 2002; Fishkin, 2010; Goeke, 2008; Kieffer & Lesaux, 2010; Leacox & Jackson, 2014) d/Dhh research (Cannon & Guardino, 2012; Gilliver et al., 2016; Trezek & Hancock, 2013)	Incorporating heritage, home, or first language in vocabulary instruction. Adding visual supports that may boost comprehension. Repeated practice in context
	Multimedia tools	DML research (Cannon & Guardino, 2012)	Incorporating technology in vocabulary instruction such as closed captioning, access to text translating applications, and visual library for images.

Skill	Strategy	Origin	Modifications for DML students*
General literacy	Word study	Hearing EL with disabilities research (Baker et al., 2016; Linan-Thompson & Hickman-Davis, 2002; Wanzek & Roberts, 2012)	Addition of visual phonics for those students who benefit from its use.
	Experiential learning	Hearing EL research (Fishkin, 2010)	Make more accessible through multiple modes of representation and visual supports. Studying and learning about concepts in literature and then experiencing and bringing them to life in an activity.
	Peer tutoring	DML research (Cannon & Guardino, 2012) Hearing EL research (Cole, 2013; Silverman et al., 2017; Thorius & Graff, 2018)	Pair students strategically to ensure effective communication and collaborative learning.
	Scaffolding	Hearing EL research (August et al., 2015; Palmer et al., 2007; Peercy, 2011).	Provide resources in the heritage, home, or native language of the learner.

(Continued)

TABLE 5.2 (*Continued*)

Skill	Strategy	Origin	Modifications for DML students*
Comprehension	Activating background knowledge	d/Dhh research (Strassman, 1997; Yurkowski & Ewoldt, 1986).	Pre-assess background knowledge prior to beginning a task or activity. Provide opportunities for students to gain background knowledge in the classroom. Use of resources in the heritage, home, or native language of the learner as a way to bridge the gap to acquisition of new knowledge and skill.
	Metacognitive strategy instruction	DML research (Cannon & Guardino, 2012). DHH research (Benedict et al., 2015; Brigham & Hartman, 2010).	Build on metacognitive strategy knowledge already developed in a heritage, home, or first language. Provide opportunities to practice and apply repair (e.g., rereading, using context clues, and looking up unknown words in the case of comprehension difficulties) strategies. Opportunities to teach others about newly acquired knowledge and/or skills.

*Some of the recommendations here are appropriate for all d/Dhh learners, not exclusively DMLs.

d/Dhh, or DML), and examples of modifications that could be appropriate for DML students.

The authors also advocate applying an approach to literacy that builds upon linguistic strengths. A strengths-based social model focuses on the benefits of areas such as ASL fluency and deaf cultural membership on academic and social outcomes of d/Dhh learners (Humphries, 2013; Ladd, 2005), which has also been found with some DMLs (Wang et al., 2016). An approach to education that focuses on strengths and assets is a paradigm shift that is argued to be important for including linguistically and culturally diverse students (Scanlan, 2007). The ultimate purpose of a strength-based approach is to leverage learner strengths to support their overall growth (Lopez & Louis, 2009).

In the areas of literacy, teachers may consider (a) whether and how much DMLs have been exposed to print in their home languages, (b) how their familial and personal language resources could impact their literacy, and (c) where opportunities may exist that allow students to develop biliteracy skills in both English and their heritage languages. Each child has their own strengths and professionals should take the time to learn about them. As such, DMLs are likely to have a wide variety of strengths that can contribute to their literacy development.

The authors recommend assembling interdisciplinary teams that include professionals with specialized strengths and knowledge that may inform the education of each DML. These teams may include individuals such as the teacher of the deaf, general education teachers, audiologists, and speech-language pathologists. Deaf adults should also be included in these teams and in classrooms with all d/Dhh children, including DMLs. Others have argued that Deaf adults are beneficial as cultural (Scott et al., 2020) and literacy models (Dostal et al., 2021). The team may also include teachers who specialize in working with English learners, reading specialists, and family outreach specialists. For instance, a reading specialist could contribute specific knowledge of reading instruction for one-on-one or small group instruction. The reading specialist may also be able to assist the team by identifying the DML's literacy strengths and needs. An EL specialist could contribute similar knowledge and experiences based on working with ELs, specifically related to utilizing language strengths and teaching English as a non-native language. A Deaf adult could provide specialized knowledge in visual communication and capitalizing on visual strengths and cultural practices of reading in deaf communities. These specialists working together would contribute a multidisciplinary perspective of strategies that could enhance the literacy instruction provided to the DML across instructional settings. A family outreach specialist may also be able to suggest activities the family could implement to support learning at home and in the community. By working together, the team actively creates a meaningful connection between home and school life. Each team member contributes their unique perspective on approaches to teaching that may be most impactful on the reading and writing abilities of the DML.

Conclusion

In this chapter, we explored instructional strategies across three fields (i.e., hearing EL education, hearing EL special education, and d/Dhh education) that appear promising for use with DMLs. Specifically, we identified (a) explicit vocabulary instruction, (b) experiential learning opportunities, and (c) peer learning as effective strategies for teaching literacy with ELs. From the field of EL special education, the use of (a) decodable texts, (b) opportunities to engage in word study, and (c) clear corrective feedback are potentially helpful when working with DMLs. Finally, we discussed the use of (a) explicit instruction, (b) activation of background knowledge, and (c) metacognitive strategy instruction as approaches utilized with d/Dhh students that may also be appropriate for DMLs. Teachers who are working with this population of students should attempt to use these practices to support literacy development.

Research has only begun to explore DMLs and the instructional approaches that might be most appropriate to ensure their success. Research is needed to better understand the multilingual and multicultural strengths and needs of this population in order to best support their literacy. As this population continues to grow, and interdisciplinary fields become more knowledgeable about these students, a strong relationship between researchers and practitioners will help ensure success for all DMLs.

Discussion Questions

1. Why are some practices used with d/Dhh students promising for use with DMLs, specifically explicit instruction, activation of background knowledge, and metacognitive strategy instruction?

2. How might experiential learning, an evidence-based practice used with English learners, support the reading development of a DML? What is one way in which this type of practice can be applied in the classroom?
3. Summarize the evidence supporting pre-teaching vocabulary before reading texts with DMLs. What makes this a promising practice?
4. Wang and colleagues (2016) found that home literacy environment, family support, a Deaf identity, and access to visual language and Deaf cultures were important for later academic success for college-age DMLs. Why might these factors be particularly important for reading and writing development?

Resources

Websites

- ¡Colorin colorado! (https://www.colorincolorado.org/): A bilingual site for educators and families of English learners.
- Described Captioned Media Program (https://dcmp.org/): Provides free access to thousands of accessible educational videos for parents and teachers working with learners who are d/Dhh. All of the videos are captioned and some videos are presented in languages other than English, such as Spanish.
- Gallaudet University's Clerc Center (https://clerccenter.gallaudet.edu/national-resources/resources/our-resources/shared-reading-project.html): Developed the Shared Reading Project to help parents and caregivers with children who are deaf or hard of hearing read to their children in a natural and productive way to help their children develop language and literacy skills.
- Global Digital Library (https://vl2storybookapps.com/digital-library): By VL2 provides a variety of children's stories presented in various spoken and signed languages.
- Teaching Vocabulary in Context (www.readworks.org): The site gives educators and families resources to practice and increase literacy skills across a variety of content areas. This site contains content specifically for English learners (Collections for ELs) and offers activities that teach language and vocabulary in context.

- University of British Columbia Global Storybooks (https://globalstorybooks.net/): This resource provides online children's textbooks in a variety of languages from around the globe.

Organizations

- Accessible Materials Project (AMP): AMP provides language and literacy support for students, professionals, and families that are or work with Deaf or Hard of Hearing individuals. AMP provides ASL versions of original resources and stories within the public domain. Some resources are available in both English and Spanish. Trade books and copyrighted materials are available under limited circumstances. Contact AMP@doe.k12.ga.us for more information.
- American Association for Applied Linguistics (AAAL; www.aaal.org): AAAL is a national organization of researchers who work in the field of applied linguistics, including topics such as bilingualism, literacy, second language teaching, and language assessment.
- International Literacy Association (ILA; www.literacyworldwide.org/): ILA is an international, teacher-centered organization that focuses on literacy skills development both in the United States and in global settings.
- National Association for Bilingual Education (NABE; https://nabe.org/): NABE is an international organization that supports the academic achievement of bilingual and multilingual learners.
- Teachers of English to Speakers of Other languages (TESOL; www.tesol.org/): TESOL is an international organization of teachers who work with children who are learning English as an additional language.

Articles and Books

- Easterbrooks, S.R., & Beal-Alvarez, J. (2013). *Literacy instruction for students who are deaf or hard of hearing.* Oxford University Press: This book explores the research-based practices in deaf education related to literacy learning.
- Easterbrooks, S. R., & Dostal, H. M. (Eds.). (2020). *The Oxford Handbook of Deaf Studies in Literacy.* Oxford University Press.
- Honigsfeld, A.M., & Dove, M.G. (2019). *Collaborating for English learners: A foundational guide to integrated practices.* Corwin Press. This

book is based upon evidence-based practices but explores these through the lens of collaboration with other professionals in order to meet the needs of English learners.

Family-Centered Brief

FAMILY-CENTERED BRIEF

CHAPTER 5
Literacy Instruction
for d/Deaf and Hard of Hearing Multilingual Learners (DMLs)

by Jessica Scott, Chidinma Amadi & Terynce Butts

PURPOSE OF THE CHAPTER
This chapter reviews approaches to teaching reading and writing with DMLs.

KEY TERMS
Important terms are highlighted in **bold** and defined within the text below

TIPS FOR FAMILIES AND TEACHERS
There is limited research published on DMLs, so try the following strategies that are known to work for English learners, English learners with disabilities, and d/Dhh students with disabilities.

- Use **explicit teaching** (clear instructions) to introduce students to important words and concepts using visual support
- Use **experiential learning** (hands-on experiences) to introduce new topics before reading or writing about them
- Use books with **decodable text** (books with words that are easy to sound out)
- Set up **peer learning** opportunities (children learn from each other)
- Teach the child to try **predicting** what will happen next
- Teach the child to try guessing a word's meaning based on **context clues** (words and pictures around the unfamiliar word)
- Teach spelling patterns and word parts
- **Activate background knowledge** (ask students to think about what they already know about a topic before teaching it)
- For students who use American Sign Language (ASL), use ASL story videos with a teacher to help the student learn new English words
- Explain a student's mistakes to help them avoid making the same mistake again

RESOURCES
University of British Columbia Global Storybooks globalstorybooks.net/

National Association of Bilingual Education special interest group for parents and community members nabe.org/about-nabe/special-interest-groups/

Deaf and Hard of Hearing Multilingual Learners: Foundations, Strategies, and Resources (2022)

References

Andrews, J. F., & Mason, J. M. (1991). Strategy usage among deaf and hearing readers. *Exceptional Children, 57*(6), 536–545.

August, D., McCardle, P., & Shanahan, T. (2015). Developing literacy in English language learners: Findings from a review of the experimental research. *School Psychology Review, 43*(4), 490–498.

Baker, D. L., Burns, D., Kame'enui, E. J., Smolkowski, K., & Baker, S. K. (2016). Does supplemental instruction support the transition from Spanish to English reading instruction for first-grade English learners at risk of reading difficulties? *Learning Disabilities Quarterly, 39*(4), 226–239. https://doi.org/10.1177/0731948715616757

Baker, S., & Scott, J. A. (2016). Sociocultural and academic considerations for d/Deaf and hard of hearing multilingual learners: A case study of a Deaf Latina. *American Annals of the Deaf, 161*(1), 43–55.

Beck, I. L., McKeown, M. G., & Kucan, L. (2002). *Bringing words to life: Robust vocabulary instruction*. Gilford.

Benedict, K. M., Rivera, M. C., & Antia, S. D. (2015). Instruction in metacognitive strategies to increase deaf and hard of hearing students' reading comprehension. *Journal of Deaf Studies and Deaf Education, 20*(1), 1–15.

Borgna, G., Convertino, C., Marschark, M., Morrison, C., & Rizzolo, K. (2011). Enhancing deaf students' learning from sign language and text: Metacognition, modality, and the effectiveness of content scaffolding. *Journal of Deaf Studies and Deaf Education, 16*(1), 79–100.

Brigham, M., & Hartman, M. (2010). What is your prediction? Teaching the metacognitive skill of prediction to a class of sixth- and seventh-graders who are deaf. *American Annals of the Deaf, 155*(2), 137–143.

Cannon, J. E., Fredrick, L. D., & Easterbrooks, S. R. (2010). Vocabulary instruction through books read in American Sign Language for English-language learners with hearing loss. *Communication Disorders Quarterly, 31*(2), 98–112.

Cannon, J. E., & Guardino, C. (2012). Literacy strategies for deaf/hard of hearing English language learners: Where do we begin? *Deafness and Education International, 14*(2), 78–99.

Cannon, J. E., Guardino, C., Antia, S., & Luckner, J. (2016). Single-case design research: Building the evidence-base in the field of education of

Deaf/hard of hearing students. *American Annals of the Deaf, 160*(5), 440–452. https://doi.org/10.1353/aad.2016.0007

Cannon, J. E., Guardino, C., & Gallimore, E. (2016). A new kind of heterogeneity: What we can learn from d/Deaf and hard of hearing multilingual learners. *American Annals of the Deaf, 161*(1), 8–16.

Carlisle, J. F., Beeman, M., Davis, L. H., & Spharim, G. (1999). Relationship of metalinguistic capabilities and reading achievement for children who are becoming bilingual. *Applied Psycholinguistics, 20*(4), 459–478.

Cole, M. (2013). Rompiendo el silencio: Meta-analysis of the effectiveness of peer-mediated learning at improving language outcomes for ELLs. *Bilingual Research Journal, 36*(2), 146–166. https://doi.org/10.1080/15235882.2013.814609

Cummins, J. (1979). Linguistic interdependence and the educational development of bilingual children. *Review of Educational Research, 49*(2), 222–251. https://doi.org/10.3102/00346 543049002222

Cummins, J. (1981). The role of primary language development in promoting educational success for language-minority students. In California State Department of Education (Ed.), *Schooling and language-minority students: A theoretical framework* (pp. 3–49). California State University.

Dewes, K. R. (2017). *The impact of See the Sound Visual Phonics has on beginning readers* [Master's thesis]. Northwestern College, Orange City, IA. http://nwcommons.nwciowa.edu/education_masters/27/

Dostal, H., Scott, J. A., Weir, J., Kang, K., Amadi, C., & Bernard, T. (2021). Literacy development at camp: Leveraging language models. *The Reading Teacher, 74*(5), 539–547.

Elbro, C., & Buch-Iversen, I. (2013). Activation of background knowledge for inference making: Effects on reading comprehension. *Scientific Studies of Reading, 17*(6), 435–452. https://doi.org/10.1080/10888438.2013.774005

Fisher, D., Frey, N., & Lapp, D. (2012). Building and activating students' background knowledge: It's what they already know that counts. *Middle School Journal, 43*(3), 22–31. https://doi.org/10.1080/00940771.2012.11461808

Fishkin, O. (2010). Effective primary literacy strategies for English language learners. *Illinois Reading Council Journal, 38*(4), 14–19.

Gallaudet Research Institute. (2013). *Regional and national summary report of data from the 2011–12 Annual Survey of Deaf and Hard of Hearing Children and Youth.* Gallaudet University.

Gay, G. (2002). Preparing for culturally responsive teaching. *Journal of Teacher Education, 53*(2), 106–116.

Gay, G. (2010). *Culturally responsive teaching: Theory, research, and practice* (2nd ed.). Teachers College Press.

Gilliver, M., Cupples, L., Ching, T. Y. C., Leigh, G., & Gunnourie, M. (2016). Developing sound skills for reading: Teaching phonological awareness to preschoolers with hearing loss. *Journal of Deaf Studies and Deaf Education, 21*(3), 268–279. http://doi.org/10.1093/deafed/enw004

Goeke, J. L. (2008). *Explicit instruction: A framework for meaningful direct teaching.* Pearson.

Gough, P. B., Tunmer, W. E. (1986). Decoding, reading, and reading disability. *Remedial and Special Education, 7,* 6–10.

Graves, D. H. (1975). An examination of the writing processes of seven year old children. *Research in the Teaching of English, 9*(3), 227–241. www.jstor.org/stable/40170631

Guardino, C., Cannon, J. E., & Eberst, K. (2014). Building the evidence-base of effective reading strategies to use with Deaf English language learners. *Communications Disorders Quarterly, 35*(2), 59–73. https://doi.org/10.1177/1525740113506932

Gunn, B., Biglan, A., Smolkowski, K., & Ary, D. (2000). The efficacy of supplemental instruction in decoding skills for Hispanic and non-Hispanic students in early elementary school. *The Journal of Special Education, 34*(2), 90–103.

Gunn, B., Smolkowski, K., Biglan, A., & Black, C. (2002). Supplemental instruction in decoding skills for Hispanic and non-Hispanic students in early elementary school: A follow-up. *The Journal of Special Education, 36*(2), 69–79.

Gunn, B., Smolkowski, K., Biglan, A., Black, C., & Blair, J. (2005). Fostering the development of reading skill through supplemental instruction: Results for Hispanic and non-Hispanic students. *The Journal of Special Education, 39*(2), 66–85.

Hall, M. L., Eigsti, I., Bortfeld, H., & Lillo-Martin, D. (2017). Auditory deprivation does not impair executive function, but language deprivation might: Evidence from a parent-report measure in Deaf native signing children. *Journal of Deaf Studies and Deaf Education, 22*(1), 9–21.

Harvey, S., & Goudvis, A. (2007). *Strategies that work: Teaching comprehension for understanding and engagement.* Stenhouse.

Humphries, T. (2013). Schooling in American Sign Language: A paradigm shift from a deficit model to a bilingual model in deaf education. *Berkeley Review of Education, 4*(1), 7–33. https://doi.org/10.5070/B84110031

International Communication Learning Institute (1996). *See the sound visual phonics.* Author.

Jaffee, A. T. (2010). Community, voice, and inquiry: Teaching global history for English language learners. *Social Studies, 107*(3), 1–13. https://doi.org/10.1080/00377996.2016.1140626

Kieffer, M. K., & Lesaux, N. K. (2010). Morphing into adolescents: Active word learning for English-language learners and their classmates in middle school. *Journal of Adolescent and Adult Literacy, 54*(1), 47–56.

Kieran, L., & Anderson, C. (2019). Connecting universal design for learning with culturally responsive teaching. *Education and Urban Society, 51*(9), 1202–1216.

Ladd, P. (2005). Deafhood: A concept stressing possibilities, not deficits. *Scandinavian Journal of Public Health, 33*(Suppl 66), 12–17. https://doi.org/10.1080/14034950510033318

Leacox, L., & Jackson, C. W. (2014). Spanish vocabulary-bridging technology-enhanced instruction for young English language learners' word learning. *Journal of Early Childhood Literacy, 14*(2), 175–197. https://doi.org/10.1177/1468798412585185

Linan-Thompson, S., & Hickman-Davis, P. (2002). Supplemental reading instruction for students at risk for reading disabilities: Improve reading 30 minutes at a time. *Learning Disabilities Research & Practice, 17*(4), 242–251.

Lopez, S. J., & Louis, M. C. (2009). The principles of strengths-based education. *Journal of College and Character, 10*(4), 1–8. https://doi.org/10.2202/1940-1639.1041

Luckner, J. L., & Handley, C. M. (2008). A summary of the reading comprehension research undertaken with students who are deaf or hard of hearing. *American Annals of the Deaf, 153*(1), 6–36. https://doi.org/10.1353/aad.0.0006

Musti-Rao, S., Kourea, L., Lynch, T. L., & Cartledge, G. (2018). Culturally responsive literacy instruction for English language learners and students with disabilities: Implications for best practice. In S. Kim (Ed.), *ESOL education: Current issues and evidence-based teaching practice*. Untested Ideas Research Center.

Office of English Language Acquisition. (2017). *Students with disabilities who are English learners*. OELA.

Palmer, B. C., El-Ashry, F., Leclere, J. T., & Chang, S. (2007). Learning from Abdallah: A case study of an Arabic-speaking child in a U.S. school. *The Reading Teacher, 61*(1), 8–17. https://doi.org/10.1598/RT.61.1.2

Palumbo, A., Kramer-Vida, L., & Hunt, C. V. (2015). Teaching vocabulary and morphology in intermediate grades. *Preventing School Failure, 59*(2), 109–115.

Park, C. C. (2002). Crosscultural differences in learning styles of secondary English learners. *Bilingual Research Journal, 26*(2), 443–459. https://doi.org/10.1080/15235882.2002.10668720

Peercy, M. M. (2011). Preparing English language learners for the mainstream: Academic language and literacy practices in two junior high school ESL classrooms. *Reading and Writing Quarterly, 27*(4), 324–362. https://doi.org/10.1080/10573569.2011.596105

Perfetti, C. A., Landi, N., & Oakhill, J. (2005). The acquisition of reading comprehension skills. In M. J. Snowling & C. Hulme (Eds.), *Blackwell handbooks of developmental psychology. The science of reading: A handbook* (pp. 227–247). Blackwell Publishing.

Proctor, C. P., Harring, J. R., & Silverman, R. D. (2015). Comparing reading profiles of biliterate Latino/a children in elementary school: Evidence from the simple view of reading. *Miriada Hispanica, 10*, 59–82.

Richels, C. G., Schwartz, K. S., Bobzien, J. L., & Raver, S. A. (2016). Structured instruction with modified storybooks to teach morphosyntax and vocabulary to preschoolers who are deaf/hard of hearing. *Journal of Deaf Studies and Deaf Education, 21*(4), 352–361. https://doi.org/10.1093/deafed/enw049

Rivera, M. O., Moughamian, A. C., Lesaux, N. K., & Francis, D. J. (2008). *Language and reading interventions for English language learners and English language learners with disabilities.* RMC Research Corporation, Center on Instruction.

Scanlan, M. (2007). An asset-based approach to linguistic diversity. *Focus on Teacher Education, 7*(3), 3–5.

Schirmer, B. R., & Schaffer, L. (2010). Guided reading approach: Teaching reading to students who are deaf and others who struggle. *Teaching Exceptional Children, 42*(5), 52–58.

Scott, J. A., Kasun, G. S., & Bedolla, F. R. (2020). "We have conflicting cultures here": Transnational third spaces in international deaf education. In Q. Wang & J. Andrews (Eds.), *Literacy and deaf education: Toward a global understanding* (69–87). Gallaudet University Press.

Silverman, R. D., Martin-Beltran, M., Peercy, M. M., & Hartranft, A. M. (2017). Effects of a cross—age peer learning program on the vocabulary and comprehension of English learners and non-English learners in elementary school. *The Elementary School Journal, 117*(3), 485–512.

Smith, A., & Wang, Y. (2010). The impact of visual phonics on the phonological awareness and speech production of a student who is deaf: A case study. *American Annals of the Deaf, 155*(2), 124–130.

Strassman, B. (1997). Metacognition and reading in children who are deaf: A review of the research. *Journal of Deaf Studies and Deaf Education, 2*, 140–149.

Thorius, K. A. K., & Graff, C. S. (2018). Extending peer-assisted learning strategies for racially, linguistically, and ability diverse learners. *Intervention in School and Clinic, 53*(3), 163–170. https://doi.org/10.1177/1053451217702113

Trezck, B. J., & Hancock, G. R. (2013). Implementing instruction in the alphabetic principle within a sign bilingual setting. *Journal of Deaf Studies and Deaf Education, 18*(3), 391–408. https://doi.org/10.1093/deafed/ent016

Trussell, J. W., & Easterbrooks, S. R. (2015). Effects of morphographic instruction on the morphographic analysis skills of deaf and hard-of-hearing students. *Journal of Deaf Studies and Deaf Education, 20*(3), 229–241. https://doi.org/10.1093/deafed/env019

US Department of Education. (2014–15). *Number and percent of children ages 3 through 5 and 6 through 21 served under IDEA, part B, by LEP status and state*. Retrieved August 3, 2017, from https://www2.ed.gov/programs/osepidea/618-data/static-tables/2014-2015/part-b/child-count-and-educational-environment/1415-bchildcountandedenvironment-4.xlsx.

Vygotsky, L. S. (1978). *Mind in society: The development of higher psychological processes*. Harvard University Press.

Wang, Q., Andrews, J., Liu, H. T., & Liu, C. J. (2016). Case studies of multilingual/multicultural Asian deaf adults: Strategies for success. *American Annals of the Deaf, 161*(1), 67–88. https://doi.org/10.1353/aad.2016.0012

Wanzek, J., & Roberts, G. (2012). Reading interventions with varying instructional emphases for fourth graders with reading difficulties. *Learning Disability Quarterly, 35*(2), 90–101. https://doi.org/10.1177/0731948711434047

Williams, C., Phillops-Birdson, C., Hufnagel, K., Hungler, D., & Lundstrom, R. P. (2009). Word study instruction in the K-2 classroom. *The Reading Teacher, 62*(7), 570–578. https://doi.org/10.1598/RT.62.7.3

Yurkowski, P., & Ewoldt, C. (1986). A case for the semantic processing of the deaf reader. *American Annals of the Deaf, 131*(3), 243–247. https://doi.org/10.1353/aad.2012.0795

6
Leadership and Collaboration in School Settings for d/Deaf and Hard of Hearing Multilingual Learners

Lianna Pizzo

Learning Objectives

Readers will:

1. Learn about the five components of the Essential Instructional Supports Framework and how they can support d/Deaf and hard of hearing multilingual learners (DMLs).
2. Understand the important roles that leaders play in creating supportive, welcoming, and trusting environments for DMLs and their families.
3. Learn about strategies leaders can use to promote praxis and reflection in their schools or programs to support the learning of DMLs.
4. Explore considerations for working with culturally and linguistically diverse families of d/Dhh children in programs and schools.
5. Reflect on one's own perspectives and experiences of cultural and linguistic diversity within d/Dhh education.

Data from the Gallaudet Research Institute (GRI, 2013) indicates that up to 35% of d/Dhh children in school in the United States are d/Deaf or hard of hearing children (d/Dhh) who come from a home where

DOI: 10.4324/9781003259176-6

a language other than English or American Sign Language (ASL) is used, also known as d/Deaf and hard of hearing multilingual learners (DMLs). To date, there is very little research on the education of children who are DMLs, but the topic has been an increasing focus of researchers in recent years (Cannon et al., 2016). One area less recognized, but deserving of attention, is the leadership and collaboration strategies needed to adequately support school staff to serve learners who are DMLs and their families.

Educational leadership is an important component of high-quality education for children in early childhood through 12th grade. Leaders set and act on a vision for the school and/or program (Drago-Severson, 2012) and facilitate school improvement and school reform (Boscardin, 2005; Hannay et al., 2013; Khalifa et al., 2014). They also support the instruction and learning of children (Branch et al., 2013), including those who are traditionally marginalized (Frattura & Capper, 2007; Marshall & Oliva, 2006). Without adequate leadership, programs and schools struggle to coordinate the instruction, services, and programming necessary to meet the needs of the learners they serve.

Terminology

This chapter uses the term "learners" to denote individuals aged birth through 22 years in an educational setting. These learners are educated in a variety of settings beyond pre-K-12 schools, such as early intervention home visits, community-based centers, transition programs, and after-school programming. In addition, the term "families" will be used over the term "parents", in order to recognize and honor non-traditional family configurations. The term "educators" is used over "teachers", as not all personnel who work with children who are DMLs are classroom teachers. Finally, the term "leaders" is used to denote the wide array of school and/or program leadership, including principals, directors, coaches, educator-leaders, and superintendents.

Conceptual Framework

Culturally responsive school leadership strategies that apply to pre-K through grade-12 schools have been identified in the research literature.

For leaders that serve DMLs, culturally responsive practices are an important component, but not enough to sustain the kinds of educational environments and practices necessary to create a truly responsive environment. A framework is needed that is (a) culturally responsive, (b) linguistically responsive, and (c) supports the unique needs of DMLs. This requires drawing upon disparate bodies of literature for key findings that apply to this population, including culturally responsive practices, linguistically responsive practices, special education, d/Dhh education, and the small bodies of research specifically addressing DMLs. For the purposes of this chapter, the Essential Instructional Supports Framework (Pacchiano et al., 2016) will be used as an organizational tool to categorize the findings across these literatures in a meaningful way.

Although Essential Instructional Supports Framework was originally designed with early childhood settings in mind, its components apply to all age levels. This framework consists of five key supports: (a) Inclusive and Instructional Leadership; (b) Routine Teacher Collaboration; (c) Child-Centered Supportive Learning Environments; (d) Ambitious Interactions and Instruction; and (e) Strong Ties and Partnerships Among Families, Schools, and Community. By examining the literature through this framework, it is possible to identify key supports that can impact the quality of education for DMLs.

Inclusive and Instructional Leadership

The Essential Instructional Supports Framework begins with *Inclusive and Instructional Leadership*, as leadership is the driver of change within schools and programs (Pacchiano et al., 2016). This component focuses on (a) establishing a vision for the program or school, (b) building trusting and respectful relationships with educators, (c) cultivating shared leadership practices, (d) hiring teachers, and (e) managing resources. See Table 6.1 for full definition and associated strategies and Box 6.1 for a vignette about establishing a mission statement at a school for the deaf with a large population of DMLs.

> Box 6.1 Inclusive and Instructional Leadership
>
> In a school for the deaf in a major city on the east coast of the United States, 80% of the school population are DMLs. Languages represented in the school are Spanish, Arabic, Creole, Portuguese, Vietnamese, Khmer, and English. The languages of instruction are ASL and English. The school also includes programming for children who are d/Dhh with disabilities.
>
> The school leadership recently decided to revise the school's mission statement to reflect the changing needs and priorities of the school. At a school-wide professional development session, the staff reviewed the current mission statement and brainstormed their thoughts on what should be included or taken out. Detailed notes were taken and the leadership team, including representatives from early childhood, elementary, and middle secondary, drafted a version of the mission. They brought the mission back to the staff and the principal asked the following questions: Does this mission accurately reflect the many cultures of our children? Have we discussed the home language and culture? What about our students with more than one disability? As the discussion progressed, the statement was amended and revised. At the annual family event, the school had multiple language interpreters and translated the mission statements, while cultural workers and community members elicited input from all families about the mission statement. The statement was then revised one last time and sent home to families for input before being put to a vote by the entire school faculty and staff.

Establishing Vision

Leaders are responsible for establishing the vision and mission of a school or program. In schools for d/Dhh children, this vision needs to explicitly include aspects of educational programming that are specific for children who are DMLs. In public schools, DMLs should be considered as one of the diverse groups that the school or program may be serving. One successful example of developing a vision including DMLs was at a school for the d/Deaf. In this case, the instructional leadership team developed a vision for their school for the d/Deaf through the establishment of a strategic planning committee. This committee consisted of a selection of school leadership, teachers, and specialists, including those who were deaf, Deaf, and hard of hearing themselves. Local public-school leadership, the commission for the d/Deaf and hard of hearing, university faculty, and parents were also invited to participate in this committee. Over the course of two years, the group met monthly to address the major needs of the school. After five major themes for school improvement were identified, the team would break into working groups to operationalize the proposed strategies to address the needs. At the end of each discussion, the principal asked the group to address two questions: (a) Is there anything specific that our DMLs need in addition to this list? (b) Are there any additional ideas to make families feel more welcome in our school? Although the vision was developed through collaboration, the leaders are responsible for encouraging and energizing the group toward realization of their goals.

Building Trusting and Respectful Relationships with Educators

Effective leaders develop an environment that promotes trust with and among educators. Trust between educators and their administrators is associated with a developed sense of community, higher morale, and lower teacher absenteeism (Crowther et al., 2009). When negative interactions among educators and administrators increase, teacher satisfaction suffers and teachers may leave the site or even the profession (e.g., Bickmore & Bickmore, 2010). Without trust, educators may not feel comfortable collaborating with others, sharing their thoughts or opinions, and/or seeking advice about their practice.

Establishing trust is especially important when discussing sensitive topics, such as language, culture, and/or identity (Scanlan & Lopez, 2012), all of which are areas that are essential to the education of DMLs. Trust requires strong attention to relationship building and maintenance.

Leaders must work to know their staff by making time for discussions and thoughtful listening (e.g., taking time to make conversations with teachers about their lives). Trusting environments support a climate where educators can discuss sensitive topics around culture and language in earnest (e.g., addressing challenges during common planning time as a group).

Cultivating Shared Leadership Practices

The literature supports the use of shared leadership strategies as a way to strengthen programs and schools (Hargreaves & O'Connor, 2018; Harris, 2013). Shared leadership, or also known as distributed leadership, requires leaders to actively work to support and develop the leadership of others (Harris, 2013). Shared leadership has been linked, directly or indirectly, with school culture, school conditions, and student outcomes (Day et al., 2009). Shared leadership strategies include the opportunity to lead meetings, develop programs, conduct professional development, and/or contribute to the content of strategic goals.

Shared leadership strategies for programs that educate DMLs include opportunities for stakeholders to share their knowledge and experience. Adults who are DMLs should be recruited to share their own experiences with language and culture when appropriate. Educators with expertise in working with DMLs should be encouraged to share their knowledge with others. For example, a program for d/Dhh children invited one of their paraprofessionals to discuss her experience living across multiple cultures and languages. The theme of the presentation was: What do I wish my teachers knew about me?

Providing a space for families of DMLs to have a voice in the school or program is also a key component of shared leadership that can support the education of DMLs. Parental input can be critical, especially at sites where few people have experiences working with DMLs and their families. Gathering information from families can be formal (e.g., asking them to share their goals for their children on a questionnaire) or informal (e.g., collecting small amounts of information over time at drop off or pick up). Regardless, engaging families in thoughtful conversations about their children can be a powerful exercise for leaders.

Hiring Teachers and Managing Resources

Leaders are responsible for the management of personnel and resources. For DMLs, effort needs to be directed at hiring staff who are competent in working with this population, who have given thought to their practice for this population, and/or who are DMLs themselves. While in certain geographic areas it is not always possible to find candidates with the relevant experience, it is important to actively recruit individuals who have the orientations and pedagogical skills necessary to support English language learners (Lucas & Villegas, 2013), including DMLs. Collaborating with teacher preparation programs, providing competitive salaries, and offering opportunities to develop educators' practice are all potentially successful recruitment strategies. When unable to recruit personnel with the prerequisite skills, finding personnel that possess some degree of linguistically responsive orientations (e.g., sociolinguistic consciousness, value for linguistic diversity, and inclination to advocate for diverse learners) and pedagogical knowledge and skills (e.g., a repertoire of strategies for learning about the background of learners, understanding of dual language development, ability to identify language demands of a task, and repertoire of scaffolding strategies) is a priority (Lucas & Villegas, 2013). As such, questions about the teacher's orientations and pedagogical knowledge and skills need to be included in any hiring interview or teaching demonstration.

In terms of resource allocation, there are many components of building a culturally and linguistically responsive budget that are necessary. Not all leaders will have control over their own budgets; however, many principals, vice principals, or school superintendents will have the ability to allocate financial resources. In some large school districts in the United States, even curriculum directors may have a budget to buy new school supplies, such as books, technology, and intervention materials. As a comprehensive approach to creating an educational program equipped to work with DMLs and their families, each component of this leadership framework has associated resources required to support it effectively. Family programming, professional development, culturally relevant curricula, technology, and staffing are all areas that may require devoted resources to support the work envisioned in this chapter.

Leaders will need to prioritize their budgets to meet the needs of all children in their schools; however, considering the specific needs of children who are DMLs and their families may enhance the educational experiences for these children and everyone in the school. For example, allocating money to buy books that support positive images of cultural diversity is essential. In addition, ensuring that high-quality interpreters are present at family events is an important part of building family relationships and an inclusive environment in the school. Interpreters, for both spoken and sign languages, require devoted financial resources.

One real-world example of using resources to support DMLs was a principal who allocated funds to support a curriculum development project. This principal paid two teachers to work a set number of hours during the summer to create extension lessons for existing curriculum units. These units focused on developing concepts of identity and culture that were: (a) integrated into the curriculum; (b) addressed understandings of heritage culture, Deaf culture, and identity; and (c) leveraged technology to introduce positive Deaf role models from various communities and cultures around the world. The work started with grades 3rd to 5th and was expanded over the next two years during grade-level common planning time.

Routine Teacher Collaboration

Teacher collaboration is a cornerstone of the educational system as it has been linked to improved student achievement (e.g., Ronfeldt et al., 2015), educator effectiveness (e.g., Leana, 2011), educator motivation and retention (e.g., Papay & Kraft, 2017), and outcomes of student-centered problem-solving teams (Sheridan et al., 2004). Collaboration in special education has served to support eligibility determination and placement, instructional practice, and the resolution of challenges for specific students (Burns et al., 2005). The Essential Instructional Supports Framework characterizes *Routine Teacher Collaboration* as leaders using strategies to build professional capacity, establish school improvement efforts, and promote regular collaboration among professionals (Pacchiano et al., 2016). In *Routine Teacher Collaboration*, leaders protect time for professional learning, build routines to support self-reflection, and support collaboration at all levels (Pacchiano et al., 2016).

For leaders who serve DMLs, many of the collaboration strategies that have been recognized as supporting the larger population also apply. However, successful collaboration and job-embedded professional learning occurs when a trusting environment is established and when considerations of language and culture (in the educational setting, at home, and in the community) are made at every opportunity. See Table 6.1 for full definition and associated strategies and Box 6.2 for an example of routine teacher collaboration in a general education school setting in Australia.

Collaboration Strategies

Collaboration in educational settings occurs when educators work together with each other, family members, and/or the community to support the learning of children. It is characterized by behaviors that reflect respect and trust (Fullan, 2008; Hallam et al., 2015; Knight, 2007). These behaviors include (a) thoughtfully listening to each other, (b) sharing responsibility for important decisions, (c) clearly communicating with each other, and (d) developing mutual goals (Friend & Cook, 2017; Fullan, 2008; Knight, 2007; Patterson et al., 2012). In addition to collaboration among colleagues, special educators need to be able to employ these strategies with families (Blue-Banning et al., 2004), especially in the context of planning individualized education. Collaboration with families is particularly important during times of great stress, such as the transition across educational settings and/or schools. For example, in the United States, high-stress transitions for children and their families include the transition from Part C (Early Intervention) to Part B (Early Childhood Special Education) services at age three, or changes of placement as the result of academic or behavioral concerns (Childre & Chambers, 2005; Hanson et al., 2000; Individuals with Disabilities Education Act, 2004, 2015; Lovett & Haring, 2003).

Leadership that promotes collaboration is respectful of the diversity present in the school and community. Sometimes the gestures leaders can make are simple. For example, when a nervous family showed up for their first meeting with their child's new educational team, a school

TABLE 6.1 Essential Instructional Supports Framework

Essential	Definition	Leading for DMLs
Inclusive and Instructional Leadership	"Leaders establish a strategic focus on children's health, learning, development and school readiness, and they support teachers to be effective in their work. They hire staff determined to continuously improve learning opportunities and outcomes for young children and families. They establish a vision for ambitious pedagogical practice and children's development, learning, and comprehensive [learning]. In daily interactions, they build and maintain mutually *trusting and respectful relationships* and build strong collective responsibility for and *enlist teachers' in improvement efforts*. They *galvanize staff activity*, programs, and resources towards a vision for sustained	*Establishing vision:* • Consider cultural and linguistic diversity as part of vision of the school and/or program • Include goals for supporting language proficiency (e.g. Scanlan & Lopez, 2012) • Focus on strengths-based language that values what language and culture diversity can bring to the school community • Include support structures that allow educators to develop their own pedagogical skills and/or practice for DMLs (e.g. Khalifa et al., 2016) • Develop the vision in collaboration with educators (e.g. Fullan, 2008; Hargreaves & O'Connor, 2018) *Build trusting relationships with educators:* • Work to establish relationships with educators (Scanlan & Lopez, 2012)

Essential	Definition	Leading for DMLs
	improvement. They practice *shared leadership* and cultivate a cadre of leaders among teachers, parents, and community. They support professional advancement for faculty and staff. They manage resources for sustained program improvement." (p. 16)	• Create a climate where educators feel safe to discuss topics of language and culture (Scanlan & Lopez, 2012) • Thoughtfully listen to educators' input and/or concerns *Cultivating shared leadership practices—* • Provide opportunities for adult DMLs to share their experiences • Encourage those with expertise on DMLs to present or lead professional development • Include the perspectives and voices of families when establishing vision and creating programming *Hiring teachers and managing resources:* • Hire a diverse teaching staff • Hire staff that have the orientations and pedagogical skills to support DMLs (Lucas & Villegas, 2013) • Build a culturally and linguistically responsive budget that includes considerations of family programming, professional development, culturally relevant curricula, technology, and/or staffing

(*Continued*)

TABLE 6.1 (Continued)

Essential	Definition	Leading for DMLs

Routine Teacher Collaboration	"Leaders use supervisory resources, relationship resources, performance feedback, and ongoing professional development to build professional capacity. They work together with staff to define their strategic focus for improvement and to solve systemic-organizational problems impacting effectiveness and improvement efforts. Leaders protect time for job-embedded professional learning opportunities, and design and facilitate routines for staff to reflect on and examine practice, review data on practice and children's progress, and collaborate towards practice improvements. All staff work in collaboration to promote their own and their colleagues' professional growth. In such schools and centers, teachers and staff are active partners in school/center improvement; they are committed to the school/center, each other and families; and focused on professional learning towards continuous improvement of teaching and learning." (p. 16)	*Collaboration strategies:*
		• Respectfully discuss diversity in the education setting
		• Explicitly consider language and culture when planning
		• Communicate clearly
		• Develop mutual goals
		• Limit generalizations about cultures and/or their practices
		• Engage in authentic interactions with others
		• Actively listen to families
		• Include families in decision-making
		• Create spaces for families to ask questions (See Chapter 2; Bowen & Baker, 2022)
		Job-embedded professional learning opportunities:
		• Include programming that addresses:
		  ○ Dual and multiple language development (Pizzo, 2016; Wang et al., 2016)
		  ○ Sociocultural influences on language development (Baker & Scott, 2016)
		  ○ Working with families who speak diverse languages (Bowen, 2016)
		  ○ Creating welcoming learning spaces (Baker & Scott, 2016)

Essential	Definition	Leading for DMLs
		○ Identity development (Pizzo, 2016) ○ Linguistically responsive instructional practice (Lucas et al., 2008) that supports ambitious instruction • Moving beyond introductory content to support mastery • Providing opportunities for reflection on one's own beliefs and biases • Setting high expectations for children • Using protocols to structure productive conversations about practice (e.g. McDonald et al., 2013)
Child-Centered Supportive Learning Environments	"[A]ll adults build supportive relationships with each other, with children and their families—the most basic prerequisite for learning . . . it is critical that children experience child-centered supportive learning environments in order to develop a positive sense of themselves, trust in others, and successful approaches to	*Physical environments:* • Include considerations for visual accessibility, distractibility, acoustics, and environmental materials in professional development. • Provide ongoing feedback on physical environments in coaching and supervision activities • Empower d/Dhh itinerant teachers to provide coaching on physical environments for general education teachers

(*Continued*)

TABLE 6.1 (*Continued*)

Essential	Definition	Leading for DMLs
	learning. Leaders use resources and establish policies that ensure all adults in the school community create consistently child-centered supportive learning environments. All adults attend daily to how they use physical space, materials, daily structure and routines, continuity of care, group size and ratio to create child-centered supportive environments. This foundation supports adults to create an emotional climate allowing children to consistently feel safe, liked, able to build relationships and actively explore. Teachers are trust-worthy and responsive to children's individual emotional and intellectual needs, they hold high expectations for children's capacity to relate, learn, and develop; and they affirm and promote children's exploration, friendships, engagement, and persistence." (p. 16)	*Emotional climate:* • Provide opportunities for interactions with adult and peer social models (Oliva & Lytle, 2014) • Develop family programming that helps families sign well (Desselle, 1994) • Eliminate communication barriers to promote connections between individuals (Antia & Kreimeyer, 2015) • Create opportunities for developing friendships and social networks (Oliva et al., 2016) • Integrate children's cultural influences into school experiences through the use of their background experiences and funds of knowledge (González, 2001)

Essential	Definition	Leading for DMLs
Ambitious Interactions and Instruction	"All adults are provided guidance articulating the what and how of teaching and learning. As a result, all adults endorse and use early learning and development standards, population-specific learning goals (e.g., special needs, dual language learners, and other vulnerable populations), and assessment information on children's progress to design, implement, reflect and refine meaningful learning opportunities for young children. This guidance scaffolds teachers to (a) develop content-based curriculum that deepens children's background knowledge and uses and develops early-literacy and -math skills; (b) differentiate instructional goals, materials, and activities; and (c) reflect and plan intentionally for their role in facilitating children's learning through interactions that are emotionally	*Continuous quality improvement strategies:* • Create systems that allow educators to use child data to understand performance and inform instruction (Pizzo & Chilvers, 2016; Pizzo & Ford, this volume) • Encourage the use of culturally responsive and collaborative protocols to reflect on and inform teaching *Professional advancement through coaching, mentoring, and supervision strategies:* • Understand the nuanced differences between coaching (Lofthouse et al., 2010), mentoring (Varney, 2009), and supervision • Utilize coaching strategies such as: 　○ Modeling of teaching practice 　○ Use of what, how, and who questions 　○ Being an active listener (Parsloe & Leedham, 2009) • Avoid the following behaviors that may produce negative experiences in the coaching relationship: 　○ Passing judgment or engaging in harsh criticism

(*Continued*)

TABLE 6.1 (*Continued*)

Essential	Definition	Leading for DMLs
	supportive, organized, and instructionally meaningful. In addition, all adults partner with families to extend and support meaningful and effective learning opportunities for children at home and at school. A coherent guidance system supports implementation and continuous improvement of this integrated teaching systems of standards, population-specific learning goals, curriculum, assessment, and interactions. Structures for the implementation of curricula, assessments, general- and specific-pedagogical practices, and use of materials are coordinated across the program. While teachers may have substantial discretion in how these resources are used, teaching effectiveness depends on the community of practice and supervisory dialogue and feedback supporting implementation." (p. 17)	○ Interceding too frequently with one's own experience ○ Asking questions about irrelevancies in the experience ○ Focusing on providing solutions rather than listening • Provide access to mentoring opportunities that are: ○ Natural and not prescribed (Varney, 2009) ○ Designed to establish trust ○ Respectful of knowledge passed down from more experienced teachers (Portner, 2008) • Consider work with DMLs and their families as part of the supervision process by evaluating: ○ Collaboration to improve instruction ○ Creation of supportive environments that are inclusive of culture and language diversity ○ Work with families ○ The use of data practices to inform instruction

Essential	Definition	Leading for DMLs
Strong Ties and Partnerships Among Families, Schools, and Community	"Children do not exist alone; they are a member of a family that lives within a community. When families, schools, and communities focus collectively on children's needs from birth through college entrance, children are healthy, competent and motivated learners, who realize long-term social and academic success. Early parent-school partnerships shape parents' awareness and capacity for partnering with educators and advocating for their children's needs to ensure positive experiences and success in school and life. Through systematic approaches the entire staff works to build responsive, respectful relationships with families that motivate their engagement, and goal-oriented partnerships among families, schools, and the community. Parents are	*Family-centered practices:* • Provide training and professional development on using family-centered practices, especially as they relate to the IEP/IFSP processes • Create opportunities to address the orientations and dispositional components of family-centered practice, such as adopting a strengths-based perspective regarding children and their families • Address language and culture in relation to family-centered practice, including issues of power and privilege as it pertains to specific languages and cultures *Family programming:* • Establish family programming that includes topics relevant to d/Dhh and linguistically diverse families

(Continued)

TABLE 6.1 (*Continued*)

Essential	Definition	Leading for DMLs
	partners in developing and achieving goals for their child and their family. Staff value parents' perspective, participation, and are willing to be influenced by it. All staff share and seek information from families to build mutual respect and understanding. They make decisions collaboratively with parents and work cohesively across home and school to support children's participation, health, learning, and development . . . Through referrals and connections to community resources and services, staff work to reduce material hardships, promote wellbeing, and increase family capacity to engage with the children's learning and development. By building social networks among families, staff work to reduce isolation, increase social-emotional supports, and open life and learning opportunities that strengthen families and entire communities." (p. 17)	• Make family programming accessible by considering (a) time of year and time of day for programs, (b) location of programs, and (c) access to child care as factors that impact access for families (Páez et al., 2011) • Ensure all recruitment materials and programs offered are available in the necessary languages to support the diverse families of the school • Respect families and make them feel welcome to participate in school functions *Connecting with the broader community:* • Create the appropriate atmosphere and provide resources for vertical and horizontal identity development (Solomon, 2012) • Provide opportunities to connect with the home community • Provide opportunities to connect with the Deaf community

Box 6.2 Routine Teacher Collaboration

Dhaval is a 15-year-old boy who recently came to Australia from the United Kingdom (UK). His family is from Gujarat, India. He has a moderate, bilateral hearing loss. Dhaval's parents speak Gujarati, Hindi, and English. Dhaval has some proficiency in spoken Gujarati and English, but has not developed skills in Hindi. He uses Auslan (Australian Sign Language) and English in school. His current reading and writing levels are 1.5 years below grade level. He is currently placed in general education classrooms with an Auslan Interpreter, although his Auslan is still progressing. He receives speech and language services, pull-out resource support, and itinerant services from a teacher of the d/Dhh weekly.

In order to address Dhaval's needs, the educational coach for the d/Dhh program convened a meeting with the itinerant and general education teachers to review educational strategies and his program. The general education teacher raised concerns about Dhaval's ability to follow large group discussions in class, especially in history class. The educational coach introduced a protocol called "lesson study" in order to examine ways to improve accessibility of class content for Dhaval. Although there are many different adaptations and variants of lesson study, this protocol focused on reviewing a videotaped lesson from the general education classroom that required large group discussions. During this process, the general education teacher reflected on the lesson, while the coach and itinerant teacher provided constructive feedback using the specific questions on the lesson study protocol. This process resulted in the identification of certain background and cultural knowledge that Dhaval was assumed to have, but did not. When he possessed the background knowledge, he was able to follow the discussion and participate; however, without context, he struggled to understand the conversation that was occurring. Therefore, the teacher began conducting pre-assessments and pre-teaching to ensure Dhaval had the cultural knowledge necessary to access the relevant history lessons presented.

administrator greeted the family in their home language, welcomed them into her office, and asked them about their family. She then asked the family members what they hoped to get out of the meeting and what goals they had for their child that year. By the time the meeting started, the family seemed more comfortable and confident in the school setting. Creating spaces for families to ask questions without judgement can foster authentic interactions and strengthen collaborations between the educational setting and the home (see Bowen & Baker, 2022; Chapter 2).

Job-Embedded Professional Learning Opportunities

Professional learning opportunities include everything from basic knowledge dissemination to building spaces that allow educators to deepen and apply new knowledge in their practice. These opportunities include a continuum of professional development opportunities that meet participants at their level and scaffold their learning to consistently incorporate the content into their work. Leaders are tasked with making these experiences a part of the routine professional development program at their sites, including finding common times for educators to meet and collaborate during their work hours. Finally, these professional development programs also need to be relevant to the content of the educational program with opportunities to apply new knowledge and reflect on the experience.

For leaders who serve children who are DMLs, carefully constructed professional learning opportunities are essential to the development of educators and staff. These opportunities should include learning new content relevant to working with this population. In addition, allowing educators to move beyond introductory content on each topic by offering opportunities to deepen and apply new knowledge will also help to develop mastery of the content. The inclusion of experiential learning and reflection, also known as praxis, can be a powerful tool to deepen the knowledge of educators. Specifically, activities to reflect on one's own beliefs and experiences with multilingualism can help educators confront their own potential biases and how they interact with their own practice.

One specific strategy to support the above activities is the use of protocols to guide discussions and focus on specific content. A protocol is a set of steps or procedures to structure a conversation about practice or learning that can inform educational services. For example, a leader might ask a grade-level team that is finding challenges when educating DMLs to engage in a specific set of steps used to analyze learner data and design a specific lesson plan to address any gaps in knowledge. While some might feel stifled by protocols at first, research shows that when protocols are used well, they provide structures that deepen the conversation and keep it on-topic (Venables, 2015). Unfortunately, most protocols are written for the broader population in mind, and would need to be slightly modified to incorporate questions relevant to diversity, language development, and/or linguistically responsive practice when necessary.

For example, a protocol that reviews specific learners' learning profiles can be modified to include questions about how to capitalize on their strengths as multilingual and multicultural learners, which work as specific teaching strategies (e.g., asking what background knowledge a child may have on the lesson topic and creating opportunities to leverage it in the lesson). See the Resources section of this chapter for recommendations on where to find potential protocols and Box 6.3 for an example of school personnel having professional learning conversations about race.

Finally, leaders must create spaces for discussing sensitive issues of racial and linguistic diversity within the day-to-day business of their jobs. These spaces can be large or small depending on the needs of the program. They can be part of a targeted initiative to introduce professional development in the program or they could be part of the ongoing coaching and mentoring at the site. Regardless of when these conversations happen, they need to happen. Furthermore, these conversations need to move past recognizing the challenges of creating a climate welcoming of diversity and move toward the implementation of solutions focused on realizing that goal. Too often, conversations about diversity do not result in tangible changes to increase inclusivity.

Box 6.3 Professional Learning Opportunities

One urban school with a large population of d/Dhh students in a midwestern US city sent a team of nine teachers/instructional coaches (including two Deaf teachers) and four school leaders (including one

Deaf Vice Principal and one hard of hearing Curriculum Specialist) to a conference on confronting racism in education. During the day, the team learned from presentations, discussed topics, engaged in small group discussions on content, and developed plans to bring these discussions back to the school. Upon returning to the school, the attendees brought back the content to the staff. The work began with an initial training on anti-bias educational strategies. The conversations around race were awkward at first. The conversations about colorism within language minority groups were even more challenging. One teacher felt that the public sharing of experiences of racism in education was a form of "teacher shaming" and harmful to the profession. Another teacher called out the staff for too much "lip service" to the topic without a tangible action plan. One teacher even cried when challenged on her own white privilege. The school leadership provided structure to the conversation, encouraged all voices to share, and provided validation for all feelings being shared in the room, creating a safe space for the emotional content of the discussion.

At the end of the session, the vice principal led them all in an exercise, "I believe . . . therefore I will do . . ." Each teacher participated in the exercise identifying realistic behaviors they could engage in the following weeks. After this initial session about race, each grade-level team met and identified one concept they learned that they wanted to engage with more deeply. One team decided to review their in-classroom libraries for children's literature that reinforced negative racial and language stereotypes. Another team decided to create an autobiographical writing unit that encouraged learners to tell their own personal histories. Although each grade level chose their own area of emphasis, time was allotted for these discussions during the school day and/or dedicated professional development time. Instructional strategies and goals were always connected to their practice (e.g., review of children's literature related to Unit 2 happened two weeks before the unit began, etc.). Finally, each grade had the opportunity to present their work at the monthly staff meetings.

While it can be easy to acknowledge that racism or linguicism exists, pushing educators to examine their own mindsets and behaviors can result in emotional exchanges that may even hurt the school climate more than help it. Therefore, leaders need to find ways to introduce hard topics, engage in difficult conversations, and provide ongoing support to keep the conversation going over time. For example, one elementary school principal used professional development hours to have educators watch segments from "America to Me", a docuseries about the experiences of racially diverse children in public schools in the greater Chicago area. Using the website's organizer guide, leaders in the school led discussions about the series and drew parallels to their own school. Specifically, these leaders addressed issues of race not just as a set of experiences individuals have had, but as how those experiences can create a mindset that is rooted in race, language, and culture.

Child-Centered Supportive Learning Environments

Learning environments that provide the opportunity to explore and acquire new knowledge in a safe and supportive context are necessary for all children. The Essential Instructional Supports framework describes *Child-Centered Supportive Learning Environments* as knowledge of how to use physical space, program materials, structure and routines, and group size to create environments for learning (Pacchiano et al., 2016). In addition, teachers support a positive emotional climate by responding to children's individual needs, holding high expectations, and creating opportunities for children to explore and make friends (Pacchiano et al., 2016).

In the Essential Instructional Supports Framework, leaders use resources and establish policies that facilitate the establishment of these child-centered learning environments. For DMLs, there are two major components of learning environments that are particularly important in supporting their learning: the physical environment and the emotional climate of that environment. For an example of both components, review Box 6.4 to see how the playground setting and language accessibility led to a misunderstanding of behavior issues.

Box 6.4 Child-Centered Supportive Learning Environments

Clover elementary school consists of 200 students in general education and 40 students in classrooms for d/Dhh children that use ASL. The majority of students in this school has a home language that was not English or ASL. Although this setting was intended to promote collaboration and integration across general education and d/Deaf education, the school day remained relatively segregated, except for the times in the day when the whole school gathered (e.g., recess, lunch, and assemblies). The school leadership was proud to include the d/Dhh program at their school; however, minimal effort was made to create community across the programs, as leaders felt it would develop on its own. One day the school psychologist noticed an increased number of d/Dhh children being kept inside for recess due to "aggressive behaviors" on the playground. When asked about the nature of these behaviors, it appeared that there were challenges on the tetherball court due to a lack of communication between the hearing and d/Dhh children. As a result, the d/Dhh children were observed physically removing hearing children from the tetherball court when they were "out" and were subsequently punished for being physical with another student.

When brought to the leadership team, a meeting was held to brainstorm solutions. At first, the conversation focused on how to work with the d/Dhh children to improve their skills engaging with the hearing children. Then a Deaf teacher asked a question, "Why should the deaf children bear the responsibility of communication challenges across both groups of children?" No one responded until the vice principal said, "You're right, the challenge is building community, not just a simple communication exercise. Let's reframe this situation."

While the immediate communication needs were addressed in both hearing and d/Dhh classrooms, the result of the meeting was a dedicated committee charged with creating an inclusive environment. Basic lessons about Deaf and hearing cultures were introduced

> to all grade levels. The fifth-grade d/Dhh classroom was also asked to lead ASL lessons for their peers across the year. And two ASL educational interpreters were on the playground to facilitate communication among all students. Finally, the teaching staff decided to leverage the diversity of the school, creating opportunities for learners to engage with each other on topics relevant to their home languages and cultures. Through activities focused on the shared home languages and cultures of the school community, opportunities for exploring similarities allowed learners to connect with each other both inside and outside the classroom, thereby creating an equitable linguistic and culturally learning environment.

Physical Environments

Whether in the home, a community-based program, or a public school, the physical environment is a key influence in a child's ability to participate in learning activities. While there is less research about the relationship of the physical environment of the home to learning, the classroom environment has been shown to influence children's behavior, participation, and attention to academic tasks (Fullerton & Guardino, 2010; Guardino & Antia, 2012; Guardino & Fullerton, 2010). For d/Dhh children, classroom participation has been specifically linked to measures of academic achievement (Antia et al., 2007) and reduction of disruptive behaviors (Guardino & Antia, 2012).

The considerations for a supportive physical environment for DMLs include promoting language accessibility through the classroom flow, visual characteristics, and acoustic environments. For example, a high-quality classroom environment includes appropriately sized furniture and easily accessible classroom materials. Ideally, there would be materials that exist in various languages and support multiple cultures that may be present in the classroom (e.g., books, posters, manipulatives, and play items). In addition, the flow of the room needs to be set up so that children are able to easily navigate to and from activities across the day, encouraging interactions and supporting community development. In addition, aspects of visual accessibility that are important for all d/Dhh learners must be addressed. For example, visual accessibility to the teacher and other students is key; however, these students are also likely to be susceptible to visual distractibility due to the heightened use of peripheral vision by d/Dhh children (e.g., Bavelier et al., 2006; Chen et al., 2006; Dye et al., 2008). As a result, visual accessibility needs to be balanced with the reduction of visual distractions. Finally, attention needs to be paid to the acoustic environment of the classroom, as DMLs with auditory access need to have the best conditions for navigating the multiple sound systems they routinely encounter. For example, background noise can affect the use of hearing technology or the ability to distinguish certain key information above potentially distracting sounds in the environment.

High-quality leadership coaches and provides routine feedback to educators on their use of physical space in their classrooms, including considerations of visual accessibility, acoustics, and materials (see Resource section for further information). They ensure that training on the physical environments to support the learning of DMLs is a part of a teacher's professional development. Leaders also include feedback for staff regarding environmental conditions as a part of the coaching and supervision process. One leader created a small grant competition to fund a classroom improvement project. This grant was given to two classrooms per year and based on a classroom analysis of ways to improve accessibility for their learners. While there were certain limits on what the grant could and could not fund, educators were encouraged to be creative in their mindsets. The first year, both winners created dioramas of their classrooms to demonstrate the improved physical access to centers, materials, and a distraction-free zone.

Emotional Climate

Social-emotional development lays a foundation for children to learn and grow academically and personally. Schools and programs are required to provide environments that promote social-emotional development at all ages. For DMLs, it is important to provide supports that reduce isolation, low self-esteem, and marginalization (Pizzo, 2016; Wang et al., 2016). Different educational settings that serve DMLs may have unique needs.

For example, general education settings may require more professional development for working with learners who have hearing loss, including information on Deaf culture and sign languages. Programs specifically designed for d/Dhh children may need more training to support the emotional needs of DMLs as a subpopulation within the school, such as information on identity development and supporting connections to heritage languages and cultural practices. For a more comprehensive list of program options, see Table 6.1.

Regardless of the setting, leaders and educators are responsible for making sure that all d/Dhh children are considered full members of a culturally rich community (Oliva & Lytle, 2014). Leaders accomplish these tasks by modeling positive interactions with children and their families, valuing diversity in public settings, and establishing programming to promote self-esteem and identity. For example, in one high school for d/Dhh learners, leadership instituted a program called "all about me", where d/Dhh children record video biographies discussing their background, heritage, and cultural characteristics. The learners are required to do research into their own background and complete a series of reflection tasks before filming their videos. Two-to-three videos are showcased each week during the school's weekly announcements.

Ambitious Interactions and Instruction

Teaching and learning are at the heart of the educational system. Leaders are tasked with supporting educators as they engage in rigorous but supportive teaching practice. The Essential Supports Framework describes *Ambitious Interactions and Instruction* as the intentional use of a content-based curriculum, differentiation of instruction which involves adapting that curriculum to meet specific learners needs, and reflection on their practice including their interactions with children during instructional time (Pacchiano et al., 2016). Given the large scope of what constitutes *Ambitious Interactions and Instruction*, this section will include a focus on what leaders need to accomplish to support teachers to be ambitious in their instructional practice with DMLs. Specifically, leaders need to build structures that support continuous improvement efforts related to curricula, instructional strategies, and assessments through supervision, coaching, and/or mentoring (Pacchiano et al., 2016). See Table 6.1 for full definition and associated strategies.

Continuous Quality Improvement Strategies

Continuous improvement uses evidence-based quantitative and qualitative methods to improve the effectiveness, equity, and implementation of educational strategies. Continuous improvement strategies include using child data to understand performance and inform instruction. For DMLs, considerations during the data-based decision-making process need to include a child's language background, current language level, and the cultural relevance of the lessons to the child's experiences. The use of culturally responsive and collaborative protocols can be one way to structure these exercises to maximize learning and inform teaching (for more information on protocols, see *Job-Embedded Professional Learning Opportunities* above). For example, one curriculum director led the school in an initiative to provide opportunities to fill in missing information and reinforce knowledge. This school dedicated two days at the end of a unit for additional practice in a center-based learning platform. In these classrooms, the teachers gathered the end-of-unit assessments and determined what information a learner might not have mastered in the unit. The learners in the classroom were then assigned to a center-based activity to review and reinforce that information.

Coaching, Mentoring and Supervision Strategies

Although often used interchangeably, coaching, mentoring, and supervision are distinct components of leadership. Coaching supports educators to develop specific skills to enhance their practice to include reflection, problem solving, and modeling, and will often create spaces for experimentation with new strategies (Lofthouse et al., 2010). Goals for the coaching experience are created together, but driven by the coachee. Coaching is typically completed by someone who is not in the line of supervision or evaluation of the coachee. For example, in a school for the d/Deaf, an ASL specialist was assigned by school leadership to provide coaching to a new teacher of the d/Dhh. One of the goals created by the pair addressed the use of diverse children's literature and advanced features of sign language to promote both language development and positive self-esteem for the DMLs in the classroom.

Mentoring is considered a more personal relationship that develops between a mentor and a protégé over a long period of time (Varney, 2009). Mentors are invested in the well-being of their protégés and create nurturing relationships with them that impact their identity development as an educator as they are socialized into the field (Mullen, 2011). Traditional mentoring occurs by passing down knowledge and skills across generations of teachers (Portner, 2008). Trusting relationships are the cornerstone of the mentoring process. Artificial, mandatory, and prescribed mentoring practices do not produce the same level of benefits as mentoring that includes voluntary components and natural interactions (Varney, 2009). For instance, one teacher with ten years of experience began stopping by a new teacher's classroom during their preparation block to check in. These conversations evolved over time to issues of instruction and planning. The school leadership noticed the collaboration and when assigning classrooms for the next school year, gave the two teachers adjoining rooms to provide increased opportunity for mentorship. For another example of mentorship that may be beneficial when working with DMLs, see Box 6.5, where we meet Xiaoqin and her teacher, who has a mentor in her school to guide her in literacy instruction.

Supervision is the act of overseeing educators and conducting formal evaluations of their performance. Supervision is the most high-stakes of all three processes, as these evaluations can have implications for job security. Supervisors may take on other roles in the lives of educators, such as mentor or confidant, but the power they hold by being a supervisor can never be fully removed from the equation. A challenge in the area of supervision has been that traditional measures of teacher effectiveness have not always been linked to the teachers' ability to teach (Darling-Hammond, 2010), which limits the ability for supervisors to provide meaningful feedback that can improve practice. One good example of supervision that could support DMLs and other diverse d/Dhh learners was demonstrated by a leader who required one professional goal per year to be devoted to inclusivity and/or diversity. That goal was then evaluated within every supervision cycle for the year.

> BOX 6.5 AMBITIOUS INTERACTIONS AND INSTRUCTION
>
> Xiaoqing is a middle-school girl who moved to Canada when she was five. She has a mild-to-moderate hearing loss. Her parents speak Cantonese. They also have basic skills in conversational English. She is placed in a general education school setting and is pulled out of class to work with a specialist for academic support during designated times of the day. She uses primarily English at school, as she only knows a handful of basic ASL signs. She speaks Cantonese at home. She attends Saturday school to learn how to read and write Chinese characters.
>
> Xiaoqing's classroom teacher is currently being mentored by a master teacher. Recently, Xiaoqing's teacher was concerned about her reading comprehension in English. The teacher brought her concerns to her mentor for advice. The mentor listened closely, looked at the assessment data, asked relevant and timely questions about her classroom engagement, and offered a similar case she had a few years ago. The conversation provided the teacher with some initial strategies to try, but the classroom teacher still found planning and implementing lessons for Xiaoqing a challenge.
>
> The mentor offered to conduct an observation and the school administration found coverage for the mentor's classroom to make it possible. As a result of the observation, the mentor provided some thoughts and additional strategies. Although the teacher felt comfortable with the majority of the strategies discussed, there was one with which she felt needed more development: close reading. As the mentor had more experience with the task, she suggested contacting the school's literacy coach to conduct a model lesson with Xiaoqing to illustrate the lesson structure. The coach agreed to conduct a model lesson and helped the teacher to plan a follow-up lesson using the demonstrated technique. After employing close reading in her class for a month, the classroom teacher reassessed to monitor Xioaqing's skill development related to comprehension and noticed a marked improvement.

Coaching, mentoring, and supervising educators to work with DMLs is a challenging task. Without more research on what it means to effectively educate DMLs, it is hard to know which instructional strategies to recommend or look for during coaching, mentoring, and supervision processes. Therefore, it is important to consider the wide range of strategies employed across the educators' practices that promote inclusivity, value diversity, and employ individualized instructional strategies, as well as to consider the cultural and linguistic diversity of the practitioners working and supervising DMLs.

Strong Ties and Partnerships Among Families, Schools, and Community

Working with families is a key aspect of education for both d/Dhh and linguistically diverse children. *Strong Ties and Partnerships Among Families, Schools, and Community* is described as a collective focus on children's needs through goal-oriented partnerships with families and the community (Pacchiano et al., 2016). Educators work to build responsive and respectful relationships with families and have a willingness to be influenced by the goals and perspectives of families in their own work (Pacchiano et al., 2016). For DMLs, it is important to consider research on working with families from sociocultural perspectives, as well as from the literature in special education. For the purposes of this chapter, three major categories of family engagement will be addressed: family-centered practices, family programming, and connecting with the larger community. See Table 6.1 for a full definition and associated strategies.

Family-Centered Practices

Family-centered practices are rooted in a collaborative partnership between the family, the educator, and the child (Swafford et al., 2015). Family-centered educational services have been linked to higher levels of self-efficacy, perceived self-competency, and increased feelings of control (Dunst & Dempsey, 2007; Epley et al., 2011). Educators that engage in these practices are trustworthy, honest, respectful, non-judgmental, caring, and attentive listeners (Woods et al., 2011). These educators are collaborative problem-solvers that discuss issues with families and do not dictate what they should do. These educators also recognize that the perspectives of the family might not match their own and are willing to accept those perspectives rather than try to refute the families' experiences.

Leaders need to support educators in understanding and engaging in family-centered practices. As family-centered practices place an emphasis on characteristics of educators, leaders also need to support activities that allow educators to adopt strengths-based perspectives, reflect on their work, and/or consider ways to partner with families more equally. For leaders who serve DMLs, issues of language and culture need to be addressed, as they may produce structural inequities in family partnerships due to associated issues of status and power. For example, in the broader society, some languages or cultures are considered more desirable than others; as such, if these biases infiltrate the school, some families may be engaged more fully than others.

Family Programming

When creating family programming, understanding the needs of families being served is a prerequisite. The more relevant families feel the program is, the greater the likelihood of their participation. Needs assessments can help to gather information from families about what they want and see as their primary needs. For families of d/Dhh children, family programming may include information about ASL, hearing technology, educational services, community services, and/or vocational services. For children who are bilingual, family literacy programming has been shown to increase the families' understanding and use of language and literacy practices in the home (Páez et al., 2011; Paratore, 2001; Shanahan et al., 1995). For DMLs, family programming that addresses both hearing loss and language use may be the most beneficial.

The content of family programming can be stellar; however, family programming is only as good as its accessibility. Páez and colleagues (2011) indicated that family programming "must be aligned with families' lives" (p. 144). The time of year and time of day for programs, the location of programs, and access to child care should be considered as factors that impact access for families (Páez et al., 2011). The languages used in family program sessions and recruitment materials should align with the languages of the families in order for linguistically diverse families to feel welcomed in these programs.

As many of these non-negotiable considerations may come with a cost, leaders will need to consider these factors when designing the program budget for the year. For example, one large urban school district in the United States offered parent programming that addressed content concerning hearing loss, language development, and sign language instruction. The program provided child care, interpreters, and two levels of ASL instruction (introductory and intermediate). The day of the week was selected through a parent questionnaire. There was always a portion of the program devoted to family socialization. After a year of the program, one parent reported that while he once felt an almost adversarial relationship with the school, he now felt like *he* belonged there too, not just his daughter.

Connecting with the Broader Community

Leaders who create strong connections with the broader community are fostering identity development and growth, a key component of culturally and linguistically responsive educational practices (Khalifa et al., 2016). For DMLs, both vertical and horizontal identities are especially important. Vertical identities are the culture and values handed down to the child across generations and horizontal identities are developed through interactions with others that share a common trait with the child (Solomon, 2012). For DMLs, the culture of the family, or heritage culture, is an important influence in developing their vertical identities. Learning about a child's background and culture is essential to the support of a vertical identity in the classroom. Horizontal identities occur when a child has a trait that is not shared by his parents and as a result is cultivated across a peer group (Solomon, 2012). For example, sexual orientation, disability, or specific life experiences can provide a connection for people to develop their horizontal identities (see Resource section for organizations that school leaders can access for more information and to find role models to connect with students).

There are two broader communities that help to support DMLs and their identity development from birth through graduation: the home community and the Deaf community. By valuing the home culture, educators are demonstrating respect for the family and strengthening family engagement for families of DMLs. These educators are also supporting the development of children's vertical identities and encouraging diversity in d/Dhh identity development (Bat-Chava, 2000). For children who are DMLs, their home communities and cultural needs should be balanced with experiences and exposure to Deaf culture. Providing opportunities to engage in activities with Deaf peers, Deaf adults, and culturally relevant curricular material (e.g., alphabet and number stories, ASL poetry, and Deaf theatre arts) are all essential to supporting the horizontal identities of d/Dhh children in educational programs. Once again, leaders play a key role in supporting positive conceptions of the learners' heritage cultures, as well as creating opportunities for children to participate in Deaf culture and community. See Box 6.6 for an example of an adult role model who is a DML, Isabella, who presents information to her school about family engagement.

Box 6.6 Strong Ties and Partnerships Among Families, Schools, and Community

Isabella is a 26-year-old third-grade teacher in a school for d/Dhh children in the Southwest United States. She was born in Arizona, but her parents are from Mexico. Isabella has a severe-to-profound, bilateral hearing loss. She attended California State University, Northridge for her teaching degree. She teaches high school classes in American Sign Language (ASL) and written English. Isabella can also read and write in Spanish. She is active in the Deaf community and the Mexican-American community. She is close with her family, especially her cousins, even those who are not proficient in ASL. She is passionate about multiple identities and is proud to be a Mexican-American Deaf woman.

Isabella was asked by her principal to present at a family engagement program on: (a) intersectional identity development, including horizontal and vertical identities; and (b) the importance of language and cultural diversity in the school. She was nervous to undertake this endeavor, as she was one of the youngest teachers in the school. The principal listened to her fears and shared her confidence in Isabella. She agreed to review the content before the presentation and provide feedback.

During the session, Isabella engaged families in a variety of cultural mapping activities where they were able to identify their most cherished traditions, values, and ideals. She affirmed their various experiences and backgrounds, while providing opportunities for questions across families as well. Isabella also had parents identify the most important aspects of their vertical identities that they want to pass onto their children, while at the same time asking parents to identify ways they can interact with and validate their children's horizontal identities. Families were asked to share out, but only if they felt comfortable.

Conclusion and Cross-Cutting Recommendations

While each component of the Essential Instructional Supports is distinct and includes specific components necessary to support the learning of DMLs in schools, there are certain cross-cutting themes that leaders can implement to create the conditions that support DMLs. These are high-leverage leadership activities that can engage this population on multiple levels simultaneously:

- Create a climate that **values** and **respects** diversity in the educational program by developing the educators' **orientations** to their work;
- Promote strategies of thoughtful **reflection** and **praxis** for educators to consider their own professional identities and potential biases;
- Create **trust** among educators and families;
- Make families feel **welcomed, respected**, and **valued** in all aspects of their child's educational setting;
- Listen to the **voices** of families even (or especially) when they disagree with your own;

- Make all programs and classrooms *accessible*;
- Provide opportunities to *collaborate* at all levels to enhance the educational program;
- Use *protocols* to structure discussions about curriculum, pedagogy, and working with families that include an emphasis on examining the influences of *language* and *culture* on learning.

By creating environments that are respectful, engaging, accessible, and conducive to collaboration, leaders can positively impact learning and identity formation on a daily basis. Strengths-based approaches such as these have the potential to support the development of robust, competent, and diverse d/Deaf children in our schools.

Regardless of how leadership chooses to begin incorporating responsive practices into their programs, leaders need to consider how they are planning, implementing, and evaluating strategies for inclusivity on a routine basis. Addressing the needs of DMLs requires a specific focus and effort to create a climate of support and learning. Ignoring issues of race, language, and culture will only serve to reinforce the status quo and be a disservice to all learners in the program. While effort will be needed in the beginning to keep DMLs in the forefront of the leadership process, over time, and with practice, inclusivity and responsiveness will hopefully become a natural part of the school climate.

Discussion Questions

1. Describe the five components of the Essential Instructional Supports Framework.
2. Identify some strategies for engaging in shared leadership.
3. What are the differences between coaching, mentoring, and supervision?
4. What are the considerations for making family programming accessible?
5. How do you develop an atmosphere of trust in your school?
6. Define vertical and horizontal identities.
7. Reflect on your experiences leading and being led by others. How did it compare to the ideas presented in this chapter? Moving forward, how might you incorporate a focus on linguistic and cultural diversity in your program and/or school?

Resources

Readings

- Hargreaves, A., & O'Connor, M. (2018). *Collaborative professionalism: When teaching together means learning for all.* Corwin.
- Kendi, I. (2019). *How to be an antiracist.* One World.
- Khalifa, M. (2018). *Culturally responsive school leadership.* Harvard Education Press.
- Lindsey, R. B., Robins, K. N., & Terrell, R. D. (2009). *Cultural proficiency: A manual for school leaders* (3rd ed.). Corwin.
- McDonald, J., Mohr, N., Dichter, N., & McDonald, E. (2013). *The power of protocols: An educator's guide to better practice* (3rd Ed.). Teachers College Press.
- Picower, B., & Kohli, R. (Eds.) (2017). *Confronting racism in teacher education.* Routledge.
- Solomon, A. (2012). *Far from the tree: Parents, children and the search for identity.* Scribner.

Websites

- America to Me—Real Talk (www.americatomerealtalk.com)
- Celebrating Black Deaf Families (www.csd.org/stories/online-communities-for-deaf-api/)
- Culturally Responsive Leadership (http://culturallyresponsiveleadership.com)
- Deaf Asian National and International Organizations (www.csd.org/stories/online-communities-for-deaf-api/)
- Deaf women throughout history (www.csd.org/stories/six-firsts-deaf-women-history-month/)
- Online Communities for Deaf Hispanics and Latinx (www.csd.org/stories/online-communities-for-latinx-deaf/)
- Online communities for LGBTQ+ (www.csd.org/stories/online-groups-for-the-deaf-lgbtqia-community/)
- National Association of Elementary School Principals, The Principal's Guide to Building Culturally Responsive Schools: (www.naesp.org/principal-s-guide-building-culturally-responsive-schools)

- UnboundEd toolkit—Disrupting Inequity: Having Brave Conversations About Bias (https://blog.unbounded.org/bias-toolkit/)

Family-Centered Brief

FAMILY-CENTERED BRIEF

CHAPTER 6
Leadership and Collaboration in School Settings for d/Deaf and Hard of Hearing Multilingual Learners (DMLs)

by Lianna Pizzo

PURPOSE OF THE CHAPTER
This chapter outlines ways to support the learning of DMLs through the clarification of team roles and collaborative efforts.

DEFINING KEY TERMS

School leadership
People at school who make decisions that affect staff and students

Family-centered practice
Making decisions about curriculum with input from family

Family needs assessment
Formally discuss the goals and wishes of the family with regards to their child

Family programming
Planning school activities that include family members

SCHOOL PERSPECTIVES THAT ARE CRITICAL FOR SUPPORTING DMLS

VALUES:
- diversity and inclusion
- strength-based learning
- collaboration between educators
- time for educators to reflect
- family inclusion

COLLABORATION means...
(School, Family, Community)
- listening to each other
- sharing responsibility for important decisions
- practicing clear communication
- developing mutual goals

HOW FAMILIES CAN BE INVOLVED IN SCHOOL LEADERSHIP

- Conduct a 'needs assessment' with families before planning family programming
- Seek input from family on ways to support the DML
- Offer opportunities for the family to learn about school supports and how their child learns

RESOURCES
Communication Service for the Deaf www.csd.org/stories/
- CSD website hosts resources for online communities of Deaf Asian, Black, Hispanic, LatinX, LGBTQ+

Solomon, A. (2012). Far from the tree: Parents, children and the search for identity. New York, NY: Scribner.

Deaf and Hard of Hearing Multilingual Learners: Foundations, Strategies, and Resources (2022)

References

Antia, S., Sabers, D., & Stinson, M. (2007). Validity and reliability of the Classroom Participation Questionnaire with deaf and hard of hearing students in public schools. *Journal of Deaf Studies and Deaf Education, 12*, 158–171. https://doi.org/10.1093/deafed/enl028.

Antia, S. D., & Kreimeyer, K. H. (2015). *Social competence of deaf and hard-of-hearing children.* Oxford University Press.

Baker, S., & Scott, J. (2016). Sociocultural and academic considerations for school-age d/deaf and hard of hearing multilingual learners: A case study of a deaf Latina. *American Annals of the Deaf, 161*(1), 43–55.

Bat-Chava, Y. (2000). Diversity of deaf identities. *American Annals of the Deaf, 145*, 420–428.

Bavelier, D., Dye, M., & Hauser, P. (2006). Do deaf individuals see better? *Trends in Cognitive Sciences, 10*, 512–528. https://doi.org/10.1016/j.tics.2006.09.006.

Bickmore, S. T., & Bickmore, D. L. (2010). Revealing the principal's role in the induction process: Novice teachers telling their stories. *Journal of School Leadership, 20*(4), 445–469.

Blue-Banning, M., Summers, J. A., Frankland, H. C., Nelson, L. L., & Beegle, G. (2004). Dimensions of family and professional partnerships: Constructive guidelines for collaboration. *Exceptional Children, 70*, 167–184. https://doi.org/10.1177/001440290407000203

Boscardin, M. L. (2005). The administrative role in transforming secondary schools to support inclusive evidence-based practices. *American Secondary Education*, 21–32.

Bowen, S. K. (2016). Early intervention: A multicultural perspective on d/Deaf and hard of hearing multilingual learners. *American Annals of the Deaf, 161*(1), 33–42.

Bowen, S. K., & Baker, S. (2022). Family engagement: Developing partnerships for d/Deaf and hard of hearing multilingual learners. In J. E. Cannon, C. Guardino, & P. V. Paul (Eds.), *Deaf and hard of hearing multilingual learners: Foundations, strategies, and resources* (pp. 30–66). Routledge.

Branch, G., Hanushek, E., & Rivkin, S. (2013). School leaders matter: Measuring the impact of effective principals. *Education Next, 13*(1), 62–69.

Burns, M. K., Vanderwood, M. L., & Ruby, S. (2005). Evaluating the readiness of pre-referral intervention teams for use in a problem solving model. *School Psychology Quarterly, 20,* 89–105. https://doi.org/10.1521/scpq.20.1.89.64192

Cannon, J. E., Guardino, C., & Gallimore, E. (2016). A new kind of heterogeneity: What we can learn from d/Deaf and hard of hearing multilingual learners. *American Annals of the Deaf, 161*(1), 8–16. https://doi.org/10.1353/aad.2016.0015

Chen, Q., Zhang, M., & Zhou, X. (2006). Effects of spatial distribution of attention during inhibition of return (IOR) on flanker interference in hearing and congenitally deaf people. *Brain Research, 1109,* 117–127. https://doi.org/10.1016/j.brainres.2006.06.043

Childre, A., & Chambers, C. (2005). Family perceptions of student centered planning and IEP meetings. *Education and Training in Developmental Disabilities, 2005, 40*(3), 217–233.

Crowther, F., Ferguson, M., & Hann, L. (2009). *Developing teacher leaders: How teacher leadership enhances school success* (2nd ed.). Corwin.

Darling-Hammond, L. (2010). *Evaluating teacher effectiveness: How teacher performance assessments can measure and improve teaching.* Center for American Progress.

Day, C., Sammons, P., Leithwood, K., Harris, A., & Hopkins, D. (2009). *The impact of leadership on pupil outcomes* [Final Report]. DCSF.

Desselle, D. D. (1994). Self-esteem, family climate, and communication patterns in relation to deafness. *American Annals of the Deaf, 139*(3), 322–328.

Drago-Severson, E. (2012). New opportunities for principal leadership: Shaping school climates for enhanced teacher development. *Teachers College Record, 114,* 1–44.

Dunst, C. J., & Dempsey, J. (2007). Family-professional partnership and parenting competence, confidence, and enjoyment. *International Journal of Disability, Development and Education, 54,* 305–318. https://doi.org/10.1080/10349120701

Dye, M., Hauser, P., & Bavelier, D. (2008). Visual attention in deaf children and adults: Implications for learning environments. In M. Marschark & P. C. Hauser (Eds.), *Deaf cognition: Foundations and outcomes.* Oxford University Press.

Epley, R. H., Summers, J. A., & Turnbull, A. P. (2011). Family outcomes of early intervention: Families' perceptions of need, services, and outcomes. *Journal of Early Intervention, 33*, 201–219. https://doi.org/10.1177/105381511142593

Frattura, E., & Capper, C. (2007). *Leadership for social justice in practice: Integrated comprehensive services for all learners.* Corwin.

Friend, M., & Cook, L. (2017). *Interactions: Collaboration skills for school professionals* (8th ed.). Pearson.

Fullan, M. (2008). *The six secrets of change: What the best leaders do to help their organizations survive and thrive.* Jossey-Bass.

Fullerton, E. K., & Guardino, C. (2010). Teacher and students' perceptions of a modified inclusion classroom environment. *Electronic Journal for Inclusive Education, 2.* Retrieved from www.cehs.wright.edu/resources/publications/ejie/WinterSpring2010/winter_spring10.html

Gallaudet Research Institute August (2013). *Regional and national summary report of data from the 2011–12 annual survey of deaf and hard of hearing children and youth.* GRI, Gallaudet University.

González, V. (2001). The role of socioeconomic and sociocultural factors in language minority children's development: An ecological research view. *Bilingual Research Journal, 25*(1–2), 1–30.

Guardino, C., & Antia, S. (2012). Modifying the classroom environment to increase engagement and decrease disruption with students who are Deaf or hard of hearing, *The Journal of Deaf Studies and Deaf Education, 17*(4), 518–533, https://doi.org/10.1093/deafed/ens026

Guardino, C., & Fullerton, E. (2010). Changing behaviors by changing the environment: A case study of an inclusion classroom. *Teaching Exceptional Children, 42*, 8–13.

Hallam, P. R., Smith, H. R., Hite, J. M., Hite, S. J., & Wilcox, B. R. (2015). Trust and collaboration in PLC teams: Teacher relationships, principal support, and collaborative benefits. *NASSP Bulletin, 99*, 193–216. https://doi.org/10.1177/0192636515602330

Hannay, L., Jaafar, S. B., & Earl, L. (2013). A case study of district leadership using knowledge management for educational change. *Journal of Organizational Change Management, 26*, 64–82. https://doi.org/10.1108/09534811311307914

Hanson, M. J., Beckman, P. J., Horn, E., Marquat, J., Sandall, S. R., Greig, D., & Brennan, E. (2000). Entering preschool: Family and professional experiences in this transition process. *Journal of Early Intervention, 23*(4), 279–293.

Hargreaves, A., & O'Connor, M. (2018). *Collaborative professionalism: When teaching together means learning for all.* Corwin.

Harris, A. (2013). *Distributed leadership matters: Potential, practicalities and possibilities.* Corwin.

Individuals with Disabilities Education Act (IDEA) of 2004, 20 U.S.C. §§ 1400–1482. (2015). https://sites.ed.gov/idea/statute-chapter-33

Khalifa, M. A., Gooden, M., & Davis, J. (2016). Culturally responsive school leadership: A synthesis of the literature. *Review of Educational Research, 86*(4), 1272–1311. https://doi.org/10.3102/0034654316630383

Khalifa, M. A., Jennings, M. E., Briscoe, F., Oleszweski, A. M., & Abdi, N. (2014). Racism? Administrative and community perspectives in data-driven decision making: Systemic perspectives versus technical-rational perspectives. *Urban Education, 49,* 147–181. https://doi.org/10.1177/0042085913475635

Knight, J. (2007). *Instructional coaching: A partnership approach to improving instruction.* Corwin.

Leana, C. (2011). The missing link in school reform. *Stanford Social Innovation Review,* 30–35. Retrieved from https://www2.ed.gov/programs/slcp/2011progdirmtg/mislinkinrfm.pdf

Lofthouse, R., Lear, D., Towler, C., Hall, E., & Cummings, C. (2010). *Improving coaching: Evolution not revolution.* National College for Leadership in Schools and Children's Services, Nottingham.

Lovett, D. L., & Haring, K. A. (2003). Family perceptions of transitions in early intervention. *Education and Training in Disabilities, 38*(4), 370–377.

Lucas, T., & Villegas, A. M. (2013). Preparing linguistically responsive teachers: Laying the foundation in preservice teacher education. *Theory Into Practice, 52*(2), 98–109.

Lucas, T., Villegas, A. M., & Freedson-Gonzalez, M. (2008). Linguistically responsive teacher education: Preparing classroom teachers to teach English language learners. *Journal of Teacher Education, 59*(4), 361–373.

Marshall, C., & Oliva, M. (2006). Building the capacities of social justice leaders. In C. Marshall & M. Oliva (Eds.), *Leadership for social justice: Making revolutions in education* (pp. 1–15). Pearson.

McDonald, M., Kazemi, E., & Kavanagh, S. S. (2013). Core practices and pedagogies of teacher education: A call for a common language and collective activity. *Journal of Teacher Education, 64*(5), 378–386.

Mullen, C. (2011). New teacher mentoring: A mandated direction of states. *Kappa Delta Pi Record, 47*(2), 63–67.

Oliva, G. A., & Lytle, L. R. (2014). *Turning the tide: Making life better for deaf and hard-of-hearing schoolchildren*. Gallaudet University Press.

Oliva, G. A., Lytle, L. R., Hopper, M., & Ostrove, J. M. (2016). From social periphery to social centrality: Building social capital for deaf and hard-of-hearing students in the 21st century. *Diversity in Deaf Education* (pp. 325–354). Oxford University Press.

Pacchiano, D., Klein, R., & Hawley, M. S. (2016). *Reimagining instructional leadership and organizational conditions for improvement: Applied research transforming early education*. Ounce of Prevention Fund.

Páez, M., Bock, K., & Pizzo, L. (2011). Supporting the language and early literacy skills of English language learners: Effective practices and future directions. In S. Neuman & D. Dickenson (Eds.), *Handbook of early literacy research* (Vol. 3, pp. 136–152). Guilford.

Papay, J., & Kraft, M. (2017). Developing workplaces where teachers stay, improve, and succeed. In D. E. Quintero (Ed.), *Teaching in context: How social aspects of school and school systems shape teachers' development & effectiveness* (pp. 15–35). Harvard Education Press.

Paratore, J. (2001). *Opening doors, opening opportunities: Family literacy in an urban community*. Allyn & Bacon.

Parsloe, E., & Leedham, M. (2009). *Coaching and mentoring: Practical conversations to improve learning*. Kogan Page.

Patterson, K., Grenny, J., McMillan, R., & Switzler, A. (2012). *Crucial conversations*. McGraw-Hill.

Pizzo, L. (2016). d/Deaf and hard of hearing multilingual learners: The development of communication and language. *American Annals of the Deaf, 161*(1), 17–32. Retrieved from www.jstor.org/stable/26235248

Pizzo, L., & Chilvers, A. (2016). Assessment and d/Deaf multilingual learners: Considerations and promising practice. *American Annals of the Deaf, 161*(1), 56–66.

Pizzo, L., & Ford, L. (2022). Developing a comprehensive language profile to support learning: The Assessment of d/Deaf and hard of hearing multilingual learners. In J. E. Cannon, C. Guardino, & P. V. Paul (Eds.), *Deaf and hard of hearing multilingual learners: Foundations, strategies, and resources* (pp. 67–105). Routledge.

Portner, H. (2008). *Mentoring new teachers* (3rd ed.). Corwin.

Ronfeldt, M., Farmer, S., McQueen, K., & Grissom, J. (2015). Teacher collaboration in instructional teams and student achievement. *American Educational Research Journal, 52*(3), 475–514.

Scanlan, M., & Lopez, F. (2012). ¡Vamos! how school leaders promote equity and excellence for bilingual students. *Educational Administration Quarterly, 48*(4) 583–625.

Shanahan, T., Mulhern, M., & Rodríguez-Brown, F. V. (1995). Project FLAME: Lessons learned from a family literacy program for linguistic minority families. *Reading Teacher, 48*(7), 586–593.

Sheridan, S. M., Erchul, W. P., Brown, M. S., Dowd, S. E., Warnes, E. D., Marti, D. C., . . . & Eagle, J. W. (2004). Perceptions of helpfulness in conjoint behavioral consultation: Congruence and agreement between teachers and parents. *School Psychology Quarterly, 19*, 121–140. https://doi.org/10.1521/scpq.19.2.121.33308

Solomon, A. (2012). *Far from the tree: Parents, children, and the search for identity.* Scribner.

Swafford, M., Wingate, K., Zagummy, L., & Richey, D. (2015). Families living in poverty: Perceptions of family-centered practices. *Journal of Early Intervention, 37*(2), 138–154.

Varney, J. (2009). Humanistic mentoring: Nurturing the person within. *Kappa Delta Pi Record, 45*(3), 127–131. https://doi.org/10.1080/00228958.2009.10517302

Venables, D. (2015). The case for protocols. *Educational Leadership, 72*(7). Retrieved from www.ascd.org/publications/educational-leadership/apr15/vol72/num07/The-Case-for-Protocols.aspx

Wang, Q., Andrews, J., Liu, H., & Liu, C. (2016). Case studies of multilingual/multicultural Asian deaf adults: Strategies for success. *American Annals of the Deaf, 161*(1), 67–88. Retrieved from www.jstor.org/stable/26235252

Woods, J., Wilcox, M., Friedman, M., & Murch, T. (2011). Collaborative consultation in natural environments: Strategies to enhance family-centered supports and services. *Language, Speech, and Hearing Services in Schools, 42*, 379–392.

7
d/Deaf and Hard of Hearing Multilingual Learners With Disabilities: A Case Study of a Learner Who Is Deaf With Autism Spectrum Disorder and From an Immigrant Family

Eun Young Kwon, Caroline Guardino, and Joanna E. Cannon

Learning Objectives

Readers will:

- Recognize the prevalence of disabilities amongst students who are d/Deaf and hard of hearing (d/Dhh) multilingual learners (DML) with a disability or disabilities (DML-D).
- Understand the perspectives of parents and/or caregivers who are culturally and linguistically diverse with children who are DML-D regarding the eligibility, placement, and intervention processes for their children.
- Realize the educational perspective of various service providers who work with children who are DML-D.
- Understand linguistic and educational considerations for families with learners who are DML-D, as described through a detailed case study;

DOI: 10.4324/9781003259176-7

and acknowledge the cultural nuances that a culturally and linguistically diverse family experienced when coming to an English-dominant country.
- Identify community-based and educational supports for families with learners who are DML-D.
- Apply the Tenants of Effective Practice for learners who are d/Dhh with disabilities (DWD) to students who are DML-D in order to provide supports for the learners and their families.

Little is known about d/Deaf and hard of hearing (d/Dhh) multilingual learners (DML) with a disability or disabilities (DML-D), because of the dearth of research and publications specific to this population. Demographic data on learners who are DML-D indicate a population whose size is consistent, if not growing. However, precise data for this population of learners is difficult to ascertain.

Terminology

Who are DML-D learners? First, these students are d/Dhh and come from homes where their parents do not speak English nor use American Sign Language (ASL). Second, they are learners who have a disability or disabilities (e.g., autism spectrum disorder, learning disability, or emotional behavioral challenges). One might argue that the student's disability is more prominent in presenting academic, social, or behavioral challenges, than in the fact that they are multilingual learners. However, when referring to this population, the authors and editors of this text believe that the language, identity, culture, and heritage of the learner should define the student, more so than the disability; therefore, we intentionally highlight their linguistic competence prior to the disability, using the term DML-D.

Demographic & Prevalence Data

Demographic data of DMLs *or* students who are d/Dhh with a disability (DWD) have been reported as a significant portion of the total population of d/Dhh students (≈18–47%, respectively; Gallaudet Research Institute [GRI], 2000–2013). The data can be disaggregated by the percent of students who are DMLs *or* students who are DWD, yet the percentage of students who are DML-D has not been reported. Figure 7.1 is a Venn

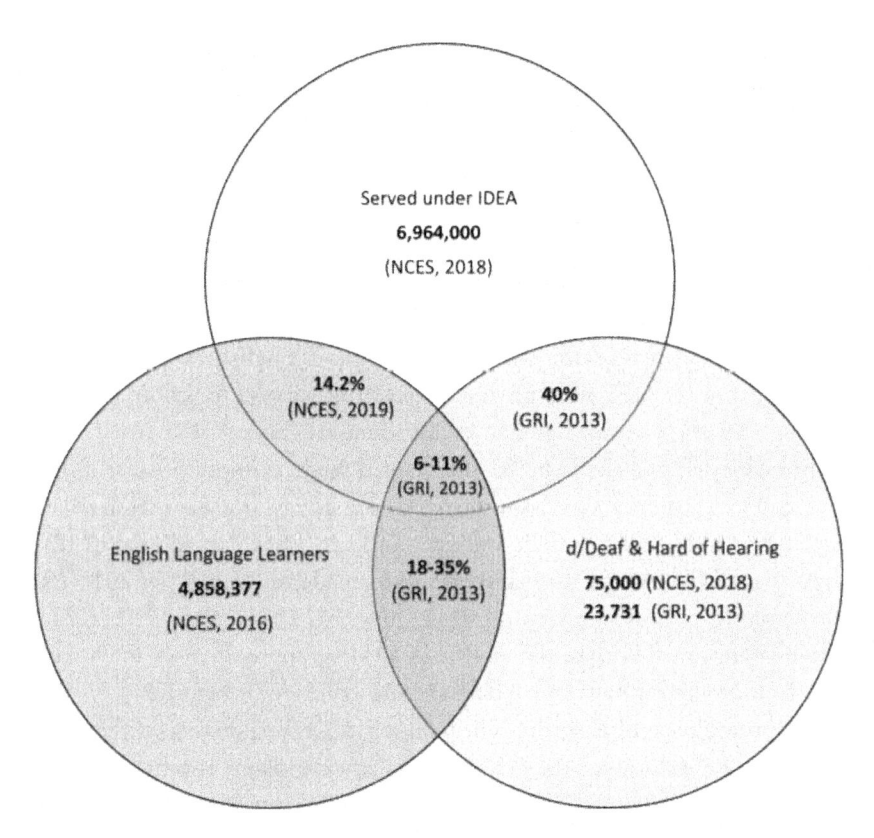

FIGURE 7.1 Visual Representation of Demographics Disaggregated

diagram illustrating the complexities of gathering accurate data across multiple sources and populations to reflect these learners. Figure 7.1 contains the most recent US demographic data regarding students who have disabilities, who are English Language Learners, and who are d/Dhh, as well as the overlap of all three of these populations. Zehler et al. (2003) reported that approximately 9% of the students with Limited English Proficiency were receiving special education services. Approximately 16 years later, as of May 2019, the National Center for Education Statistics reported that 14.2% of the total population of English language learners also receives special education services.

The Venn Diagram shows disaggregated USA data of students who qualify for special education under IDEA (approximately seven million), English Language Learners (ELL) (approximately five million), and students who are d/Dhh (approximately 75,000). ELL students with special needs account for 14% of the special education population. Approximately 40% of students who are deaf have disabilities. And 18–35% of students who are d/Dhh are also ELL learners. The center of the diagram depicts students who are d/Dhh with disabilities and ELLs, approximately 6–11% of the deaf and hard of hearing K-12 population.

What percentage of the 14.2% of students who are English language learners with disabilities are d/Dhh? The only source of information that collected data on students who are d/Dhh and English language learners was from the GRI who previously sent out surveys to school districts throughout the United States to collect data on learners who are d/Dhh nationwide. The data must be interpreted with caution because 2012 was the last year the GRI administered the survey, the data from 2012 was never published on their website, and no other data source of this type is available. After a special request was made to the GRI in 2015 (R. Winiarczyk, personal communication, June 16, 2015), their 2011/2012 survey data revealed that of the 19,444 DMLs, approximately 6.3% had one or more disabilities. These data are also reflected in Figure 7.1.

The prevalence of each disability among d/Dhh students is difficult to ascertain. By examining the GRI survey, for example, it is estimated that approximately 2.2% of d/Dhh students have Autism Spectrum Disorder (ASD). This is not too different from the Centers for Disease Control's (CDC) report (2018) as well as Szymanski and colleagues' (2012) which reported the prevalence rate of ASD among the general population to be one in 59 children. The CDC report (2018) also indicated that ASD occurs at a similar rate among d/Dhh individuals as those with typical hearing. Presumably, a similar rate of students with ASD would be found in the DML-D population.

There are several caveats with the reliability of the GRI data: (a) professionals were not obligated to complete the survey; (b) professionals may not have received the survey; (c) many students may be in inclusive settings and their general education teacher may not have the information to complete the survey questions; (d) some students attend private schools which are not a part of the public school system and therefore may not have received the survey; (e) smaller or new programs within a district may not have been identified within the GRI database and therefore did not receive it; and (f) teachers or administrators may not have the time to complete the survey (Mitchell, 2004).

Theoretical Frameworks & Approaches

Guardino and Cannon (2022) created the framework *Tenets of Effective Practice for Learners who are DWD* (*TEP*; see Figure 7.2). We assert this framework is also applicable with students who are DML-D, as it contains the necessary elements or "structures" that support these learners and families. The foundation of the framework is Vygotsky's (1978) sociocultural theory. This theory emphasizes the importance of providing natural experiences that reflect the cultural beliefs and practices of the DML-D and their families. These experiences build background knowledge in the context of the learner's heritage culture. The sociocultural theory also accentuates the need for professionals to examine their cultural competence so

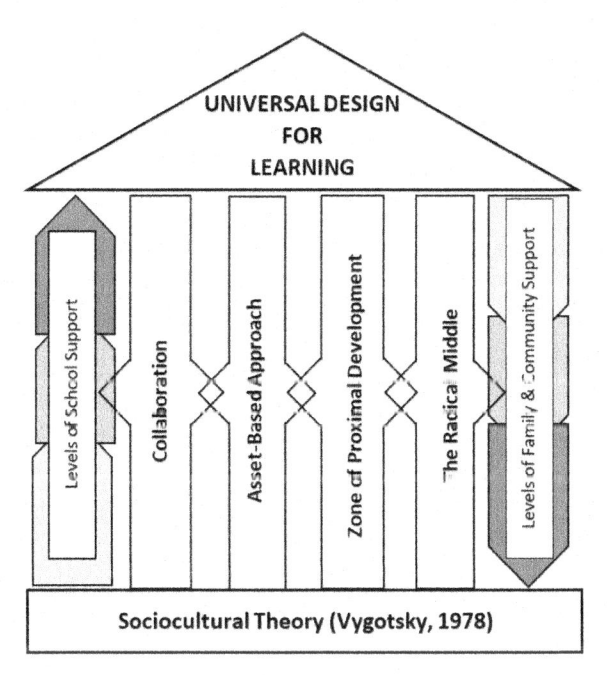

Figure 7.2 Tenets of Effective Practice Applied to DML-D (Guardino & Cannon, 2022)

they can effectively understand, communicate, and interact with DMLs and their families.

A structure that looks like a house, supported by four pillars labeled (from right to left), "Collaboration, Asset-based Approach, Zone of Proximal Development, and The Radical Middle". The walls of the house have arrows pointing up and down showing levels of school, family, and community support. The foundation is Vygotsky's Sociocultural Theory. A roof labeled "Universal Design for Learning" protects the house.

The framework contains four pillars: (a) collaboration, (b) asset-based approach, (c) Zone of Proximal Development (Vygotsky, 1978), and (d) The Radical Middle (Easterbrooks & Maiorana-Basas, 2015; Gardiner-Walsh & Lenihan, 2017). Collaboration can take place through a variety of formats (e.g., face-to-face, virtually, and via emails or texts) to increase communication options between professionals and families. Collaboration requires a team approach, involving the family members as an integral part of the collaborative process. Team members should use an asset-based approach, believing the DML-D learners are capable of learning, thriving, and growing in their homes, communities, and educational environments. Through a collaborative, asset-based approach, team members are able to share their successes, as well as strategies used to overcome challenges as they arise.

In Box 7.1 we are introduced to one of three vignettes provided within the chapter to highlight the variety of learners being discussed. For example, Tomas is from Portugal, exposed to two languages, and uses an assistive communication device. Tomas' educational team works together to use an asset-based approach that actively involves his family in the process. They ensure interpreters are available and all materials are translated into the home language of the family, with extra time for discussion during the meeting. These activities also increase the cultural competence of the team working with students with multiple needs from Portugal, such as Tomas.

Vygotsky's Zone of Proximal Development is a theoretical approach with practical implications to working with DML-Ds. The Zone of Proximal Development helps professionals recognize the learner's potential and use this information to scaffold learning and increase academic, social, cognitive, and behavioral outcomes (Vygotsky, 1978). And finally,

> ### Box 7.1 Tomas
>
> Tomas is a 19-year-old male with a moderate conductive hearing level and Down syndrome. His family emigrated five years ago from Porto, Portugal to New York City, New York because of his sister's work. Tomas' parents died when he was 12 years old and he has been living with his older sister since that time. Tomas' sister, her husband, and their two daughters all use Portuguese in the home. Tomas is nonverbal and uses an Augmentative Alternative Communication application on his tablet to communicate with others. Tomas attends a general education school and spends time in the general education classrooms, as well as a small group class with other students with special needs. In both classrooms his family and teachers are focused on involving Tomas in all academic and social activities with instructional focus on functional skills that will benefit Tomas in future work placements. Tomas will be eligible to remain in school until he is 22 and his Individualized Education Plan (IEP) team is working to determine the type of jobs and/or activities Tomas would like to do after he graduates so they can support him acquiring the necessary skills and supports. His family is very involved in all decision-making and even though they have been in the country for five years, they always request a Portuguese interpreter for all meetings, translation of all documents, and extra time during meetings to ensure they are making an informed decision. The IEP team also works with Tomas to be involved in any decisions and to make sure he understands the goals and activities suggested by the team.

The Radical Middle is a holistic approach that respects the DML-D individual and family as well as professional and personal opinions of each team member. The common goal of those who adhere to The Radical Middle approach is to apply a variety of strategies, regardless of their own professional training, orientation, and positionality, to determine what will best support the DML-D to have a positive trajectory in their academic, social, and behavioral outcomes. The Tenets of Effective Practice framework illustrates pillars as the supporting approaches by which we implement instruction, housed under the "roof" of Universal Design for Learning. Universal Design for Learning is the manner in which we offer access to information in the classroom with careful consideration of various learning styles and skill levels (Rose & Gravel, 2010).

Components of the framework require careful introspection of our own beliefs (i.e., The Radical Middle), planning for *all* learners (i.e., Universal Design for Learning) while incorporating culturally responsive teaching (Kieran & Anderson, 2019); understanding the cultural beliefs and practices of others (i.e., Vygotsky's sociocultural theory); and thus making the framework applicable to DML-D. The authors also examined the broader field of bilingual and special education to obtain information on educational eligibility, placement, intervention processes, language, and communication considerations.

Educational Issues & Considerations

We examine the issues surrounding educational eligibility, placement, intervention, and language and communication considerations for DML-D. This information guided the formulation of our research questions into better understanding the unique characteristics of students who are DML-D.

Eligibility

The process of identifying and determining eligibility of a student who is culturally and linguistically diverse or DML-D is complex because they may have "greater exposure to the gestational and environmental factors, including prior to school entry, that increase the risk for cognitive, behavioral, or physical impairments" (Morgan et al., 2018, p. 262). These predisposed factors often cause students who are culturally and linguistically diverse to be susceptible to misdiagnosis, mislabeling, or misidentification, thus causing over- and under-representation of diverse students in special education (Artiles et al., 2005; Claycomb et al., 2004; Samson & Lesaux, 2009; Van den Bergh & Marcoen, 2004). Many students who are d/Dhh are also predisposed to genetic and environmental factors, which can cause varying disabilities (Bruce et al., 2022). We can see an example of environmental factors in Box 7.2, as we meet Ballabh who was born in Nepal with minimal resources.

Professionals in special education have concerns about how to differentiate between pre-dispositional factors that cause delays and the factors that determine eligibility for support services. The answer is partially through

---

Box 7.2 Ballabh

Ballabh recently immigrated from Nepal to Liverpool, United Kingdom with his mother, father, two aunts, and four younger siblings. Ballabh is five years old, deaf with an unknown hearing level, and has never received formal schooling. Ballabh's family members speak and are literate in Nepali, the official language of Nepal. Ballabh was born at home when resources were limited and no medical professionals were available to assist in the birthing process. His mother experienced complications during childbirth that resulted in Ballabh's developmental complications soon after birth. Ballabh demonstrated signs of a developmental delay when he did not meet developmental milestones (e.g., poor head and neck control and walking at two years old). His family had four more children within the next four years, and his parents noticed Ballabh's delays as the other children advanced past him in motor and cognitive abilities. Because of political unrest and turmoil within the city in which Ballabh's family resided, their parents sought the right of asylum through the United Kingdom parliament. After moving to Liverpool, Ballabh and his brothers and sisters attended the neighborhood school and began learning English and the culture of their new environment. The school personnel formed a transdisciplinary team that included early intervention experts in developmental delay and educators with experience working with learners who are deaf and have a developmental delay. The team sought assistance from an audiologist, school psychologists, a Nepali interpreter, and a cultural broker to provide Ballabh's family with information about his hearing level, receptive and expressive language, and areas in need of support.

varying types of assessment; however, psychoeducational testing is controversial when conducted with students who are DWDs and/or DMLs (Cawthon, 2015; Leigh & Andrews, 2016; Pizzo & Chilvers, 2016).

Although assessments exist that test cognitive, language, and literacy skills, these tests do not account for individual differences including family, academic, and social experiences (McCain & Farnsworth, 2018). Standardized assessments for students who are English language learners should be provided in the home and in the first language of the learner; however, not all are available in multiple translations and/or various sign languages (e.g., Philippine Sign Language or Mexican Sign Language; Cawthon, 2015). In addition, standardized assessments are known to lack cultural sensitivity and results should be considered with caution when making eligibility decisions. For example, test items may contain pictures and references a student who is culturally and linguistically diverse has not been exposed to, depending on their cultural background (Farnsworth, 2016). Multiple assessments including culturally and linguistically responsive tests, administered by various professionals (e.g., teacher, school psychologist, and social worker), in addition to interviews of the child and their family members, are the most accurate forms of identifying students who are DML-Ds (Pizzo & Chilvers, 2016). After a student is determined to be eligible for services for English language learners and students with special needs, the next step is finding the least restrictive environment that will meet the multifaceted needs of the learner.

Educational Placement

While there are multiple services available for students who are culturally and linguistically diverse and are d/Dhh, determining what is the least restrictive learning environment for students who are DML-Ds is complex. The most important aspect to the least restrictive environment is having educators and service providers who are trained in linguistically and culturally responsive pedagogy and practices. Involving the family in the educational placement decision-making process is crucial to providing the services and supports a DML-D may need at school. Providing spoken and sign language interpreters, cultural brokers, community cultural workers, and advocates for students with exceptionalities may provide the family with the support needed to understand the referral, educational placement, and services process (Cannon & Guardino, 2022; see Chapter 1). The vignette provided in Box 7.3 discusses the use of interpreters and cultural brokers to assist a family in better understanding a school system outside of their home country and culture. The limited level of understanding of the IEP process, combined with a possible lack of knowledge of the predominant cultural language, are barriers for many families who have recently immigrated to English-speaking countries. These barriers must be overcome before they can begin to comprehend the information about their children's academic and social development, especially those of children with multiple linguistic and special needs, as demonstrated within the vignette provided.

> Box 7.3 Naamah
>
> Naamah is a ten-year-old female who recently immigrated to Dunedin, New Zealand from Pattaya, Thailand, with her parents and siblings (one younger sister and one older brother). Due to complications during birth, Naamah was born with a moderate-to-severe bilateral hearing level and moderate spastic cerebral palsy. Naamah's family spoke Thai in the home and began learning a modified version of Modern Standard Thai Sign Language that was accessible for Naamah (full accessibility was difficult due to fine and gross motor coordination required for some signs). Naamah expresses herself using some speech, but her primary mode of communication is Thai Sign Language with approximations, along with home signs. Naamah uses a motorized wheelchair to travel long distances, and two crutches when she is at home, in the classroom, or playing outside. When Naamah became school-age she went to the Sotpattana School for the Deaf in Pattaya, but her family is relocating to Dunedin, New Zealand where many of their family members live. Before moving to New Zealand, the family began English classes at their local community center and watched videos online of New Zealand Sign Language (NZSL). They also called their family members who have children in the school district where they will move to better understand the policies and procedures for enrolling their children and what supports will be available for Naamah in her transition.

Intervention

Strategies and supports for working with students who are DMLs or DML-Ds should follow the principles of culturally responsive pedagogy (Gay, 2010; Higgins & Liberman, 2016; Humphries, 2004; Lucas et al., 2008; McCain & Farnsworth, 2018; Pizzo & Chilvers, 2016). Teachers who implement culturally responsive pedagogy use explicit instruction and embrace the learners' assets to build receptive and expressive language skills. Culturally responsive pedagogy includes strategies to engage families as active participants in their children's development by teaching them how to promote language-rich experiences at home. Most importantly, in a classroom with students who are DML-Ds, the teacher researches and understands both the student's disability and culture in order to: (a) build positive relationships, (b) encourage students to integrate their culture and experiences into their learning, (c) differentiate instruction to meet the varying learning styles, (d) connect topics to the strengths of the students, and (e) scaffold instruction to make learning manageable rather than overwhelming (Espinosa, 2013; McCain & Farnsworth, 2018; Pizzo & Chilvers, 2016).

Linguistic and Communication Considerations

Students who are DML-Ds may have unique communication and language considerations depending upon their exceptionality, strengths, and needs. Students who are DWD may use various communication modes or modalities such as listening and spoken language, sign language, and/or combinations of the two. Physical disabilities may result in limitations surrounding the use of spoken language and/or sign language (e.g., those with cerebral palsy affecting the limbs utilizing two-handed signing; Bonvillian et al., 2020a; Bonvillian et al., 2020b, Davis et al., 2010; Westling & Fox, 2000). Developmental delays may limit the d/Dhh individual's capacity for communication in one or more modes (Bruce & Borders, 2015). Augmentative and alternative communication devices (e.g., speech production devices, communication books, and clickers/switches) are an option for some learners (see Box 7.1). A family-centered approach to all communication and language decisions is important to understand the goals for the learner and ways the family can support language and communication acquisition (see Boxes 7.1–7.3).

Where Do We Begin?

After a search of 247 different combinations of the terms associated with deafness, disabilities, and English Language Learners, only 11 publications about DMLs surfaced, none specifically pertaining to students who are both DML-Ds. In an effort to understand how the complexities of educational eligibility, placement, intervention, and communication and language impact the success of a student who is a DML-D, the authors conducted an intrinsic case study (see Methodology; Baxter & Jack, 2008; Stake, 1995). This case study will assist in building a repository of information about learners who are DML-Ds with ASD, where parents and professionals can gain a better understanding of how to effectively meet these learners' needs.

Methodology

An intrinsic case study (Baxter & Jack, 2008; Stake, 1995) was conducted due to the interest in understanding a case because of its uniqueness, not necessarily because it represents the population as a whole. In addition, an intrinsic case study is not generalizable across a population of learners; rather it represents a picture of one case, which researchers can build upon to understand a larger population of learners. Ultimately, the intrinsic case study presented within this chapter addresses the research questions through interviews with parents, teachers, and educational assistants (EAs).

The researchers examined the perspectives of parents and service providers who have or work with a child who is a DML-D. Their perspectives regarding the educational eligibility, placement, intervention, and communication and language considerations were explored. The following research questions guided the case study:

1. What are the perspectives of parents and/or caregivers who are culturally and linguistically diverse with children who are DML-Ds regarding the eligibility, placement, and intervention processes for their children?
2. What are the educational perspectives of service providers who work with children who are DML-Ds?

3. What are the linguistic and communication considerations when working with students who are DML-Ds and their families?

Participants

Inclusionary criteria for this study were parents, teachers, and EAs of a child who is d/Dhh, has been diagnosed with a disability (e.g., ASD or intellectual delays), and whose home language is neither English nor ASL. A convenience sampling method was utilized and prospective participants who met the inclusionary criteria in a region of the Pacific Northwest were recruited. A family whose home language is Korean and has a son who is deaf with ASD was contacted and agreed to participate in the study. The son, who is the primary subject of the interviews, was in a third-grade general education classroom when the case study was conducted. He was given the pseudonym "Jimin" and will be referred to as such throughout the chapter.

Upon permission from the parents, the child's teachers and EAs were recruited for the study. Three teachers (i.e., teacher of the d/Dhh, special education teacher, and general education classroom teacher) and two EAs (past and present) agreed to participate and were interviewed. All of the educators had worked with the child for at least two years in the same school. Detailed demographic information about the teachers and EAs is presented in Table 7.1.

Procedures and Setting

The consent forms and interviews were provided in the participant's preferred language. The child's teachers and EAs preferred English, whereas the parents preferred Korean. Interviews of all the participants were audio-recorded and transcribed. Semi-structured interviews ranged from 60 to 90 minutes and were conducted over the course of five months. The parents were interviewed on two different days at the father's office. The educators were interviewed once in a quiet classroom of their choice in Jimin's school building. Two different sets of interview questionnaires were developed based on the research questions and provided to the participants: one for the parents and the other for the educators.

Learners With Disabilities 233

TABLE 7.1 Demographics of Educational Participants

Participants	Roles & Responsibilities (described by them)	Relevant Experience	Grades worked with Jimin	Instructional Setting
Teacher of the Deaf and Hard of Hearing (TDHH)	• District itinerant teacher • Provides language sessions through 1:1 session or with Speech Language Pathologist (SLP)	Five years as teacher of the deaf and hard of hearing	K–2	30–60 minutes weekly
Special Education Teacher (SET)	• Case manager in the school • Coordinates and writes IEP • Provides resources and support to the team (e.g., CT, EA, TDHH) • Communicates with parents as a liaison to the district	>Ten years as SET & CT, taking a master's degree in Special Education.	K–present	Ongoing observation and supervision; no individual teaching
Classroom Teacher (CT)	• Ensures *the curriculum is modified for Sam to help create a place where the child is welcomed and accepted* with his EA	>Ten years as classroom teacher	1–2	Daily classroom teaching; no individual teaching
Educational Assistant 1 (EA)	• Provides 1:1 support • Teaches him signs	Ten months of full ASL immersion program	K–1	Daily
Educational Assistant 2	• Provides 1:1 support • Facilitates Picture Exchange Communication System (PECS) under the direction of TDHH & SLP	Previously worked as a Behavioral Interventionist; learning ASL	2–present	Daily

Data Analysis

A semantic thematic analysis (Braun & Clarke, 2006) of the transcripts was conducted by all three authors using NVIVO 12 during coding and the analysis (QSR, 2018). As described by Braun and Clarke (2006, 2012), a semantic thematic analysis involves a systematic process for identifying, organizing, and offering insight into patterns of themes across a data set. This analysis allows researchers to (a) identify commonalities among participant responses, (b) organize the collective or shared meanings and experiences as themes, and (c) offer answers to each research question.

The six phases of thematic analysis by Braun and Clarke (2006) were utilized in an inductive approach to coding and analyzing the data. Once familiarized with the data (phase 1), the authors generated initial codes and collated data relevant to each code (phase 2; e.g., educational diagnosis, placement, intervention, and linguistic and communication considerations). From those codes, the authors independently searched for potential themes (phase 3). The authors then triangulated the results by reviewing and refining the initial analysis into a coherent set of themes that captured the most important elements for answering each research question (phase 4). During the analysis, the researchers saw themes emerge and overlap across the six interviews. Themes that emerged included: cultural considerations, qualifications, availability, and collaboration. These themes aligned with the codes and helped to further analyze the data set to better understand the overall story of the case study (phase 5). The results and discussion sections that follow are the final phase of the analysis (phase 6) and include explicit examples of the case as related to the literature and the research questions.

Results

What Are the Perspectives of Parents Regarding the Eligibility, Placement, and Intervention Processes for Their Child?

The parents' perspective on the educational diagnosis, placement, and interventions are reported here in depth. Additional underlying themes that emerged throughout the interview included: collaboration, community, and psycho-emotional aspects. We begin by providing demographic information of Jimin and his family, then moving into a presentation of the aforementioned themes.

DML-D and Their Family

Jimin is a child who is deaf, has ASD, and was born in Canada to parents who immigrated from Korea one years before Jimin was born. Jimin has three siblings, two older brothers and a younger sister, and the primary language in the home is Korean. His siblings are bilingual and regularly use English and Korean. The family had no experience with d/Dhh individuals and were unaware of Deaf culture and sign languages at the time of Jimin's birth.

Educational Eligibility

Jimin's hearing loss was identified via Newborn Hearing Screening. When he was three months old, he was diagnosed with a profound bilateral hearing loss due to significant bilateral cochlea and auditory nerve abnormalities. The etiology was unknown. His parents felt puzzled, but his mom "thought that technology might help for him to hear better and cope with his hearing loss".

When Jimin was one-and-a-half-years old, his parents took him to South Korea for cochlear implant surgery. Over the next 11 months of use of a cochlear implant, Jimin did not show any response to auditory input. A professional at an Audiology Clinic at a local hospital referred Jimin to the Infant Development Program. Consequently, an Infant Development Worker visited Jimin's home twice a month over the course of two years, from age one to three years old. At the age of two-and-a-half, Jimin stopped using amplification devices and his parents began using basic ASL to communicate with him. During this time, the Infant Development Worker was concerned about Jimin's developmental delays, as he displayed some restrictive patterns of behavior, unusual sensory interest, and limited nonverbal social communication. These concerns led the parents to request several diagnostic assessments by the Hearing Loss Team at a local children's hospital.

Jimin, at 3.7 years old, was diagnosed with ASD. With this diagnosis, his parents were shocked and confused. They had "believed that his delay or ASD symptoms were caused by his hearing loss" and thought that "once he is able to hear us, his autistic symptoms would be gone". Jimin's dad reported that "the more I learned about autism as a disability not related to deafness and that there will be no cure in his entire life, the more I felt dismayed". Jimin's mom stated:

> At the beginning, I thought we could solve this problem [ASD] too with help, like hearing loss. The more I had learned about ASD, however, the more I was shocked. I came to realize that this condition will be a burden in my entire life.

This diagnosis changed their choices when considering preschool settings for Jimin.

Educational Placement

From the time Jimin was identified with ASD and until entering Kindergarten, he received applied behavior analysis (ABA) therapy twice a week and attended two preschools: one where ASL was the primary language of instruction and another that was an inclusive general education program. The ASL program was housed in a non-profit organization and one of two programs in the province where Deaf educators taught d/Dhh children and/or their siblings in ASL. They did not have a specific unit for d/Deaf children with disabilities. His parents described the preschool staff as looking "burdened" and "embarrassed", and that they did not seem to know what to do with Jimin because of his behaviors and complex needs. Jimin's mom also reported that "it was hard for me to communicate with the [Deaf] teachers who used ASL as well as the hearing teachers", as a Korean language interpreter was not always available to the parents. Due to limited staffing, Jimin was only allowed to attend the specialized preschool two half days per week. Jimin attended a general education preschool program for the other three days of the week where none of the staff knew ASL and communication was limited. Jimin's parents reported that his behaviors escalated on the days he attended this program.

After attending the preschool that used ASL, Jimin entered kindergarten at the local school for the deaf. Jimin's eligibility to be placed at the school for the deaf was decided by a committee who determined that he would attend the school for one year, conditional upon his behavior and ability to communicate in ASL. At the end of the school year, the committee determined that he was not eligible to continue in the program based on the supports they determined he required (e.g., placement in a resource room supporting students with autism, services of a behavioral consultant, a peer group of deaf students, and opportunities for his family to develop fluency in ASL). The parents did not agree with this decision. The committee advised the parents to send him to a district resource program for students with ASD. When the parents called the school district principal to inquire about the ASD program, they were told that there was no room for Jimin and no ASL support available in the resource room. When summer concluded, Jimin's parents registered him for a repeat kindergarten year in a general education school where his siblings also attended.

The local kindergarten class consisted of 22 students and a classroom teacher. Under the supervision of the special education teacher in the school, an assigned EA who had signing skills worked with Jimin one-on-one the entire school day. An itinerant teacher of the d/Dhh (TDHH) visited Jimin approximately once a week to support his language and communication development. Because Jimin had three years of instruction in this academic setting, the professionals working with Jimin were able to develop intervention strategies to address his needs.

Interventions

The parents reported the different types of interventions used with Jimin, including ABA therapy and a Picture Exchange Communication System (PECS) combined with ASL. The parents realized the importance of these interventions when his negative behavior decreased and his ability to communicate using ASL increased. The school personnel implemented these interventions, but the parents were not always provided the resources or information to use them with Jimin at home.

There were instances when Jimin's mother requested information regarding strategies to use with Jimin, yet her inquiries were not answered. She reported:

> During the IEP meetings I asked them to share the materials they used at school with Jimin so that I could use them at home. They said

yes, but it never happened. Maybe they have forgotten. They did not suggest or send me any materials.

When she asked the school staff about the interventions they were using with Jimin, she was not sure if she communicated her intention clearly. Jimin's mom noted, "Once I asked them [EA or special education teacher] regarding what they were doing with Jimin and what Jimin was learning, they looked uncomfortable. I was afraid that my questions were giving them the wrong impression, so I stopped asking those kinds of questions." His mom offered a potential solution during the interview:

> I wish they would take videos (even one or two-minutes long) of what they are doing with Jimin and send them to me, rather than writing or speaking to me since I don't understand English well. However, it would be much easier for me to understand if I could see the videos and to try the interventions or strategies at home, if it is not a matter of confidentiality.

Sharing intervention information was not the only area of uncertainty for the parents. Collaboration was also intermittent and disjointed.

Collaboration and Community

While there was limited collaboration with the school staff, the parents found the most comfort from collaborating with community members in their neighborhood and local church. Jimin's mom shared that "[m]any people from the church community, especially parents whose children have ASD, shared their stories and encouraged my family" and "A TDHH who speaks Korean has helped me understand the school services available for the future".

At times, collaboration across professionals and community members revealed an imbalance of services and inability to meet Jimin's needs. Certain children who were deaf with disabilities and attended the same preschool as Jimin received more services than he did. The mother attributed the inequity to parents who "raised their voices strongly". His parents were frustrated that the professionals working with their son seemed unqualified and potentially biased. Jimin's mom reported, "[T]heir concerns were always about his behaviors. They did not know what to do with his behaviors" and "the regular preschool expressed their difficulties in educating my child due to their limited staff." Jimin's dad stated that "it was very obvious that they did not know what to do with [his] child." This was not the only time where the parents shared the psycho-emotional aspects of having a child with a disability, as well as being culturally and linguistically diverse.

Cultural Considerations

The parents spoke of their perspective of being immigrants from South Korea in a predominantly English-speaking country (i.e., Canada) and having a child with a disability. Jimin's mom stated:

> A thought came to my mind often: what if I was white or deaf, would they treat me the same way? I am actually in their blind spot. They might think that because we don't speak English well and cannot communicate with ASL either.

She reported incidents where she was uncertain of her English comprehension: "As an immigrant, I am often guessing while listening to or reading their instructions. Does it mean they did this this way or not? I am often uncertain of what they are saying." Jimin's dad also reflected:

> I felt that [the camp for families with deaf child(ren)] was for only white people. They did not show any consideration for my child. Jimin did not know ASL much and had behaviors. It was very obvious that they did not know what to do with my child.

Jimin's challenging behaviors, coupled with the parents' difficulty learning English and ASL simultaneously, resulted in a feeling of isolation and incongruity with the Deaf (ASL users) and hearing (English speakers) communities that surrounded them.

Jimin's mother equated her experience of learning language to the needs of her son:

> I talked to them [the Education Committee]. Just as I am an English language learner, the more I am exposed to English speaking

environment, the more fluent I become. My child would be the same. If he had to stay in a hearing school, how would my child access language and be exposed to his language [ASL]?

In addition to these struggles, the mother also shared that she suffered from depression for a one-to-two-year period when Jimin was young.

To answer the first research question, the data analyses revealed the following parent perspectives about their son's eligibility, placement, and intervention experiences in school: (a) Jimin's early intervention settings did not have personnel with training in special education and ABA techniques; (b) finding a primary school educational placement for Jimin with access to instruction in ASL *and* professionals trained in ABA techniques was challenging and complex; (c) Jimin's parents did not have a strong understanding of the Canadian school system and the district's referral and placement process; (d) the family and professionals working with Jimin identified ABA, and PECS combined with ASL as effective interventions; (e) although collaboration was limited between the parents and school personnel, they found comfort in their community; and (f) the parents perceived linguistic and cultural barriers when they attempted to express their concerns and advocate for their child.

What Are the Educational Perspectives of Teachers and Service Providers Who Work With Children Who Are DML-Ds?

Table 7.1 shows the demographic data of the previous and current IEP team members who participated in this study. Across the five educators who were interviewed, common themes emerged in five different areas: educational placement, qualifications, collaboration, intervention strategies, and psycho-social aspects.

Educational Placement

The educational team shared three concerns regarding Jimin's educational placement: (a) Jimin would benefit from instruction in an ASL-English bilingual classroom, (b) the educational referral and placement process was not clear, and (c) an ideal placement does not exist in the area where Jimin's family resides.

The educators believed Jimin would benefit the most from being immersed in an educational setting where all students and staff communicated using ASL. The TDHH saw Jimin "getting tiny and tiny better language directly every day from an EA who is not proficient in signs". She stated: "we knew he needed a certain level of language [to attend the school for the deaf] . . . [and] we struggled to even give him that level of language, so we were caught in limbo because we couldn't get his language up because of lack of exposure." The classroom teacher was also concerned about Jimin's current placement: "most people in the classroom cannot speak his language. So, he's in silence. There's a deficit in language." The second EA (EA2) pointed out that this language deficit "is exacerbating other challenges that he has" such as behaviors and socialization.

As mentioned above, however, when the educators were seeking a way to fully immerse Jimin in "his first language", the team felt frustrated over the referral process which was not clear to them. The special education teacher reported:

> I don't understand what their criteria is and how they evaluated him. It just seems like it's sort of we went through the motions, and then it just kind of stopped. So, I don't know if there's been an official reapplication and an official rejection or what.

When an ASL specialist came to visit Jimin to assess his language skills, the results were incongruent from the team's observations. While the classroom teacher and EA2 saw Jimin learn some signs and engage in basic communication, the specialist did not report the same findings. The EA2 pointed out:

> [the specialist] didn't have the skills to communicate with a kid with autism who needs quite a different approach, so they [are]coming in and just meeting him the first time or the first couple of times, they didn't have a lot of luck getting any response from [Jimin].

The team discussed the ideal placement for Jimin. As stated by the special education teacher, the parents and team members wanted "him in an environment where he can succeed with full immersion of sign". Ideally, they suggested that Jimin should be amongst other deaf children, with and without ASD, who use ASL/English bilingual instruction throughout the day. In addition, many team members agreed that this "ideal" classroom would need to have a professional trained in ABA to assist with challenging behaviors.

Qualifications

The team members working with Jimin had varied expertise, rather than the comprehensive skillset needed to effectively serve Jimin. The needed skills included: (a) knowledge and use of ASL and ABA techniques, and (b) a firm understanding of those who are d/Dhh and have ASD. Many of the team members reported their inability to confidently serve Jimin. The TDHH stated:

> It definitely the autism piece was a part that I did not know . . . this case was so severe I knew that behaviors were getting in the way of language but I did not know necessary how to reduce his behaviors with ABA techniques so I found that challenging. . . . very multifaceted and overwhelming for me.

Coupled with the teachers' feeling of needing further training, there were no other professionals with both ABA and ASL communication skills in the school district. Currently, the EA2 has ABA training and is learning ASL while working with Jimin. The special education teacher expressed concern:

> As a teacher, I could tell you where a kid's at and where he needs to go next and what kind of strategies work for that. I don't have that skill set for ASL, and the EA doesn't have that . . . we're going to hit a, hit a ceiling of the skill sets we have.

Not only did the educators feel unprepared and underqualified to work with Jimin, their situation was exacerbated by the lack of time to collaborate.

Collaboration

The educators reported the challenges and successes they had when collaborating together as a team and working with other specialists. The main challenge reported was the lack of multi-dimensional expertise in understanding and meeting the complex needs of the learners who are d/Dhh with ASD. The team members had some knowledge about special education, but with minimal professional guidance in terms of ASD support and ASL assessment; as such, they struggled to have a comprehensive picture of how to meet Jimin's unique needs. A district specialist in ASD provided consultation for the team; however, more frequent collaboration with the TDHH was needed to meet Jimin's needs surrounding his ASD and deafness. Furthermore, the team had limited time to work in a cohesive manner with professionals regarding intervention strategies. The TDHH mentioned that "it was hard on the heart because you wanted to make progress and you wanted to give everything but everyone at the table only had limited time and limited resources" while "knowing the child deserves more".

Successful collaboration occurred when the team members met regularly to design and implement a specific intervention. The TDHH stated: "in the third year, the speech-language pathologist, and I, and EA worked as a team in every session to focus on language development and extending the student's attention to be able to sit longer. The speech-language pathologist provided the PECS", the TDHH paired the PECS with ASL, and the EA gathered evidence of how Jimin used this combination. The TDHH reported: "so, we decided to go on the same day, for the same session, and that's when we started to make the most progress." Accordingly, this collaboration led to positive outcomes for Jimin. Another collaboration included an ASL specialist who worked with Jimin's EA2 virtually via live streaming and taught the EA2 ASL signs to use during instruction. Although the team's collaborative work was limited and challenging at times, they continuously made efforts to address Jimin's needs through a variety of intervention strategies.

Interventions

The team has worked on improving Jimin's language, behavior, social, and academic skills as his IEP indicated. The team reported that Jimin made steady progress in the third year when ABA skills were consistently utilized in his routines through ASL. The special education teacher stated: "it is structured with visuals, paired with signs, and he [Jimin] responds to it. He's very strong at copying the signs, and you can see him trying them out spontaneously from time to time". His EA2 accredited consistency and strong repetition as the key factors to Jimin's improvement: "[we're] having an activity that's just the same every day, and then you change it slowly over time as he's mastering targets . . . so that consistency and repetition and predictability [is] very important for him". Once the functions of his behaviors were understood and his sensory needs were satisfied and managed, his language started to improve.

The team also noticed that Jimin became more engaged in class activities and motivated to socialize with his peers when his EA2 assisted him to systematically and repeatedly interact with them during activities (i.e., Circle Time). The classroom teacher reflected that "the ABA things, the structure, the very structured way of doing things, having a motivator even just a high five" were successful to get Jimin engaged in her classroom. She worked to ensure that "Jimin was just part of the classroom" and acknowledged that "we're communicating with Jimin too as part of the class" using "sign language". However, she admitted that there was a heavy reliance on the EA2 as it was he who systematically set up Jimin's routines, directly implemented interventions, and continuously collected data (e.g., videos) as evidence of his language development in the classroom.

Psychosocial Aspects

Jimin seemed to be well-accepted by his hearing peers thanks to, as his EA1 stated, "his giggling and peaceful nature", although his EA2 also observed that "he seems to prefer being on his own anyway and quite happy in his own world doing his own thing". Throughout Jimin's third year in his general education placement setting, his EA2 noted:

> He [Jimin] was showing more and more interest in his peers and wanting to, there were kids he would gravitate towards in the class. He would, his ability to interact meaningfully or in a complex way with them is very limited, of course, but he would go after them and touch their arms and give them hugs and stuff. So, you know, he was becoming increasingly social, even if he didn't have the skills to do that properly.

However, Jimin's special education teacher observed that, as Jimin was the only deaf student in a hearing classroom, "he started to be drawn to the kids and teachers with sign" in the hallway and playground which were shared with the school for the deaf.

His classroom teacher perceived that "they [the class] seem to be more caring; they're forgiving, like he's accepted, and kids were still interested in being near him". Due to his sensory-seeking behaviors, such as nose picking and playing with his saliva, "there were some kids who were a bit less comfortable about that"; however, as his EA2 stated, "there were a handful of kids who are really keen to be involved with Jimin, they'd tell [sign] him, 'oh, it's time to come and line up now' and he'd follow their instructions." The classroom teacher also reported that she was more connected to Jimin as he showed responses to her signs and asked for her attention.

To answer the second research question regarding the perspectives of the educational team, the analysis revealed that the team determined that an educational environment where personnel have knowledge of deafness, ASL, ABA techniques, and learners with ASD would most benefit Jimin's linguistic, social, and behavioral goals. Collectively they felt unqualified to fully assess his language skills and that they needed more support and resources to effectively teach Jimin. None of the team members had a firm understanding of ASD combined with deafness. There were no experts or EAs who possessed both ABA and ASL skills within the district. Successful collaboration to implement interventions occurred only when the team members systematically planned and met with district specialists. Although Jimin was well-accepted by his peers in the general education classroom, the team agreed that his current setting did not provide him with sufficient ASL language exposure.

What Are the Linguistic and Communication Considerations When Working With Students Who Are DML-Ds and Their Families?

Linguistic considerations included any language-related factors that were discussed and shared, including language choices for Jimin (while at school) and his parents (during meetings with school personnel). Communication considerations were defined as any response that involved a reference to communication between the parents, educational team, and/or district specialists.

Linguistic Considerations

When Jimin did not respond to listening and spoken language after receiving his cochlear implant, his parents began using ASL to communicate with him. His mom took some ASL courses but often struggled with English vocabulary. PECS was introduced for a brief time during Jimin's preschool years, but was not successful. Once Jimin's receptive comprehension of ASL began during his first three years of elementary school, his disruptive behaviors decreased and communication with his peers and staff increased. PECS was then reintroduced in combination with ASL, which proved to be successful when implemented consistently.

Jimin's parents and many of the educators working with him were aware of his linguistic needs. His parents strongly advocated for Jimin to be immersed in a signing environment because they believed that "more exposure would bring more language proficiency". The special education teacher described that Jimin was "at a critical point he needs to move to an immersed language environment" and noticed that "he was starting to be drawn to signing peers and adults on the playground". The TDHH and EA2 used labeling (e.g., book, paper, and friend) and requesting signs (e.g., eat, write, and go) with Jimin.

In Jimin's classroom, he did not have ASL role models to promote opportunities for learning language and social interactions. Jimin did not have occasions to acquire language through incidental learning—the act of watching or hearing others use the language in which one is learning. His EA1 noted:

> He needs to be in a social situation and see signing as a conversation, not just me giving him directions . . . so conflict resolution, how you know kids cause hurt with other kids and that kind of things, so it's the conflict resolution between the students, it's how an adult will deal with situation with the student, all of that is missing. He's not getting any of that. So, he has no idea if in our classroom, we have a situation that needs to be resolved [but nobody tells him].

Communication Considerations

The Parent's Perspective. Jimin's parents reported that the most challenging aspect of Jimin's education has been communicating in both English and ASL with him and school personnel. When Jimin's mom began learning ASL she was often confused because she was simultaneously learning English. She describes this experience as the following:

> In the beginning of learning ASL, when each basic sign was introduced word by word, I thought I could learn that language. However, when the deaf teacher wrote the vocabulary for the signs people did not understand, I actually did not know the English vocabulary either. I could not laugh with the other classmates. The textbook was filled with unknown English vocabulary and the deaf teacher did not understand why I needed to look at my electronic dictionary instead of practicing signing during the class. I did not have time to do both.

There were also communication challenges with spoken language interpreting services. Jimin's mom reported that the English-to-Korean spoken language interpreters often seemed unqualified and became disruptive in meetings because they "did not know appropriate terminologies and not have relevant knowledge"; she also reported that "some interpreters did not interpret all the words they heard and they skipped unfamiliar parts". To remediate the situation, Jimin's mom attempted to bring a friend who was bilingual to the meetings, but they were not a trained spoken language interpreter nor were they familiar with special education terminology. During meetings in Jimin's early intervention years, his mom stated that she "understood 20–30% at the beginning" of the discussion. She chose to "just try to understand the most important parts, like conclusion, future direction, what to do, etc." without having a Korean language interpreter.

Because communication was a challenge, Jimin's mom and dad both reported that they felt they could not properly advocate for Jimin. His dad shared that he struggled with both English and ASL. With regards to communicating with Deaf staff, his mom stated: "I missed lots of information even through the ASL to English interpreter because of my poor English. I had to email her when I felt I did not fully understand the conversation.

The most difficult part was to advocate my child on the spot." As stated above, Jimin's mom tried to reconcile her lack of understanding by following up meetings with emails. However, she disclosed:

> Emailing did not work because they wanted to make a decision on the spot and I could not tell them what my child needed properly. After those meetings I was upset and often cried at home. There were so many meetings that I could not find help for each time.

Daily communication with the staff became easier by the third year of school; however, it was still challenging for the parents to understand the information exchanged quickly during meetings, especially when the team discussed educational placement options for Jimin. His mom shared that she "understood up to 80%-ish [of the meetings]."

Educators' Perspective. The educational team members felt that they could comfortably converse with Jimin's mom, more so than with his dad. Typically, his mom attended school meetings alone. The educators perceived that Jimin's mom did not have difficulty communicating about the day-to-day matters; yet, in meetings, her expressions sometimes indicated a lack of understanding.

The teachers stated that collaborating with parents is very important, especially when developing goals and implementing strategies. The TDHH and special education teacher made some efforts to provide information about school interventions (e.g., why and how PECS would work to improve Jimin's ASL), but stated that insufficient time in meetings limited these discussions.

At times, the professionals did not agree about the levels of Jimin's language and communication skills. In part, this seemed to be caused by the lack of expertise in both ASD and deafness, which led to different judgements and assumptions of Jimin's language skills and behavioral challenges. For example, the TDHH noted:

> The speech-language pathologist and I agreed that he [Jimin] was doing some form of babbling with his signs and the ASL specialist felt that it was stimming, not babbling. But they never saw what we saw

and we could never catch a video of it to show them so there were so many different opinions of what it could be.

Team members were frustrated that the work they were doing with Jimin was not leading to a more appropriate educational setting that provided continuous ASL exposure. His EA2 admitted: "yeah it's very frustrating how what seems like, what should be, even the two schools are just intermeshed as they are, how difficult it was for a deaf student to get access to a deaf classroom."

In summary, the linguistic and communication considerations of both the parents and educators were analyzed to answer the third research question. Results revealed the importance of providing information in the families' home language. Jimin's parents were overwhelmed when trying to learn two new languages simultaneously (English and ASL), while also adjusting to new educational terminology (e.g., audiogram, intervention, IEP, and ABA). Unqualified interpreting services caused communication breakdowns and misunderstandings. Both the parents and educators agreed that when ASL was paired with PECS, Jimin's disruptive behaviors decreased and communication with peers and staff emerged. Clear, transparent communication among the professionals, as well as with the parents, was essential for effective services to be implemented.

Discussion

The purpose of this case study was to understand the perspectives of the parents and the educators of a deaf child with ASD whose home language is Korean, regarding eligibility, placement, intervention, and linguistic and communication considerations. With minimal research to guide our practice, a case study can provide a foundation to understanding critical considerations that may influence the educators' practice and the parents and/or caregivers' decision-making process. Furthermore, case studies provide a basis in which to build the research base for larger and more complex studies. From this case study, the following codes and themes emerged: educational eligibility, placement, intervention strategies, linguistic and communication considerations (codes) and psychosocial/emotional impact, qualifications, availability, and collaboration (themes).

Educational Eligibility

The parents reported a drastic change in educational choices when Jimin's ASD was diagnosed. Finding professionals who had experience and knowledge of DMLs with ASD was extremely difficult. A transdisciplinary approach across educators and professionals revealed their knowledge of ASD, ABA techniques, ASL instruction and assessment, and working with d/Dhh learners, yet none had training across all niches. Assessing ASL, including differentiating between babbling and self-stimulating behaviors, how to assess and progress-monitor ASL with PECS support, and how to support the parents in reinforcing all these factors in the home setting were the academic and behavioral challenges experienced by all participants. Jimin's transdisciplinary team may benefit from recommendations in the literature to include d/Dhh mentors and cultural brokers as well as educators who have experience working with learners who are DWD or DML-D (see Box 7.2; Jackson et al., 2015).

Placement Considerations

Borders et al. (2017) has noted that d/Dhh students with ASD often have a different trajectory between educational placements, as exemplified by Jimin's case. Jimin experienced multiple early intervention settings: a kindergarten class at the school for the deaf and then three years in a general education classroom with a full-time EA. The educational team from his current setting, including the parents, perceived that Jimin would be better served in a signing educational environment. Ewing and Jones (2003) asserted that the best educational setting is one that emphasizes the unique strengths and needs of an individual child rather than their categorical eligibility label. Wehmeyer (2009) reminds parents and professionals: "The most salient characteristic of current efforts to promote inclusion and access to the general education curriculum is that the focal point has shifted primarily from *where* a student receives his or her educational program, to *what* and *how* the student is taught" (p. 262). The authors would add that of equal importance is the qualifications and preparedness of *whom* is teaching the child in the placement options available.

Placement in a general education classroom alone will not guarantee improved outcomes for students with severe disabilities (Kurth et al., 2015). Students who are DML-D may need a classroom with support for learning and participation, with special consideration given to the students' culture, disability, and mode of communication chosen by the family (Leigh et al., 2020). Utilizing Universal Design for Learning during instructional planning may provide this type of learning environment and follows the Tenets of Effective Practice framework (Guardino & Cannon, 2022; Rose & Gravel, 2010).

In Jimin's case, qualified professionals who are fluent in ASL and have experience working with learners who are d/Dhh and have ASD should be involved in the planning and placement decisions. The referral and placement process for Jimin may be enhanced if his parents were able to locate a cultural broker and/or advocate in special education that would assist them in navigating the process. Jimin's transdisciplinary team may also consider connecting with nearby school districts to see if they have personnel with the expertise to provide further insight into placement options.

Intervention

All of the educators who participated in the study felt unqualified to fully assess Jimin's language skills and determine effective interventions. Borders et al. (2016) reinforced this notion by recognizing that professionals who work with children with ASD are often inadequately prepared to provide services to those who are d/Dhh because of the children's unique needs with a dual-sensory diagnosis. The educators working with Jimin were implementing PECS combined with ASL, which appeared to be increasing Jimin's expressive and receptive language skills. Repetition and consistency also appeared to be effective in Jimin's understanding routines and classroom activities. Although the educational team felt unprepared, they worked together to determine the most effective interventions for Jimin. His parents also seemed unprepared about how to best use interventions in the home. Jimin's mother had a helpful suggestion to video-record examples of how the EA and the teachers implement interventions with Jimin so that she has a visual, non-linguistic resource to refer to when she is at home and working with Jimin. In addition, she is able to share the intervention videos with siblings and Jimin's father so they can participate in the development of targeted skills.

Linguistic and Communication Considerations

Many families who are culturally and linguistically diverse and recent immigrants struggle to acquire English and acclimate to a new country. As Jimin's parents struggled with their own language barriers and unfamiliarity with the Canadian medical and education systems, they struggled to cope with Jimin's deafness and ASD. His parents believed that Jimin's hearing could be improved or "fixed" with a cochlear implant as they did not have a full understanding of the technology and physiological factors related to hearing loss (Spencer & Marschark, 2003). Although they were informed about the risks and the limitations of surgery, as well as the slim likelihood that the cochlear implant would be successful, due to auditory nerve damage, they decided to go forward with the surgery. Their decision was more likely influenced by their Korean culture, which may consider them uncaring if they did not attempt all possible avenues for Jimin's future.

When Jimin's parents chose ASL as his primary mode of communication, they too pursued learning the language, yet struggled when attending ASL classes. Instructors who use English-based vocabulary to make a correlation or connection to signs in ASL should be aware that parents who are culturally and linguistically diverse may also be learning English while taking ASL courses. In which case, these learners need more time to process and connect vocabulary.

It is also important for families of DML-Ds to have skilled language interpreters and/or cultural brokers to assist them in understanding terminology (Bowen, 2016) pertaining to their children's education and behavior. These professionals can also assist with determining and choosing appropriate educational and behavioral services, as well as their rights and responsibilities regarding those services (Akamatsu & Cole, 2003). Understanding professional discussions and advocating for their children during school meetings require parents to have an advanced English proficiency level due to the complexity of topics discussed. Cultural brokers can provide support and guidance that are culturally sensitive (e.g., explaining how the educational placement is the same and different to the process in their home country to provide context for a discussion about where their child will receive services and support). Bowen and Baker (2022; see chapter 2) stress the importance that information is communicated with parents in their preferred language and in multiple ways before they have to make any decision. This allows families to process information and discuss with extended family members, religious advisors, mental health professionals, or any other support systems the families use to make decisions and understand their children's education better.

Recommendations made to families should be feasible and realistic for them to commit to and implement. Furthermore, the parents' silence should not be understood as agreement as it could be due to a lack of understanding or their cultural practice. Schools or organizations should provide a written agenda with the names and titles of the meeting attendees prior to the meeting, especially for meetings concerning services, evaluations, and future educational placements of the child. Administrators should allot additional time during meetings so that sufficient discussion and clarification of concepts and agenda items take place during the meeting. Parents should be given additional time to make decisions, so they can confer with parent advocates, cultural brokers, and other allies to ensure that they understand the content and conditions of what has been shared with them.

Ineffective interpreters can make parents feel confused and skeptical as to whether they have all the information needed to make an informed decision about their children's education (Bowen, 2016; Steinberg et al., 2003). When Jimin's mom tried to advocate for more services from the staff at his preschool, only an ASL interpreter was provided to facilitate discussions with the teachers, although she was still developing an understanding of English. Akamatsu and Cole (2003) assert that two or more relay interpreters should be used for communication between a family that is culturally and linguistically diverse and d/Deaf teachers. One interpreter is needed to translate the family's home language to English, and another interpreter is needed to interpret English to ASL and vice versa. Ideally, the family's interpreter is also a cultural broker, who understands the cultural values, the expressive style, and the help-seeking practices of the parents (Akamatsu & Cole, 2003; Cole, 1998). By having two interpreters, professionals can better understand the family's responses, questions, and/or opinions as well as the behaviors of the DML-D child. Furthermore, with skilled interpreters and the use of a cultural broker, parents can feel more secure that they obtained the most accurate and ample information available.

Conclusion

Professionals need to develop an understanding of the personal lens through which they view and define their own culture, as well as the cultures of others (Cannon & Guardino, 2022, see Chapter 1). By doing so, they may reduce the biases and assumptions they may have about disabilities, multilingualism, and other cultures. This self-reflection aligns with the radical shift needed in our field toward respecting the needs and preferences of learners when designing research and practice (Easterbrooks & Maiorana-Basas, 2015). By examining the parents' and teachers' perspectives, professionals may better understand ways to implement more culturally and linguistically responsive practices when working with students who are DML-Ds and their families. For a child to succeed in their learning, we must be able to find ways to coordinate with the family and engage them to actively participate in their child's education (Akamatsu & Cole, 2003; Bowen & Baker, 2022, see Chapter 2; Cole, 1998; Jackson et al., 2015). As professionals, we can empower parents and build a healthy partnership with them by acknowledging their needs.

One possibility for building those partnerships, based on the results of this study, includes the idea of a network for DML-D students and their families. This recommendation is based on the parents' comment that a TDHH who is Korean was helpful for them to understand the school system. Establishing an online website where professionals who are multilingual and have cultural competence are available to provide consulting or mentoring services to the parents of DML-Ds might be helpful. Professionals could also create webinars, blogs, or forums in various languages to function as ways to create healthy dialogue between families and professionals via virtual platforms. Virtual services such as tele-practice or tele-intervention are already being used with positive outcomes to deliver audiology, early intervention services, speech-language pathologist sessions, and other services in remote communities and isolated teaching settings (Bowen & Baker, 2022, see Chapter 2; Jackson et al., 2015) and are recommended for practitioners and parents of children who are DWD (Guardino, 2015).

Another possibility for building school capacity would be for programs to hire an outreach consultant for learners who have complex needs (e.g., DWD or DML-D). The professional could (a) possess expertise in the education of learners with exceptionalities (including ABA techniques), (b) consult with school districts to form a transdisciplinary team for learners with complex needs, (c) administer comprehensive assessments and/or connect with professionals who can administer these assessments, and (d) train staff and share resources in working with learners with complex needs who are culturally and linguistically diverse. Jimin and his parents would likely benefit if an outreach consultant with these skills became a part of his transdisciplinary team.

There is a high level of diversity among the DML-D population; therefore, the concerns and challenges of each DML-D and their family are likely different than those described in the case study or vignettes presented. The DML-D child brings with them unique learning needs, background experiences and knowledge based upon the family's culture and access to education, as well as other characteristics. For example, DML-Ds vary in the form and number of languages they may use or be exposed to at home and school, as well as the type of disability(ies) they have (see vignettes in Boxes 7.1–7.3). Further case studies are needed to understand the specific needs of DML-Ds and build the research base of practices and interventions that most benefit these learners and their families (Enns, 2017).

Discussion Questions

1. What is the approximate prevalence of disabilities amongst students who are DML-Ds and why is obtaining accurate information a challenge?
2. What are some of the challenges that parents and/or caregivers who are culturally linguistically diverse with children who are DML-Ds have when they begin to explore eligibility and placement options for their children?
3. Teachers and other service providers working with students who are DML-Ds with ASD might utilize which types of interventions to target language, social, and behavioral goals?

4. What are some culturally responsive teaching practices that can be employed with families who are culturally and linguistically diverse with children who are DML-Ds? Why is implementing these practices important to the profession?
5. In what ways do community-based and educational supports for families with learners who are DML-Ds converge and diverge? (e.g., a cultural broker can help in the IEP process as well as the family's transition to a new city and community)
6. How can professionals apply the Tenants of Effective Practice for Learners who are DWD to students who are DML-Ds and their families?

Resources

- Colorado culturally and linguistically diverse and special education eligibility considerations (www.cde.state.co.us/cdesped/ta_criticalquestion-scld): This handout covers caveats of referring culturally and linguistically diverse students to special education services, including safeguarding from potential biases due to language or cultural differences.
- ¡Colorin colorado! Overview of English language learners and Special Education (www.colorincolorado.org/school-support/special-education-and-english-language-learners): This is a bilingual site for professionals and families of students who are culturally and linguistically diverse. The site has multiple articles, interviews, and resources pertaining to the referral, eligibility, assessment, and intervention process with students who are DML-Ds.
- Colorin Colorado ELL and Special Education Resources (www.colorincolorado.org/special-education-ell/resources): This is a bilingual site for professionals and families of culturally and linguistically diverse students. The site has multiple resources such as articles, blogs, books, a toolkit, and various state resources to use with students who are DML-Ds.
- Deaf Students with Disabilities Network by Laurent Clerc National Deaf Education Center (https://clerccenter.gallaudet.edu/national-resources/info/info-to-go/deaf-students-with-disabilities.html): This online network is designed to provide resources, tools, and information

to parents and professionals who have or work with students who are DWD. The site includes discussion forums designed to promote information sharing and ongoing opportunities to engage with others living and working with students who are DWD.
- Guidelines and Resources: Special Education Assessment Process for CLD Students (http://5c2cabd466efc6790a0a-6728e7c952118b70f16-620a9fc754159.r37.cf1.rackcdn.com/cms/Special_Education_Assessment_Process_for_Culturally_and_Liguistically_Diverse_(CLD)_Students_with_logos_and_links_1489.pdf): These are guidelines for professionals who specialize in the assessment and evaluation of students who are d/DML-Ds.
- Hear and Now Community Society (http://eng.hereandnowca.org): This is a non-profit organization that provides community inclusion programs and parent consultations to Korean-speaking families in Canada whose family members have disabilities. Parents may find information regarding day programs and shared living opportunities being provided in Korean available in the Greater Vancouver area.
- Lifeprint (www.lifeprint.com/): Free online resource to learn and practice ASL.
- Milal Mission (www.milalmission.com): This is a non-profit organization with 100 branches around the world to serve people with disabilities who are Korean-speaking in their local areas. This site helps families connect with other families and provides information related to events such as camps for students with disabilities and Korean sign language courses.
- Texas School for the Deaf Outreach Center (www.tsd.state.tx.us/apps/pages/soc): This website contains multiple resources in both English and Spanish.
- The Radical Middle (https://radicalmiddledhh.org/): This is a platform for researchers, practitioners, families, and members of d/Deaf and hard of hearing communities to communicate and collaborate with others who have a variety of expertise across modalities and educational practices.
- US Department of Education ELL Toolkit (www.colorincolorado.org/sites/default/files/eltoolkit_0.pdf): The toolkit is written to assist state and local education agencies in providing support to CLD families and

their children during the entire educational process from referral to transition.

Family-Centered Brief

FAMILY-CENTERED BRIEF

CHAPTER 7
d/Deaf and Hard of Hearing Multilingual Learners with Disabilities
by Eun Young Kwon, Caroline Guardino & Joanna E. Cannon

PURPOSE OF THE CHAPTER
This chapter brings attention to the unique considerations and supports in place for learners who are d/Deaf or hard of hearing, are multilingual and who also have one or more disabilities (**DML-D**).

DML-D make up 6-11% of all DHH students

KEY TERMS
Culturally and Linguistically Diverse
Having diverse cultures, ethnic backgrounds, traditions, societal structures, and religious practices ... typically used when these differ from those of the community in which they live

TIPS FOR PARENTS

- You can ask for an **interpreter** so that you understand
- You can ask for **translations** of school messages so that you understand
- Tell the teachers about the **behaviours** you see in your child at home
- Ask the teacher to teach you **activities** you can do at home with your child

Culture, Language
DML-D
Hearing, Disability

TIPS FOR EDUCATORS

- There is **very little research** to guide teaching these learners!
- Learn about the **family's perspectives** on disability and hearing ability
- There are many **cultural nuances** in your school system that families might find confusing
- Learn about **community supports** and share them with the learner's family

RESOURCES
¡Colorín Colorado! Overview of ELL and Special Education
www.colorincolorado.org/school-support/special-education-and-english-language-learners

National Deaf Children's Society www.ndcs.org.uk/information-and-support/parenting-and-family-life/parenting-a-deaf-child/deafness-and-autism/

R Deaf and Hard of Hearing Multilingual Learners: Foundations, Strategies, and Resources (2022)

References

Akamatsu, C. T., & Cole, E. (2003). Deaf immigrant and refugee children: A different kind of multiculturalism? In C. Ester & J. A. Siegel (Eds.), *Effective consultation in school psychology* (2nd ed., pp. 296–321). Hogrefe & Huber.

Artiles, A. J., Rueda, R., Salazar, J. J., & Higareda, I. (2005). Within group diversity in minority disproportionate representation: English language learners in urban schools. *Exceptional Children, 71*, 283–300. https://doi.org/10.1177/001440290507100305

Baxter, P., & Jack, S. (2008). Qualitative case study methodology: Study design and implementation for novice researchers. *The Qualitative Report, 13*(4), 544–559.

Bonvillian, J., Lee, N., Dookey, T., & Loncke, F. (2020a). *Simplified signs: A manual sign communication system for special populations. Vol. 1: Principles, background, and application.* Open Book Publishers. https://doi.org/10.11647/OBP.0205

Bonvillian, J., Lee, N., Dookey, T., & Loncke, F. (2020b). *Simplified signs: A manual sign communication system for special populations. Vol. 2: Simplified sign lexicon, descriptions, and memory aids.* Open Book. https://doi.org/10.11647/OBP.0220

Borders, C.M., Bock, S. J., & Probst, K.M. (2016). A Review of Educational Practices for Deaf/Hard of Hearing Students with Comorbid Autism, *Deafness & Education International, 18*(4), 189-205, https://doi.org/10.1080/14643154.2016.1255416

Borders, C. M., Bock, S. J., Probst, K., & Kroesch, A. (2017). Deaf/hard of hearing students with disabilities. In S. Lenihan (Ed.), *Preparing to teach, committing to learn: An introduction to educating children who are deaf/hard of hearing.* www.infanthearing.org/

Bowen, S. K. (2016). Early intervention: A multicultural perspective on d/Deaf and hard of hearing multilingual learners. *American Annals of the Deaf, 161*(1), 33–42. https://doi.org/10.1353/aad.2016.0009

Bowen, S. K., & Baker, S. (2022). Family engagement: Developing partnerships for d/Deaf and hard of hearing multilingual learners. In J. E. Cannon, C. Guardino, & P. V. Paul (Eds.), *Deaf and hard of hearing multilingual learners: Foundations, strategies, and resources* (pp. 30–66). Routledge.

Braun, V., & Clarke, V. (2006). Using thematic analysis in psychology. *Qualitative research in psychology, 3*(2), 77–101.

Braun, V., & Clarke, V. (2012). Thematic analysis. In H. Cooper, P. M. Camic, D. L. Long, A. T. Panter, D. Rindskopf, & K. J. Sher (Eds.), *APA handbook of research methods in psychology, vol. 2: Research designs: Quantitative, qualitative, neuropsychological, and biological* (pp. 57–71). American Psychological Association.

Bruce, S. M., & Borders, C. (2015). Communication and language in learners who are deaf and hard of hearing with disabilities: Theories, research, and practice. *American Annals of the Deaf, 160*(4), 368–384. https://doi.org/10.1353/aad.2015.0035

Bruce, S. M., Nelson, C., & Stutzman, B. (2022). Understanding the needs of children who are d/Deaf or hard of hearing with disabilities due to generic causes. In C. Guardino, J. E. Cannon, & P. V. Paul (Eds.), *Deaf and hard of hearing learners with disabilities: Foundations, strategies, and resources* (pp. 96–132). Routledge.

Cannon, J. E., & Guardino, C. (2022). Learners who are d/Deaf or hard of hearing and Multilingual: Perspectives, Approaches and Considerations. In J. E. Cannon, C. Guardino, & P. V. Paul (Eds.), *Deaf and hard of hearing multilingual learners: Foundations, strategies, and resources* (pp. 1–29). Routledge.

Cawthon, S. (2015). From the margins to the spotlight: Diverse deaf and hard of hearing student populations and standardized assessment accessibility. *American Annals of the Deaf, 160*(4), 385–394.

Centers for Disease Control. (2018). *Autism Spectrum Disorder (ASD): Data & statistics.* www.cdc.gov/ncbddd/autism/data.html

Claycomb, C. D., Ryan, J. J., Miller, L. J., & Schakenberg-Ott, S. D. (2004). Relationships among attention deficit hyperactivity disorder, induced labor, and selected physiological and demographic variables. *Journal of Clinical Psychology, 60*, 689–693. https://doi.org/10.1002/jclp.10238

Cole, E. (1998). Immigrant and refugee children: Challenges and opportunities for education and mental health services. *Canadian Journal of School Psychology, 14*, 36–50.

Davis, T., Barnard-Brak, L., Dacus, S., & Pond, A. (2010). Aided AAC systems among individuals with hearing loss and disabilities. *Journal of*

Developmental and Physical Disabilities, *22*, 241–256. https://doi.org/10.1007/s10882-009-9180-6.

Easterbrooks, S. R., & Maiorana-Basas, M. (2015). Literacy and deaf and hard-of-hearing Students. In H. Knoors & M. Marschark (Eds.), *Educating deaf learners: Creating a global evidence base* (pp. 149–172). Oxford University Press.

Enns, C. (2017). Making the case for case studies in deaf education research. In S. Cawthon & C.L. Garberoglio (Eds.), *Research in deaf education: Contexts, challenges, and consideration* (pp. 203-224). Oxford University Press. https://doi.org/10.1093/oso/9780190455651.001.0001

Espinosa, L. M. (2013). PreK-3rd: Challenging common myths about dual language learners: An update to the seminal 2008 report. *Foundation for Child Development PreK-3rd Policy to Action Brief, No. 10*, August. Foundation for Child Development.

Ewing, K. M., & Jones, T. W. (2003). An educational rationale for deaf students with multiple disabilities. *American Annals of the Deaf*, *148*, 267–271. https://doi.org/10.1353/aad.2003.0019

Farnsworth, M. (2016). Differentiating second language acquisition from specific learning disability: An observation tool assessing dual language learners' pragmatic competence. *Young Exceptional Children*, *21*(2), 92–110. https://doi.org/10.1177/1096250615621356

Gardiner-Walsh, S., & Lenihan, S. (2017). Communication options. In S. Lenihan (Ed.), *Preparing to teach, committing to learn: An introduction to educating children who are deaf/hard of hearing* (pp. 1–18). EHDI Learning Center.

Gay, G. (2010). Acting on beliefs in teacher education for cultural diversity. *Journal of Teacher Education*, *61*(1–2), 143–152.

Guardino, C. (2015). Evaluating teachers' preparedness to work with students who are deaf and hard of hearing with disabilities. *American Annals of the Deaf*, *160*(4), 415–426. https://doi.org/10.1353/aad.2015.0030

Higgins, M., & Liberman, A. M. (2016). Deaf students as a linguistic and cultural minority: Shifting perspectives and implications for teaching and learning. *Journal of Education. 196*(1), 9–18. https://doi.org/10.1177/002205741619600103.

Humphries, T. (2004). The modern Deaf self: Indigenous practices and educational imperatives. In B. Brueggemann (Ed.), *Literacy and deaf people: Cultural and contextual perspectives* (pp. 29–46). Gallaudet University Press.

Jackson, R. W., Ammerman, S. B., Trautwein, B. A. (2015). Deafness and diversity: Early intervention. *American Annals of the Deaf, 160*(4), 356–367.

Kieran, L., & Anderson, C. (2019). Connecting universal design for learning with culturally responsive teaching. *Education and Urban Society, 51*(9), 1202–1216.

Kurth, J. A., Lyon, K. J., & Shogren, K. A. (2015). Supporting students with severe disabilities in inclusive schools: A descriptive account from schools implementing inclusive practices. *Research and Practice for Parents with Severe Disabilities, 40*(4), 261–274. https://doi.org/10.1177/1540796915594160

Leigh, I. W., & Andrews, J. F. (2016). *Deaf people and society: Psychological, sociological and educational perspectives* (2nd ed.). Routledge. https://doi.org/10.4324/9781315473819

Leigh, I. W., Andrews, J. F., & Harris, R. L. (2020). *Deaf culture: Exploring Deaf communities in the United States* (2nd ed.). Plural Publishing.

Lucas, T., Villegas, A., & Freedson-Gonzalez, M. (2008). Linguistically responsive teacher education: Preparing classroom teachers to teach English language learners. *Journal of Teacher Education, 59*(4), 361–373. https://doi.org/101177/0022487108322110

McCain, G., & Farnsworth, M. (2018). *Determining difference from disability: What culturally responsive teachers should know*. Routledge.

Mitchell, R. (2004). National profile of deaf and hard of hearing students in special education, from weighted results. *American Annals of the Deaf, 148*(4), 336–349.

Morgan, P. L., Frakas, G., Cook, M., Strassfeld, N. M., Hillemeier, M. M., Hung Pun, W., Wang, Y., & Schussler, D. L. (2018). Are Hispanic, Asian, Native American, or language-minority children overrepresented in special education? *Exceptional Children, 84*(3), 261–279.

Pizzo, L., & Chilvers, A. (2016). Assessment and d/Deaf and hard of hearing multilingual learners: Consideration and promising practice. *American Annals of the Deaf, 161*(1), 56–66.

QSR International Pty Ltd. (2018). *NVivo (Version 12), Qualitative Data Analysis Software*. Nvivo.

Rose, D. H., & Gravel, J. W. (2010). Universal design for learning. In E. Baker, P. Peterson, & B. McGaw (Eds.), *International encyclopedia of education* (3rd ed.) (pp. 119–124). Elsevier. www.udlcenter.org/resource_library/articles/udl

Samson, J. F., & Lesaux, N. K. (2009). Language minority learners in special education: Rates and predictors of identification for services. *Journal of Learning Disabilities, 42*, 148–162. https://doi.org/10.1177/002221 9408326221

Spencer, P. E., & Marschark, M. (2003). Cochlear implants: Issues and implicational implications. In M. Marschark & P. Spencer (Eds.), *The handbook of deaf studies, language, and education* (Vol. 1, pp. 434–448). Oxford University Press.

Stake, R. E. (1995). *The art of case study research*. Thousand Oaks, CA: Sage.

Steinberg, A., Bain, L., Li, Y., Delgado, G., & Ruperto, V. (2003). Decisions Hispanic families make after the identification of deafness. *Journal of Deaf Studies and Deaf Education, 8*(3), 291–314. https://doi.org/10.1093/deafed/ eng016

Szymanski, C. A., Brice, P. J., Lam, K. H., & Hotto, S. A. (2012). Deaf children with autism spectrum disorders. *Journal of Autism and Developmental Disorders, 42*(10), 2027–2037. https://doi.org/10.1007/s10803-012-1452-9

Van den Bergh, B. R., & Marcoen, A. (2004). High antenatal maternal anxiety is related to ADHD symptoms, externalizing problems, and anxiety in 8- and 9-year-olds. *Child Development, 75*, 1085–1097.

Vygotsky, L. S. (1978). *Mind in society: The development of higher psychological processes*. Harvard University Press.

Wehmeyer, M. L. (2009). Self-determination and the third generation of inclusive practices. *Journal of Education, 349*, 45–67.

Westling, D. L., & Fox, L. (2000). *Teaching students with severe disabilities* (2nd ed.). Merrill.

Zehler, A. M., Fleishchman, H. L., Hopstock, P. J., Stephenson, T. G., Pendzick, M. L., & Sapru, S. (2003). *Policy report: Summary of findings related to LEP and SPED-LEP students*. Retrieved from National Clearinghouse for English Language Acquisition website: http://www.ncela.us/files/rcd/BE021195/pol- icy_report.pdf

8

Transition for d/Deaf and Hard of Hearing Multilingual Learners: Guiding Principles and Planning Tools

John L. Luckner and Joanna E. Cannon

LEARNING OBJECTIVES

Readers will:

1. Explain the transition planning process and research-based strategies for culturally and linguistically diverse learners that may benefit d/Deaf and hard of hearing multilingual learners (DMLs).
2. Identify the guiding principles and person-centered planning tools for working with DMLs during the transition process.
3. Identify some informal and formal transition assessments to use with DMLs.
4. Explain how to involve DMLs and their families in the transition planning process.
5. Describe actions to promote preparation for postsecondary experiences and connections with adult agencies.
6. Identify opportunities for increasing cultural competence in the transition process from K-12 to postsecondary experiences.

d/Deaf and hard of hearing multilingual learners (DMLs) are defined as learners who come from homes where their families use languages

DOI: 10.4324/9781003259176-8

other than English or American Sign Language (ASL) to communicate. A DML is typically expected to learn written and spoken English and possibly ASL in the course of their academic career (Cannon et al., 2016). Although all students must transition to the next grade level, DMLs face far greater transitions throughout their academic careers (e.g., transition to a new country, school, and community that speaks a language other than their home/heart language). This chapter addresses the transition from secondary to postsecondary experiences for DMLs and their families. Considerations for professionals are also reviewed.

What Is Transition and Why Is It Important?

The general term transition refers to the passage from one form, state, style, or place to another. Transition services as they relate to DMLs who attend schools in the United States are authorized and regulated by the Individuals with Disabilities Education Act (IDEA, P.L. 108–446). In the Act, the term "transition services" means a coordinated set of activities that:

(A) is designed to be a results-oriented process, that is focused on improving the academic and functional achievement of the child with a disability to facilitate the child's movement from school to post-school activities, including postsecondary education, vocational education, integrated employment (including supported employment), continuing and adult education, adult services, independent living, or community participation;
(B) is based on the individual child's needs, taking into account the child's strengths, preferences, and interests;
(C) includes instruction, related services, community experiences, the development of employment and other post-school adult living objectives, and, when appropriate, acquisition of daily living skills and functional vocational evaluation.

Transition from school to a postsecondary education or a work setting is exciting, yet often challenging because it generally involves unfamiliar (a) people, (b) settings, (c) events, and (d) requirements. Consequently, effective transition planning and implementation is important because it (a) decreases the fear of change, (b) helps assure that appropriate services are available, (c) empowers students and families to make choices in the best interest of the student, and (d) helps students create personally fulfilling lives. In addition, research has determined that effective transition planning is directly linked to positive post-school outcomes in the areas of postsecondary education and/or training, employment, and independent living (Garberoglio et al., 2019; Test et al., 2009; Young et al., 2015).

The Individualized Education Program (IEP) team for a DML should begin addressing transition service requirements by the time the student turns 14 years old. Under the IDEA, the transition section of the IEP should include postsecondary goals based on age-appropriate transition assessments related to training, education, employment and independent living, and the transition services needed to assist the student in reaching their goals (US Department of Education, Office of Special Education and Rehabilitative Services, 2017).

Box 8.1 Mateo

Mateo is a 16-year-old male with a profound bilateral sensorineural hearing level. His parents, Santiago and Rosa, came with Mateo to Canada from El Salvador when he was six years old and his sister, Luciana, was four. Spoken Spanish, spoken English, and some Lengua de Señas Salvadoreñas, (LESSA; El Salvador Sign Language) are used in the home. He uses both American Sign Language (ASL) and listening and spoken English (at varying times and situations) to communicate outside of his home, and LESSA, Spanish, and English at home. He attends his local high school and is enrolled in general education classes with support from an itinerant teacher of the deaf and hard of hearing two times per week and an ASL interpreter present in all his academic and extracurricular subjects. Academically, he is currently on par with his peers in reading, math, and writing. Mateo has a large group of friends and plays soccer and baseball on community and school teams.

> Upon graduation from high school he wants to attend The National Technical Institute for the Deaf in Rochester, New York and complete his bachelor's degree as a Physician's Assistant, as his career goal is to work as one in a hospital. At his most recent Individualized Education Program meeting, the team decided that given his career goal, it would be best to provide him with specialized instruction in (a) completing university applications, (b) self-determination training, and (c) self-advocacy in postsecondary settings. They also suggested that Mateo begin volunteering at the local hospital to gain experience in the medical field and his team is arranging a shadowing experience of a nurse who has a visual impairment, is from El Salvador, and works in a local nursing care facility.

In Box 8.1, we are introduced to Mateo and his family, whose teacher of the deaf and hard of hearing has started the steps to ensure they feel empowered and receive appropriate supports in his transition planning. The teacher accomplishes this by understanding Mateo's goals and his family's expectations. His teacher wants to capitalize on his multilingual background and will seek out volunteer and shadowing experiences with mentors who are bilingual in Spanish and English to prepare him for postsecondary training. His family was also involved in the IEP and transition-planning process and were provided with all materials in advance in their native language of Spanish. His father suggested that Mateo's uncle could also provide him with mentorship, as he works in a hospital and is also deaf, thus serving as a culturally and linguistically diverse role model. The IEP team and his family collaborated to provide Mateo with varied experiences to ensure he has the resources to reach his transition goals.

Guiding Principles

Although a wealth of literature exists on the general topic of recommended practices in transition planning for youth with disabilities as well as culturally and linguistically diverse learners, a paucity of literature exists on the recommended practices in transition planning for DMLs and their families (Greene, 2011; Tansey et al., 2016). Consequently, until additional research is conducted, practitioners must extrapolate from the literature in the fields of education of individuals who are culturally and linguistically diverse (CLD; e.g., Gay, 2010), general special education (e.g., Kochhar-Bryant & Greene, 2009), and education of students who are d/Dhh (e.g., Luft, 2016). In the absence of research literature, it is crucial to have some guiding principles that are appropriate for DMLs. Principles adapted from Greene (2011), Leake and Cholymay (2004), and Wehmeyer and Webb (2012) are provided in Table 8.1 and will guide in extrapolating relevant practices across the aforementioned fields.

One pertinent tenet of working with students and families who are culturally and linguistically diverse is the concept of cultural competence for optimizing communication and interactions. Cultural competence is necessary to build rapport and trust with families by understanding their beliefs and values associated with their cultures and how that might impact their ability to serve as advocates for their children (McCain & Farnsworth, 2018). Lynch and Hanson (2004) identified five aspects of cultural competence to help guide professionals in their transition planning practices (see Table 8.1). Another tenet is to focus on the quality of life rather than employment outcomes, knowing the students' goals may not coincide with those of their family members or caregivers, as goals will vary across the intersectionality of the DMLs and their families (see Cannon & Guardino, 2022, Chapter 1). For example, quality of life can be measured by one's ability to: make choices, exhibit self-determination, communicate effectively, have relationships including friendships, and participate in the community in which you live (McLetchie & Zatta, 2014).

The field of special education contends that transition from school to life after high school is best facilitated when the following elements have been implemented: (a) a comprehensive assessment of strengths, needs, preferences, and interests, (b) the inclusion of transition activities and/or services in the IEP, and (c) coordination among key school and adult service agency personnel (Wehmeyer & Webb, 2012). The National Technical Assistance Center on Transition (NTACT) concurs and adds that individuals with disabilities will increase their post-school success if they and the IEP team use the following six-step process: (1) conduct transition assessments; (2) write postsecondary goals focused on education, employment

TABLE 8.1 Guiding Principles, Cultural Competence, and Transition Planning Practices

Guiding Principles (adapted from Greene, 2011; Leake & Cholymay, 2004; Wehmeyer & Webb, 2012)	Five Aspects of Cultural Competence to Guide Professionals (adapted from Lynch & Hanson, 2004)	11 Research-Based Transition Planning Practices (adapted from Gothberg et al., 2019)
(a) Transition efforts should start early.	(1) Awareness of one's own cultural limitations.	(1) School special education personnel encourage parents to participate in the entire assessment process from data gathering to verification of information, valuing the parents' cultural backgrounds and intimate knowledge of and experience with their children.
(b) Student participation throughout the process is important.	(2) Openness, appreciation, and respect for cultural differences.	(2) Parents are essential members of the transition team and are present and active partners at transition planning meetings, giving information about their children either orally or in writing.
(c) Early exposure to information about careers and facilitation of the development of behaviors related to responsibility, independence, and self-determination are necessary.	(3) View of intercultural interactions as learning opportunities.	(3) Parents are actively encouraged to engage in elections, selecting people who represent their needs and concerns to local school building committees or boards.

(Continued)

TABLE 8.1 (*Continued*)

Guiding Principles (adapted from Greene, 2011; Leake & Cholymay, 2004; Wehmeyer & Webb, 2012)	Five Aspects of Cultural Competence to Guide Professionals (adapted from Lynch & Hanson, 2004)	11 Research-Based Transition Planning Practices (adapted from Gothberg et al., 2019)
(d) Family involvement is vital.	(4) Ability to use cultural resources in interventions.	(4) Parents are provided opportunities within the school to connect with other culturally and linguistically diverse families through support groups, mentors, or community liaisons.
(e) The transition process must be sensitive to diversity.	(5) Acknowledgment of the integrity and value of all cultures.	(5) Parents are recruited to engage in peer advocacy for other culturally and linguistically diverse parents (e.g., provide IEP support or serve as interpreters at IEP meetings).
(f) Cultural brokers can be recruited to help create bridges between groups with different cultural backgrounds, such as educators and families.		(6) Culturally and linguistically diverse interpreters who are non-family members and are trained in the basics of special education, transition law, and familiar with the individual student's family culture are used at IEP meetings.

(g)	Use of professional interpreters who have experience in special education and transition.	(7)	School special education personnel know the background of an individual student's family culture including the following: languages spoken at home, styles of communication, norms for personal and social development, postsecondary goals held by the family, views on disability, family structure, and decision-making practices.
(h)	Interagency commitment and coordination are essential.	(8)	Special education school personnel are provided cultural competence training to increase their cultural sensitivity and reduce professional behaviors that are known to be deterrents to culturally and linguistically diverse parent participation in the transition planning process.
		(9)	To promote active participation in special education and transition planning meetings, training is offered to culturally and linguistically diverse parents based on their self-identified needs, which helps to increase their knowledge of school policy, practices, and procedures in special education and transition planning.

(*Continued*)

TABLE 8.1 (*Continued*)

Guiding Principles (adapted from Greene, 2011; Leake & Cholymay, 2004; Wehmeyer & Webb, 2012)	Five Aspects of Cultural Competence to Guide Professionals (adapted from Lynch & Hanson, 2004)	11 Research-Based Transition Planning Practices (adapted from Gothberg et al., 2019)
		(10) School special education personnel use person-centered planning tools for transition planning with students, including those designed for culturally and linguistically diverse students (e.g., Circles, MAPS, and PATHS).
		(11) Self-determination coursework is provided to all students at school, including culturally and linguistically diverse students, with an emphasis on postsecondary options, legal rights, effective self-advocacy, and working with transition service providers to achieve desired postsecondary goals.

and independent living; (3) develop IEP goals for the remainder of secondary school and formulate appropriate transition services; (4) list specific skills that need to be taught; (5) identify evidence-based practices that can be adapted to meet the linguistic and instructional needs of DMLs; and (6) develop data collection and evaluation procedures. In addition, Bonds (2003) recommends providing d/Dhh learners with experience in the cycle of learning (i.e., goal setting, planning, evaluating achievement, adjusting actions accordingly, and self-determination and self-advocacy).

Transition Assessment

Transition assessment should be viewed as an ongoing process and should take place over multiple years (Greene, 2011). The purpose is to gather information about abilities, attitudes, and interests; work behaviors, self-determination and self-advocacy knowledge and skills; academic, social-emotional, and independent living skills; and potential future training or education preferences (Miller et al., 2007).

Transition assessment should be student-centered, useful and understandable to all individuals involved, and sensitive to cultural, linguistic, and ethnic diversity, so that it accurately reflects the values, desires, and beliefs of DMLs and their families (Test et al., 2006). The assessment data collected provides the basis for defining goals and services to be included in an IEP and transition plan (Sitlington et al., 1997).

When conducting transition assessments with DMLs, educators should keep in mind that language is integrally connected to all aspects of assessment, including following directions, producing responses, and demonstrating content knowledge (Pizzo & Chilvers, 2016). Linguistically responsive assessment practices should be implemented by professionals with knowledge of the learners' level of first language (L1; e.g., Lengua de Señas Mexicana [Mexican Sign Language], second language [L2; Spanish], third language [L3; English], and/or fourth language [L4; ASL]), the culture of the learner and their family, the need for multiple types of assessment, and the linguistic demands of each assessment (Lucas et al., 2008; Pizzo & Chilvers, 2016). Professionals should also take into consideration the varied language experiences and possible appropriate accommodations of DMLs when planning, conducting, and reporting assessment activities (Pizzo & Chilvers, 2016).

One valuable resource for gathering information about the language proficiency of DMLs is the World-class Instructional Design and Assessment (WIDA) Can Do Descriptors. The descriptors are skill sets based on English language acquisition proficiency levels and stages of development (see Resources at the end of this chapter). The Can Do Descriptors identify what learners are capable of accomplishing at different stages throughout early childhood and K-12 contexts. The descriptors are available across grade levels and the language domains of listening, speaking, reading, and writing. The descriptors are organized by communicative purposes—recount, explain, argue, discuss, express self, and inquire—and are available in both English and Spanish. Assessment of DMLs' levels of English language proficiency can help professionals identify appropriate assessment tools and procedures. Appropriate accommodations could include changing the setting of the assessment, modifying the presentation of the materials, allowing alternate response modes (e.g., sign language, computer, or portfolio), adjusting the schedule (e.g., breaking the task into three segments), and providing additional time (Hoover & Patton, 2017).

Informal and Formal Transition Assessments

Informal transition assessments include interviews, questionnaires, observation, student work samples, and portfolios, and allow professionals to gather information to determine the students' needs, preferences, and interests relative to the anticipated post-school outcomes. One linguistically responsive informal transition assessment and planning process is referred to as Person-Centered Planning (Greene, 2011). Person-centered planning refers to an approach that brings together the student, family members, friends, and professionals to develop a plan of action so that the transition IEP goals, objectives, and action statements can easily be implemented (Clark, 2007). One of the advantages of Person-Centered Planning for DMLs is that it provides an avenue for professionals to take the time and make the effort to get to know the background of the youth and family they are working with (Leake & Black, 2005). In addition, the Person-Centered Planning process emphasizes the unique strengths of each individual family and youth, the importance of creating an equal relationship between the family, the student, and professionals, and the capacity of families and youth to share their preferences regarding future careers and other life-related areas. A life-span approach is recommended with Person-Centered Planning practices as a framework that considers the strengths, needs, and interests of the learner and what resources are necessary to achieve their goals throughout the course of their lifetime (Borders et al., 2017).

For students who are DMLs, some linguistic and cultural knowledge is necessary to answer questions and understand their options for the future. This may be a challenge for some learners with varying language and literacy skills. Vocabulary included in the questions may be difficult for some learners to comprehend and should be pre-taught and discussed, such as: "preferences", "functional", "interests", and "abilities". What does being a "fully functional member of my family and community" mean within the context of their current town, state, and/or country as well as their own family? What does "prepare for my future" mean linguistically and culturally for a DML? What are the options available for the DML regarding employment, education, etc.? How does the DML's immigration status impact their postsecondary options? What support systems are available to assist the DML and their family in understanding the transition planning process? If the learner does not have a family and is in the foster care system, how will these questions be presented? What if the learner is separated from their family and doesn't know their goals and wishes for their future? It is important to review these options because the DML may not be aware of them nor the training and education necessary for each option.

Transition assessments that are beneficial in Person-Centered Planning include the *Transition Planning Inventory* (TPI-2; Patton & Clark, 2014), composed of 57 items focusing on nine different areas (i.e., employment, further education/training, daily living, leisure activities, community participation, health, communication, self-determination, and interpersonal relationships). The assessment includes two student interests and preferences forms, a CD that contains seven additional resources, and is available in paper or computer formats.

The *Transition Assessment and Goal Generator* (TAGG; available at https://tagg.ou.edu/tagg/) is another transition assessment tool that professionals can use with DMLs. Like the TPI-2, it has three rating scales (i.e., professional, student, and family). Each version includes 34 items representing behaviors associated with postsecondary employment and education. What is unique about the TAGG is that it has an ASL video for each student item. It requires approximately 20 minutes to complete, has a minimal cost (i.e., $3.00) for one professional, student, and family version, and it generates sample goals designed to address the students' needs.

A formal transition assessment specifically developed for students who are d/Dhh is the *Transition Competence Battery for Deaf & Hard-of-Hearing Adolescents and Young Adults* (TCB; Reiman et al., 1993) and a shortened version, referred to as the Mini-TCB (Bullis et al., 1997). The longer version of the TCB has 163 items, which are organized into six video subtests, each video lasting 30–45 minutes in duration, presented by an ASL-certified interpreter. The subtests include: job seeking skills, work adjustment skills, job-related social and interpersonal skills, money management skills, health and home skills, and community awareness skills. In contrast, the Mini-TCB is considered a screening tool, is composed of 46 multiple-choice items, and takes approximately one hour to complete. Utilizing these assessments results, along with Person-Centered Planning, will increase success in the transition process, especially if the DML is involved.

Student Involvement in the Transition Process

The Division of Career Development and Transition (DCDT) of the Council for Exceptional Children (CEC) has strongly endorsed empowering all youth with disabilities to develop and demonstrate self-determination and self-advocacy (Field et al., 1988). Professionals working with DMLs should continually develop their cultural competence (see Table 8.1) to be sensitive to the differences between the individualist values of mainstream cultures and the collectivist values that are characteristic of many other cultures (Valenzuela & Martin, 2005). Therefore, professionals should engage in culturally sensitive self-determination and self-advocacy training in order to teach DMLs how to advocate and make choices for themselves. Increasing self-advocacy and self-determination skills may better prepare DMLs for navigating the expectations within their culture and the mainstream culture (Greene, 2011).

During preschool all the way through the high school years, professionals working with DMLs need to provide direct instruction in self-advocacy so they are able to understand and explain their knowledge of self, including their: hearing levels, accommodations, and modifications needed. Professionals can then scaffold instruction of the other aspects of self-advocacy (i.e., knowledge of rights, communication, and leadership; Luckner & Becker, 2013) and ensure that students have opportunities to make choices and participate in their IEP meetings. Participation in IEP meetings provides DMLs with opportunities to learn about and practice important self-advocacy and self-determination skills, including: (a) describing their hearing loss, personal strengths, needs, present level of performance, and necessary accommodations; (b) evaluating progress and developing goals; (c) preparing and delivering formal presentations; (d) communicating interests and preferences; and (e) participating in discussions about post-school goals and plans (Cote et al., 2012; Test et al., 2004).

Person-Centered Planning and linguistically responsive practices promote the participation of all learners in self-directed IEP meetings (Cote et al., 2012). Prior to the meeting, culturally responsive educators should review the steps in participating (preferably through role-play), send home materials in the family's preferred language for them to review, learn about the family's culture and language, acknowledge differences, and consider mutual goals for the DML, family, and school (Gothberg et al., 2019).

Box 8.2 Ayesha

Ayesha, who is 14 years old, was born in Palestine but has lived in the United States since she was eight-years old. Ayesha and her family speak English and Arabic at home, and she communicates with her friends at school using listening and spoken English. Ayesha is working with her itinerant teacher of the deaf and hard of hearing to prepare for her upcoming meeting to review and revise her IEP. She is role-playing what she is going to say about how she is doing in school. Later in the week they will talk about what she wants to

> do after she completes school. The itinerant teacher has given Ayesha the list of questions from the Person-Centered Planning process to think about. Simultaneously, she had the questions translated into a document in Arabic and sent it home so Ayesha and her parents could discuss them; it will also help the parents to be prepared for the meeting by providing an outline of the topic and points to be discussed. Early next week, Ayesha and the itinerant teacher will review who is going to be at the meeting and practice her responses to the questions about what she wants to do in her future as an adult. Finally, prior to the meeting they will discuss the classes or activities she wants added to her program to help her meet her goals and prepare for life after she completes high school.

In Box 8.2 we are introduced to Ayesha, her educators, and her family. Her educational team used Person-Centered Planning and select linguistically responsive practices to involve Ayesha in her IEP transition planning process. To become familiar with the cultural beliefs of Ayesha's family, the team sent home the transition questions for them to discuss and to help them prepare for the IEP meeting. Using the questions for context may reduce barriers to understanding the public-school system procedures and increase the level of critical discussion that may take place at the IEP meeting. There will also be an interpreter present at the meeting to facilitate communication. Team members should also familiarize themselves with Palestinian culture and the wishes of Ayesha's extended family. These practices build the team member's cultural competence, so that they have background knowledge about possible cultural influences. The team should be careful not to stereotype cultural, ethnic, or religious beliefs based upon the family's country of origin. Understanding that beliefs and practices vary among cultures and families is another characteristic of cultural competence that aligns with Person-Centered Planning. This understanding is important for (a) proactively finding avenues to better grasp the family's expectations for students during the transition planning process, and (b) encouraging student participation.

Culturally sensitive discussions during the IEP meeting create opportunities for professionals to encourage DMLs and their families to share their cultural values as well as their visions for the future. Involving learners in self-directed IEPs is one avenue to increasing their self-advocacy skills and ability to express their interests and goals. An incremental approach for self-directed IEP meetings, suggested by Martin et al. (2006) and adapted by Cote et al. (2012), is provided in Table 8.2. Utilizing self-directed IEPs and Person-Centered Planning also conveys respect and value of the

TABLE 8.2 Person-Centered, Self-Directed Transition IEP Meeting Process for DMLs (Adapted from Martin et al., 2006; Cote et al., 2012)

Transition IEP Meeting Process
1. Introduce yourself.
2. Introduce IEP team members and other attendees (e.g., interpreters, cultural brokers, and extended family members).
3. State the purpose of the meeting.
4. Express your interests in academic, sociocultural, extracurricular activities, and hobbies.
5. Express your academic (e.g., present levels of performance) and personal strengths and challenges.
6. Review your past IEP goals and progress including those related to transition.
7. Ask for feedback from your family and the IEP team about transition goals.
8. Ask for clarification from the participants in the meeting and ask questions if you don't understand.
9. State your future goals, including postsecondary expectations.
10. Respect differences of opinions; they may occur because everyone cares about you and your future.
11. State the support you need (e.g., accommodations and/or modifications) to facilitate success in reaching your goals.
12. Once IEP is finalized, make sure to sign the document and request a copy for you and your family to review. Request that the IEP is translated into your home language.
13. End the meeting by thanking everyone.

family's beliefs and participation. With mutual respect and cultural competence, families can feel empowered and an integral part of the transition planning process.

Family Involvement in Transition Planning

Families who are culturally and linguistically diverse bring a variety of important contributions to the transition planning process, which include: in-depth knowledge of their child's interests, strengths, and challenges; cultural funds of knowledge; community values grounded in ethnicity; perceptions about the most significant aspects of education based on cultural values; and cultural views about disability (Hoover & Patton, 2017). Research supports focusing on the family as a whole during the process, as parents may play a support role after the DML's secondary education and since more family involvement leads to better student outcomes (Gothberg et al., 2019). Furthermore, involving families and the students is a tenet of Person-Centered planning, and in the United States, under IDEA (2004), it is required in the transition planning, implementation, and evaluation process.

Intercultural differences between educators and families provide learning opportunities during the transition planning process, particularly the multifaceted intersectionality of many DMLs and their families (see Cannon & Guardino, 2022, Chapter 1). For example, professionals in countries and regions where the mainstream culture values independence, autonomy, and physical and emotional separation from parents for teenagers as they become adults, must learn the cultural values and traditions of the DML and their family (Kim & Morningstar, 2005) to demonstrate cultural competence. Some families may value interdependence, family orientation, and extended family systems within their culture, as well as various other values that are different from the dominant culture in which they live (Kim & Morningstar, 2005). For example, students may live in multi-generational households and/or work in family businesses, with expectations that their postsecondary goals will include these environments. Some DMLs and their families may value a combination of these attributes, as diversity and intersectionality increase globally. Understanding and respecting individual and collective values in the transition planning process will guide educational and vocational decisions (Gothberg et al., 2019).

Involving parents from culturally and linguistically diverse backgrounds in the transition process (Cameto et al., 2004) may be accomplished by nurturing relationships between parents and educators (Schuster et al., 2003), reducing intimidation experienced when interacting with school personnel in public school settings (Landmark et al., 2007), and increasing understanding of the transition planning process (Geenen et al., 2003). Utilizing the guiding principles, aspects of cultural competence, and research-based transition practices (see Table 8.1) may lead to increased family involvement and improved satisfaction of the process. These practices may also empower families to provide valuable and necessary knowledge during the transition process. Examples of ways to enact the guiding principles are described below.

In order to invite family involvement and to promote trust and open communication, professionals should get to know the background of the youth and their family. A few questions adapted from Greene (2011) to help determine some of the key values and background of the family are: (a) Is there anything we should know about your family or cultural community that can help us provide the best education possible for your child?; (b) What languages are used in the home and by which family members?; and (c) What goals do you have for your child after high school? When educators discuss these questions with the family, a cultural broker, or someone who can support the family's understanding of the current school culture and procedures, further trust is promoted and the family may feel more comfortable and open during the discussion.

Four strategies, adapted from Wandry and Pleet (2012), that could be utilized for engaging families of DMLs during the transition process are:

- Establish two-way communication. Seek family perspectives about their needs, concerns, hopes, and dreams for their child. Encourage open discussions during IEP meetings and provide families with resources in their native language. Utilize resources, such as the Right Question Institute's Question Formulation Technique, to assist parents in asking the questions necessary to advocating for their child's needs (see Resource section).

- Develop cultural competence. Be culturally aware and use cultural reciprocity (i.e., understanding the families' cultural beliefs and using this understanding to help promote student success) when talking with families about value-laden topics such as post-school options, self-determination, and desired outcomes.
- Engage in shared decision-making. Welcome the family and try to seek and incorporate cultural information and preferences from them. Model effective problem-solving and recognize families as partners who will collaborate in making decisions about the student's future.
- Resolve disputes. Differences in opinion about what is best for an individual's future may occur given the different information that each team member possesses and the requirement of predictive planning that the transition process necessitates. Professionals should expect disagreements and try to handle them in a respectful manner during meetings with both parents and professionals. Resources such as cultural brokers and/or liaisons, community leaders and/or informal support providers can be invited to participate in meetings in order to help plan and facilitate culturally appropriate transitions to adulthood.

Vocational Rehabilitation

One component of the coordinated set of activities undertaken by IEP teams is identifying adult agencies that can assist in the provision of transition services. For many DMLs who will enter the workforce upon graduation, the most important agency may be their state vocational rehabilitation (VR) agency, a federally designated program operated by each state and territory in the United States and in many other countries. The primary emphasis of VR programs is employment. To ensure that individuals who are culturally and linguistically diverse receive access to VR services, professionals will need to take into consideration the linguistic and cultural differences, level of knowledge of VR services and benefits, the importance of building trust through the use of culturally responsive practices by rehabilitation practitioners and potential employers, expectations of job placement, and the level of knowledge and accessibility to technology (Moore et al., 2016). Utilizing cultural competence to address these considerations with professionals can increase the benefit of VR services for individuals who are CLD and reduce barriers to services (Tansey et al., 2016).

To foster Person-Centered Planning family engagement in the transition process with DMLs and their families, it is essential that professionals explain the legal mandates regarding transition policies, practices, and procedures. To build cultural competence for the educators and the families, this explanation should be completed in a jargon-free and understandable manner, as well as in the families' home languages. Utilizing interpreters and cultural brokers or multicultural support workers to explain terminology and procedures to the families and relate them to their own cultures is an avenue to building cultural competence and trust with the families and students. Similarly, eligibility requirements for VR services can be complex and confusing, particularly with the prerequisite to complete and submit forms in order to be determined eligible to receive services. Therefore, professionals may want to help DMLs and their families understand the eligibility requirements of VR and other potential postsecondary transition services. Another example of cultural competence is for professionals to provide access to cultural community members or other DML parents to act as mentors to assist with the transition planning and implementation processes (Greene, 2011). In addition, legal forms and literature should be provided in the families' home language. If translated materials are not available, professionals should provide an explanation of such literature in the family's home language.

In the United States and many other countries, DMLs or their families need to apply for VR services if they are under 18 years old. It is recommended that this process is initiated during the students' third year of high school. Once an individual is determined to be eligible for a VR program, an Individualized Plan for Employment (IPE) can be developed, which contains employment outcome goals based on the individual's unique abilities, interests, strengths, priorities, and concerns. The IPE should list the services to be provided and who is responsible for each service, along with time frames and methods to evaluate progress. VR services will differ from person to person because they are customized to meet individual needs.

In Box 8.3 we meet Fadhili, who is d/Dhh with a disability and plans to work in the retail industry when he completes high school. The IEP team has included Fadhili's family in the transition planning process, during which they expressed their wishes for his future work. The family's support will help accomplish Fadhili's goals. The team talked with them during the meeting (using a Swahili interpreter who has experience in the school system) about increasing Fadhili's ability to make change and to answer people's questions. His parents shared that Fadhili likes to help prepare for Jamhuri Day to celebrate Kenya becoming a republic, which they celebrate with friends and family each year. The celebration will include stations in their backyard with games, food, and a raffle, and his parents will allow him to collect the raffle funds and answer questions about the prizes. This is one example of how the family can assist in building Fadhili's skills for his transition to postsecondary training, and how the IEP team can increase their cultural competence by learning more about the Kenyan culture and Fadhili's family traditions.

Box 8.3 Fadhili

Fadhili is a part of a tightly knit Kenyan family that immigrated to the United States when he was 13 years old. Currently, he is a 17-year-old student with a moderate bilateral hearing loss and has mild cognitive disabilities. He consistently uses his hearing aids and communicates using spoken English and Swahili. He is in his third year of high school. He plans to stay in high school until he is 21 years old. He is completing a specialized course of study that includes both applied academics and vocational preparation to receive a high school diploma. Fadhili lives at home with his parents and four siblings. After high school, he wants to work at a department store stocking items on the shelves and working the register. This year, he worked at a discount store stocking shelves for a few hours a week after school and did well. In order to work the register, he will have to learn to make changes independently as well as answer customer questions. He will also need to learn how to get to and from work on his own. His parents would like Fadhili to explore other jobs within the retail environment, such as janitorial tasks, organizational tasks, and jobs within the store café, while he is still in high school. Fadhili agrees with his parents that he should experience a variety of work-based options prior to leaving high school.

Life-Skills and Community-Based Instruction

Some learners may not benefit from the standard middle or high school curriculum and may need a program of study that focuses more on life-skills, which have been defined as "those skills or tasks that contribute to the successful independent functioning of an individual in adulthood" (Cronin, 1996, p. 54). A life-skills curriculum may be appropriate for some DMLs with disabilities (e.g., Autism Spectrum Disorder or Intellectual Disabilities) and those with significant language delays. Examples of life-skills include grocery shopping, food preparation, self-care, personal health and safety, functional reading, and banking.

Similar to other forms of transition-related assessments, a variety of methods are available to determine the students' present level of performance as well as to monitor and evaluate their progress on a life-skills curriculum. General types include formal testing, informal techniques such as observation, structured interviews, work sample analysis, rating scales, and performance assessments (Cronin et al., 2007). Frequently used and commercially available instruments that focus on life skills include: the *Vineland-II Adaptive Behavior Scales—Second Edition* (Sparrow et al., 2005), the *Adaptive Behavior Assessment System—Second Edition* (Harrison & Oakland, 2003), and The *Arc's Self Determination Scale* (Wehmeyer & Kelchner, 1995). Informal assessments should take place in multiple natural environments and involve a variety of individuals associated with each setting (e.g., the student, their network of family and friends, school and transition personnel, and community service providers; Greene, 2011). Assessors should be fluent in the language of the student, knowledgeable about their cultural and linguistic background, and self reflective about biases and stereotypes regarding DMLs to assure the results are a reflection of the learner and not the assessor (Gothberg et al., 2019; Pizzo & Chilvers, 2016).

Universal Design for Learning (UDL) is a helpful framework for planning and delivering lessons for a life-skills curriculum that is linguistically and culturally sensitive to the needs of every learner, especially those who are DMLs. UDL is an approach to planning instruction designed to increase accessibility by removing barriers and building in scaffolds and supports to meet the needs of diverse learners (Meyer et al., 2014). Utilizing this framework in combination with increasing the educators' cultural competence (Lynch & Hanson, 2004) may increase the benefits of a life-skills curriculum for DMLs.

Life-skills instruction that utilizes a UDL framework can occur in a variety of ways depending on the needs of the student. For example, content can be infused into existing courses, such as in a literacy class that focuses on utilizing information from simple charts, diagrams, maps, and menus. Students can be taught and practice skills related to reading public transportation schedules, locating key information on posters and other informational charts, and using menus to order meals. Another option is the development of a specific course such as "Functional Math," which could focus on topics like understanding paychecks, banking, budgeting, and paying bills. A valuable resource for educators working with DMLs who benefit from life-skills instruction provided in school is the National Technical Assistance Center on Transition (NTACT). They provide lesson plans that include objectives, settings and materials, content, teaching procedures, and evaluation information about a wide variety of evidence-based practices related to life-skills (Test et al., 2009).

While many life-skills can be taught in classroom settings, there may be advantages to learning and practicing specific skills in the natural environments in which they occur, such as the community in which the students live. Community-based instruction provides a level of applied experience that is often difficult to create in the classroom. Community-based instruction is designed to support the students' use of skills in their current or subsequent settings. Examples of community-based sites to consider include businesses (e.g., restaurants, laundromats, and groceries), services (e.g., libraries and recreation centers), government agencies (e.g., Social Security office and Department of Motor Vehicle), utilities (e.g., cable TV and electricity), and public transportation options.

The advantages of community-based instruction for DMLs may be that they have experiential learning activities which may increase their linguistic and cultural capacities through exposure to workplace people, places, materials, and experiences. UDL should be utilized to plan this transition instruction so that the students have full physical, visual, and/or auditory access as needed during the experiences. Professionals may want to solicit input from families and cultural brokers to identify culturally appropriate community settings for instruction, and be sure that spaces are visually and/or auditorily accessible for all users.

Postsecondary Education

Postsecondary education options for DMLs include adult education programs, trade and vocational schools, and two and four-year universities. Key findings from the National Deaf Center in the United States indicate that postsecondary education of any kind may narrow the employment gap between d/Dhh individuals and the general population (Garberoglio et al., 2019). Enrollment in postsecondary education has a 6% gap overall between people who are hearing and those who are d/Dhh (Garberoglio et al., 2019). For the receipt of high school diplomas and/or GED, there is a 16% gap for people who are d/Dhh and Asian, 10% gap for people who are d/Dhh and black, 9% for people who are d/Dhh and multiracial or Native American, 7% for people who are white, 4% people who are Hispanic/Latinx, and 0% for people who are Pacific Islander (Garberoglio et al., 2019). Although median earnings by educational degree are comparable for those who are hearing and d/Dhh, a significant difference exists for employment, with 53.3% of people who are d/Dhh employed compared to 75.8% of hearing people (Garberoglio et al., 2019).

DMLs who are planning to participate in postsecondary education will want to work closely with their IEP team and engage in self-directed IEP activities (see Table 8.2). Educators should utilize Person-Centered Transition Planning when working with DMLs to determine the type of postsecondary setting most appropriate for each learner. Capitalizing on the strengths and interests of the DMLs and ensuring that cultural resources are available are vital to increasing motivation and retention during the training. The IEP team should also consider the four issues that the National Deaf Center on Postsecondary Outcomes (NDC, 2018) identified that professionals should be aware of as they work to help d/Dhh learners prepare for their postsecondary programs, and could be applied to DMLs. These issues include the need to increase access to language and communication, social opportunities, and qualified and experienced professionals, while at the same time reducing negative attitudes, biases, and low expectations (NDC, 2018).

Members of the IEP team will want to capitalize on the self-advocacy and self-determination skills students developed during their school years. These skills can foster responsible behaviors and independent learning skills within DMLs to assist them in acclimating to and understanding the cultural demands and expectations of their postsecondary environments. These skills may help d/Dhh individuals by increasing their abilities to establish social support; problem-solve; state their needs to professionals; and perform in academic, personal, and social environments (Luft & Huff, 2011; Wheeler-Skruggs, 2002).

When DMLs are getting ready to leave high school, professionals can develop a Summary of Performance (SOP) document that summarizes the students' functioning in three areas: academic achievement, functional performance, and recommendations to assist students in reaching their postsecondary goals (Greene, 2011). The development of the SOP through the use of the guiding principles (i.e., Table 8.1) provides an opportunity to analyze the students' data and discuss with DMLs, their families, and the IEP team how the data show the students' strengths, areas of needs, and how the two fit together with their goals. In addition, the SOP can serve as a bridge to postsecondary education or training programs by documenting strategies, services, and accommodations that have helped the students be successful in the past. IEP teams may want to consider additional recommendations that draw from the works of Dalke (1991), Oesterrich and Knight (2008), and Tierney et al. (2009) as presented in Table 8.3.

TABLE 8.3 Recommendations for Preparing DMLs for Postsecondary Options (Includes an Adaptation of the Four Phases by Brolin & Loyd, 2004; Sitlington et al., 1997)

Recommendations for Preparing DMLs for Postsecondary Options
• Provide instruction and opportunities to practice self-advocacy. • Explore careers by shadowing culturally and linguistically diverse adults, volunteering and/or participating in service learning events, and participating in part-time employment (including work-study roles on a college campus). • Discuss cultural traditions and values with the students and their families during the transition planning process.
• Encourage and support the students' involvement in extracurricular activities and exploration of their hobbies.

- Provide d/Deaf, culturally and linguistically diverse, and/or Deaf Multilingual mentors and role models and invite community and cultural leaders to talk about attending postsecondary programs as part of the larger community.

- Assist students in finding postsecondary employment or school programs that match their qualifications, interests, cultural values, and goals (e.g., Gallaudet University, National Technical Institute for the Deaf, and Lamar University).
- Empower students to be lifelong learners who seek training and advocate for their communication needs.

- Ask families if they would like support in identifying culturally and linguistically diverse resources (e.g., family networks, cultural brokers, multicultural workers, training, language courses, and scholarships).

- Engage and support students in completing employment and/or postsecondary applications.
- Role-play different interview scenarios and review the process.

- Familiarize students and their families with campus and community organizations, agencies, and related support services (e.g., Accessibility Support Services, cultural centers, and student organizations).

The NDC (2018) encourages the establishment of work based learning programs for students who are d/Dhh. Examples of work-based learning programs are job shadowing, service learning, cooperative education, internships, and apprenticeships. These types of experiences provide opportunities for students to apply classroom knowledge in a work setting, develop specific work behaviors, improve interpersonal skills, and learn from professionals currently working. When creating work-based learning programs, NDC (2018) suggests that professionals take into consideration four key areas of focus: (a) developing partnerships with employers; (b) undertaking a variety of pre-enrollment activities with students, families, and employers prior to beginning the program; (c) carefully structuring the program by defining roles and responsibilities of students and employers; and (d) establishing an evaluation system.

Conclusion

The transition planning process for DMLs has an impact on the acquisition of knowledge and skills for achieving post-school quality of life in domains such as employment, interpersonal relationships, community participation, health and fitness, independent or interdependent living, and leisure and recreation (Greene, 2011). Transition planning for DMLs provides multiple opportunities for professionals to utilize the guiding principles, develop their cultural competence, and implement the research-based strategies provided in Table 8.1. Some of these opportunities will include: preparation for a postsecondary education with appropriate accommodations; classes designed to address transition skills such as self-determination, social skills, and career preparation; and/or a program that focuses on daily living skills and community-based instruction.

Opportunities for professionals to engage in cultural competence training (see Table 8.1) will increase cultural and linguistic knowledge, understanding, and respect for the DMLs' preferred cultures (Landmark et al., 2007). Differences in values, practices, and beliefs should be respected and treated with sensitivity to facilitate collaborative discussions during the transition planning process. Language differences and varying degrees of understanding in special education transition regulations should be mediated through the use of cultural brokers and language interpreters to ensure that the family can fully participate in meetings and decision-making (Greene, 2011) providing parent support programs across languages and cultures to connect families across similar backgrounds and/or beliefs may increase community social support. This support could empower families to work with professionals during this crucial planning period (Gothberg et al., 2019).

As the global population becomes more diversified and intersectionality is recognized across individuals, researchers have the opportunity to become inspired to reexamine transition, education, high leverage practices, and career outcomes for DMLs. Now is the time to celebrate and understand how our differences are strengths. Consequently, there is a strong need to conduct research that helps guide DMLs, their families, and educators so that they can work together to develop and implement educational programs that lead to successful adult lives.

Discussion Questions

1. Explain what transition is and describe the research-based strategies for culturally and linguistically diverse learners that may benefit DMLs.
2. Identify opportunities DMLs may encounter during the transition process.
3. Describe what must be included in the transition-age Individualized Education Program (IEP).
4. How would you incorporate the contents of Table 8.1 into the planning process?
5. Explain ways that professionals can involve DMLs and their families in the transition planning process.
6. Describe actions that can be taken to promote preparation for postsecondary education, and create linkages to adult agencies and social supports.

Resources

- American Civil Liberties Union (www.aclu.org/other/faq-educators-immigrant-students-public-schools): Provides information to public school educators about frequently asked questions about immigrant students and their rights.
- Centers for Independent Living (www.ncil.org): Community-based, non-profit organizations that help individuals with disabilities achieve and maintain self-sufficient lives. Examples of services provided include: peer support, individual and systems advocacy, and independent living skills training.
- Center for Parent Information & Resources (www.parentcenterhub.org/): A central place for materials that provide support and services to families, including a resource library organized by topics.
- Deaf Aotearoa (www.deaf.org.nz/): The national service provider for deaf people in Australia. They produced videos and the PDF of the "DEAFinitely stepping ahead project" on transition for deaf learners to postsecondary settings.
- Gallaudet University (www.gallaudet.edu/): A federally chartered private university for the education of the deaf and hard of hearing. It is located in Washington, D.C., on a 99-acre campus. Founded in 1864, Gallaudet University was originally a grammar school for both deaf and blind children.

- Inclusion.com (https://inclusion.com/path-maps-and-person-centered-planning/): Provides transition curriculum that aligns with UDL and person-centered planning tools.
- Life Centered Education Transition Curriculum (www.cec.sped.org/Publications/LCE-Transition-Curriculum): A completely online transition curriculum and assessment portal to prepare students for independent living.
- Life Skills Curricula Series (www.attainmentcompany.com/life-skills-curriculum-series): A picture-based curriculum that teaches functional skills to students, such as "Shopping Smart" and "Keeping House."
- National Center on Secondary Education and Transition (www.ncset.org/): Disseminates resources related to secondary education and transition for youth with disabilities to help prepare them for successful futures.
- National Deaf Center (www.nationaldeafcenter.org/topics/transition): Provides transition resources for students who are d/Dhh such as planning transitions, teaching self-advocacy, and how to work with vocational rehabilitation. Pre-employment Transition Services Guide: www.nationaldeafcenter.org/topics/pre-ets. Vocational Rehabilitation Professionals Toolkit: www.nationaldeafcenter.org/topics/vrtoolkit
- National Technical Assistance Center on Transition (https://transitionta.org/): Provides resources focusing on evidence-based and research-based practices for professionals helping secondary students with disabilities prepare for postsecondary education and employment.
- National Technical Institute for the Deaf (www.rit.edu/ntid/): The first and largest technological college in the world for students who are deaf or hard of hearing.
- O*Net Online (www.onetonline.org/): Sponsored by the US Department of Labor's Employment and Training Administration, this website provides information on various occupations.
- PACER's National Parent Center on Transition and Employment: (www.pacer.org/transition/learning-center/benefits/vocational-rehab.asp)
- Right Question Institute (https://rightquestion.org/schools-families/): Provides the *Right Questions School-Family Partnership Strategy* which provides teachers with tools to show parents how to ask the "right" questions to gain the outcomes they desire for their children.
- US Department of Education's College Navigator (https://nces.ed.gov/collegenavigator/): Allows students to search for colleges based on location, program, level of education, and institution type.

- World-class Instructional Design and Assessment (WIDA) Can Do Descriptors (www.wida.us): The Descriptors are skill sets based on English language acquisition proficiency levels and stages of development.
- Zarrow Center for Learning Enrichment (www.ou.edu/education/centers-and-partnerships/zarrow): Provides resources for transition, including *The Self-Directed IEP*, which includes a teacher manual, student workbook, and PowerPoint presentation.

FAMILY-CENTERED BRIEF

FAMILY-CENTERED BRIEF
CHAPTER 8
Transition for d/Deaf and Hard of Hearing Multilingual Learners (DMLs): Guiding Principles and Planning Tools

by John Luckner and Joanna E. Cannon

PURPOSE OF THE CHAPTER
This chapter discusses the specialized transition planning and strategies for children and adolescents who are **d/Deaf Multilingual Learners (DMLs)**.

Why is this important? The transition from high school to young adulthood is a critical stage for all youth. Also, transitions between grades or schools may require a transition plan. **For DMLs these transitions may require extra planning and goal setting.**

KEY TERMS

Transition plan
Section of the Individual Education Plan (IEP) that outlines transition goals and services for students.

Cultural broker
A person who can bridge the language and cultural gap between family members and school staff.

TRANSITION PLANNING
Meetings will be scheduled to create the **DML's transition plan** and will include the following people:

CRITICAL
- Student (i.e., DML)
- Family member(s)

IMPORTANT
- Teachers
- School counselor
- Other school staff (e.g., vice principal)
- d/Deaf or hard of hearing advocate
- Cultural broker

AS NEEDED (specific to the DML's context and goals)
- Local social service agencies
- Adult school-to-work programs
- Postsecondary academic advisor
- Vocational rehabilitation counselor
- Health care provider (e.g., physiotherapist)

FORMAL AND INFORMAL TRANSITION ASSESSMENTS IDENTIFY:

DML
- current functioning
- strengths & skills
- hobbies & interests
- hopes for the future

Family
- hopes for the DML's future
- understanding of what they believe their child wants for the future

RESOURCES
Center for Parent Information & Resources www.parentcenterhub.org/
PACER's National Parent Center on Transition and Employment · Vocational Rehabilitation
www.pacer.org/transition/learning_center/benefits/vocational-rehab.asp

Deaf and Hard of Hearing Multilingual Learners: Foundations, Strategies, and Resources (2022)

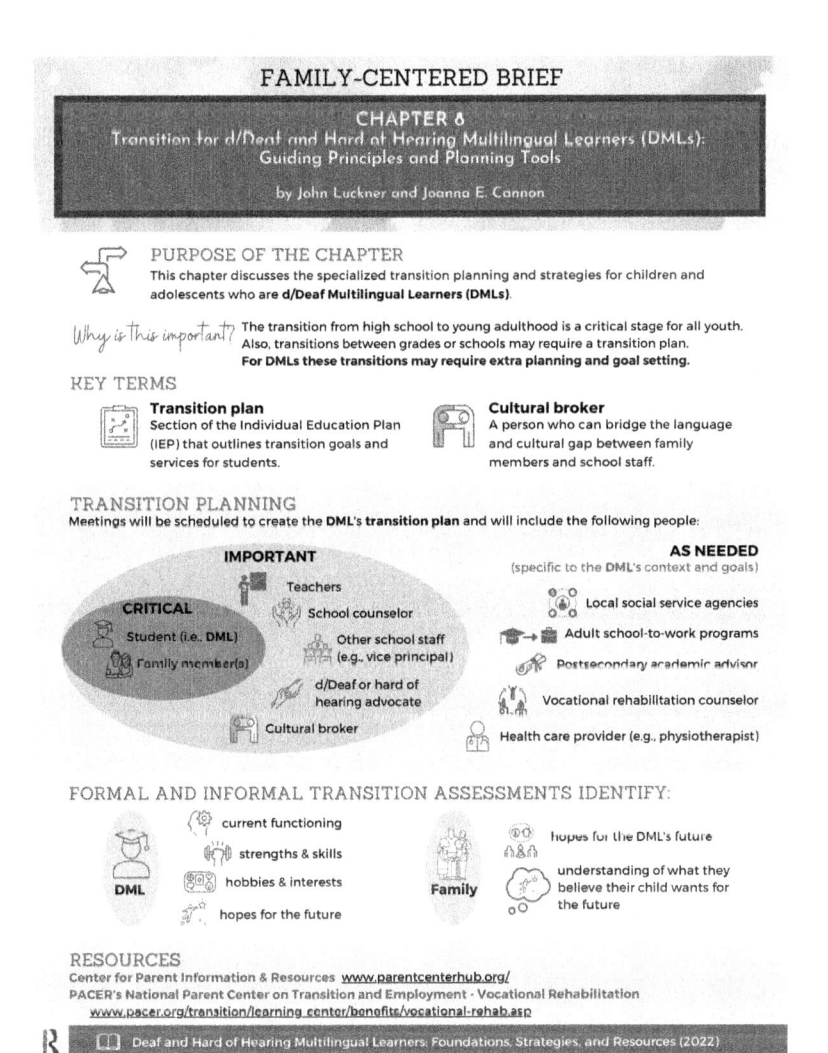

References

Bonds, B. G. (2003). School-to-work experiences: Curriculum as a bridge. *American Annals of the Deaf, 148*(1), 38–48. https://doi.org/10.1353/aad.2003.0001

Borders, C. M., Bock, S. J., Probst, K., & Kroesch, A. (2017). Deaf/hard of hearing students with disabilities. In S. Lenihan (Ed.), *Preparing to teach, committing to learn: An introduction to educating children who are deaf/hard of hearing*. www.infanthearing.org/

Brolin, D. E., & Loyd, R. J. (2004). *Career development and transition services: A functional life skills approach.* Merrill.

Bullis, M., Reiman, J. W., Davis, C., & Reid, D. (1997). National field testing of the 'mini' version of the Transition Competence Battery for adolescents and young adults who are deaf. *Journal of Special Education, 31*, 347–361.

Cameto, R., Levine, P., & Wagner, M. (2004). *Transition planning for students with disabilities.* SRI International. www.nlts2.org/reports/2004_11/index.html.

Cannon, J. E., & Guardino, C. (2022). Learners who are d/Deaf or hard of hearing and multilingual: Perspectives, approaches and considerations. In J. E. Cannon, C. Guardino, & P. V. Paul (Eds.), *Deaf and hard of hearing multilingual learners: Foundations, strategies, and resources* (pp. 1–29). Routledge.

Cannon, J. E., Guardino, C., & Gallimore, E. (2016). A new kind of heterogeneity: What we can learn from d/Deaf and hard of hearing multilingual learners. *American Annals of the Deaf, 161*(1), 8–16.

Clark, G. M. (2007). *Assessment for transition planning* (2nd ed.). PRO-ED.

Cote, D. L., Jones, V. L., Sparks, S. L., & Aldridge, P. A. (2012). Designing transition programs for culturally & linguistically diverse students with disabilities. *Multicultural Education, 20*(1), 51–55.

Cronin, M. E. (1996). Life skills curricula for students with learning disabilities: A review of the literature. *Journal of Learning Disabilities, 29*, 53–68.

Cronin, M. E., Patton, J. R., & Wood, S. J. (2007). *Life skills instruction: A practical guide for integrating real-life content into the curriculum at the elementary and secondary levels for students with special needs and who are placed at risk.* Pro Ed.

Dalke, C. (1991). *Support programs in higher education for students with disabilities: Access for all.* Aspen.

Field, S., Martin, J., Miller, R., Ward, M., & Wehmeyer, M. (1988). *Self-determination for persons with disabilities: A position statement of the Division of Career Development and Transition.* Council for Exceptional Children.

Garberoglio, C. L., Palmer, J. L., Cawthon, S., & Sales, A. (2019). *Deaf people and employment in the United States: 2019.* Washington, DC: US Department of Education, Office of Special Education Programs, National Deaf Center on Postsecondary Outcomes.

Gay, G. (2010). *Culturally responsive teaching: Theory, research, and practice.* Teachers College Press.

Geenen, S., Powers, L., Lopez Vasquez, A. L., & Bersani, H. (2003). Understanding and promoting the transition of minority adolescents. *Career Development and Transition for Exceptional Individuals, 26,* 27–46.

Gothberg, J. E., Greene, G., & Kohler, P. D. (2019). District implementation of research-based practices for transition planning with culturally and linguistically diverse youth with disabilities and their families. *Career Development and Transition for Exceptional Individuals, 42*(2), 77–86. https://doi.org/10.1177/2165143418762794

Greene, G. (2011). *Transition planning for culturally and linguistically diverse youth.* Brookes.

Harrison, P., & Oakland, T. (2003). *Adaptive behavior assessment system* (2nd ed.). Psychological Corporation.

Hoover, J. J., & Patton, J. R. (2017). *IEPs for ELs and other diverse learners.* Corwin.

Individuals with Disabilities Education Act (IDEA) of 2004, 20 U.S.C. §§ 1400–1482 (2015).

Kim, K. H., & Morningstar, M. E. (2005). Transition planning involving culturally and linguistically diverse families. *Career Development for Exceptional Individuals, 28*(2), 92–103. https://doi.org/10.1177/08857 288050280020601

Kochhar-Bryant, C. A., & Greene, G. (2009). *Pathways to successful transition for youth with disabilities: A developmental process* (2nd ed.). Merrill/Pearson.

Landmark, L. J., Zhang, D. D., & Montoya, L. (2007). Culturally diverse parents' experiences in their children's transition: Knowledge and involvement. *Career Development and Transition for Exceptional Individuals, 30*(2), 68–79.

Leake, D., & Black, R. (2005). *Essential tools: Improving secondary education and transition for youth with disabilities: Cultural and linguistic diversity: Implications for transition personnel.* National Center on Secondary Education and Transition.

Leake, D., & Cholymay, M. (2004). Addressing the needs of culturally and linguistically diverse students with disabilities in postsecondary education. *Information Brief, 3*(1). National Center on Secondary Education and Transition, University of Minnesota. Retrieved from www.ncset.org/publications/viewdesc.asp?id=1411

Lucas, T., Villegas, A., & Freedson-Gonzalez, M. (2008). Linguistically responsive teacher education: Preparing classroom teachers to teach English language learners. *Journal of Teacher Education, 59*(4), 361–373. https://doi.org/10.1177/0022487108322110

Luckner, J. L., & Becker, S. J. (2013). Fostering skills in self-advocacy: A key to access in school and beyond. *Odyssey: New Directions in Deaf Education, 14*, 34.

Luft, P. (2016). *Promoting positive transition outcomes: Effective planning for deaf and hard of hearing young adults.* Gallaudet University Press.

Luft, P., & Huff, K. (2011). How prepared are transition-age deaf and hard of hearing students for adult living? Results of the Transition Competence Battery. *American Annals of the Deaf, 155*(5), 569–579. https://doi.org/10.1353/11d.2011.0000

Lynch, E. W., & Hanson, M. J. (2004). *Developing cross-cultural competence: A guide for working with children and families* (3rd ed.). Brookes.

Martin, J. E., Van Dycke, J. L., Christensen, W. R., Greene, B. A., Gardner, J. E., & Lovett, D. C. (2006). Increasing student participation in IEP meetings: Establishing the self-directed IEP as an evidence-based practice. *Exceptional Children, 72*(3), 299–316.

McCain, G., & Farnsworth, M. (2018). *Determining difference from disability: What culturally responsive teachers should know.* Routledge.

McLetchie, B., & Zatta, M. (2014). *To live, to love, to work, to play: Blending quality of life into the curriculum.* www.perkinselearning.org.

Meyer, A., Rose, D. H., & Gordon, D. (2014). *Universal design for learning: Theory and practice.* CAST.

Miller, R. J., Lombard, R. C., & Corbey, S. A. (2007). *Transition assessment: Planning transition and IEP development for youth with mild to moderate disabilities.* Allyn & Bacon.

Moore, C. L., Wang, N., Eugene-Cross, K., & Washington, A. L. (2016). Immigration trends' impacts on state vocational rehabilitation agency minority application rates: An empirical forecast model demonstration study. *Journal of Vocational Rehabilitation, 45*(2), 197–212. https://doi.org/10.3233/JVR_160823

National Deaf Center on Postsecondary Outcomes. (2018). *Root causes of gaps in postsecondary outcomes for deaf individuals.* www.nationaldeafcenter.org/sites/default/files/Root%20Causes%20of%20Gaps%20in%20Postsecondary%20Outcomes%20of%20Deaf%20Individuals.pdf

National Technical Assistance Center on Transition. (nd). *From assessment to practice: Model for teachers.* https://transitionta.org/system/files/effectivepractices/Assessment_to_Practice_Model_FINAL.pdf?file=1&type=node&id=1256&force=

Oesterrich, H. A., & Knight, M. G. (2008). Facilitating transitions to college for students with disabilities from culturally and linguistically diverse backgrounds. *Intervention in School and Clinic, 43*(5), 300–304.

Patton, J. R., & Clark, G. M. (2014). *Transition planning inventory* (2nd ed.). PRO-ED.

Pizzo, L., & Chilvers, A. (2016). Assessment and d/Deaf and hard of hearing multilingual learners: Considerations and promising practices. *American Annals of the Deaf, 161*(1), 56–66.

Reiman, J., Bullis, M., & Davis, C. (1993). *Transition competence battery for deaf adolescents and young adults.* James Stanfield.

Schuster, J. L., Timmons, J. C., & Moloney, M. (2003). Barriers to successful transition for young adults who receive SSI and their families *Career Development and Transition for Exceptional Individuals, 26,* 47–66.

Sitlington, P. L., Neubert, D. A., & LeConte, P. J. (1997). Transition assessment: The position of the division of career development and transition. *Career Development for Exceptional Individuals, 20,* 69–79.

Sparrow, S. S., Cicchetti, D. V., & Balla, D. A. (2005). *Vineland-II adaptive behavior scales* (2nd ed.). American Guidance Service.

Tansey, T. N., Dutta, A., Kundu, M., & Chan, F. (2016). From admiration of the problem to action: Addressing the limited success in vocational rehabilitation of persons from diverse racial and cultural backgrounds. *Journal of Vocational Rehabilitation, 45*(2), 117–119. https://doi.org/10.3233/JVR_160816

Test, D. W., Aspel, N., & Everson, J. (2006). *Transition methods for youth with disabilities.* Merrill/Prentice Hall.

Test, D. W., Mason, C., Hughes, C., Konrad, M., Neale, M., & Wood, W. (2004). Student involvement in individualized education program meetings. *Exceptional Children, 70,* 391–412.

Test, D. W., Mazzotti, V. L., Mustian, A. L., Fowler, C. H., Kortering, L., & Kohler, P. (2009). Evidence-based secondary transition predictors for improving postschool outcomes for students with disabilities. *Career Development for Exceptional Individuals, 32,* 160–181.

Tierney, W. G., Bailey, T., Constantine, J., Finkelstein, N., & Hurd, N. F. (2009). *Helping students negotiate the path to college: What high schools can do: A practical guide* (NCEE #2009–4066). Washington, DC: National Center for Education Evaluation and Regional Assistance, Institute of Education Sciences, US Department of Education. http://ies.ed.gov/ncee/wwc/publications/practiceguides/.

US Department of Education, Office of Special Education and Rehabilitative Services. (2017). *A transition guide to postsecondary education and employment for students and youth with disabilities.* Author.

Valenzuela, R. C., & Martin, J. E. (2005). Self-directed IEP: Bridging values of diverse cultures and secondary education. *Career Development for Exceptional Individuals, 28*(1), 4–14.

Wandry, D. L., & Pleet, A. M. (2012). Family involvement in transition planning. In M. L. Wehmeyer & K. W. Webb (Eds.), *Handbook of transition for youth with disabilities.* (pp. 102–118). Routledge, Taylor & Francis Group.

Wehmeyer, M. L., & Webb, K. W. (2012). An introduction to adolescent transition education. In M. L. Wehmeyer & K. W. Webb (Eds.), *Handbook of transition for youth with disabilities* (pp. 3–10). Routledge, Taylor & Francis Group.

Wehmeyer, M., & Kelchner, K. (1995). *The Arc's Self-Determination Scale, Adolescent Version.* The Arc of the United States. www.thearc.org/document.doc?id=3670 or www.ou.edu/education/centers-and-partnerships/zarrow/self-determination-assessment-tools/arc-self-determination-scale

Wheeler-Skruggs, K. (2002). Assessing the employment and independence of people who are deaf and low functioning. *American Annals of the Deaf, 147*(4), 11–17. https://doi.org/10.1353/aad.2012.0260

Young, A., Squires, G., Oram, R., Sutherland, H., & Hartley, R. (2015). Further education as a post-secondary destination for deaf and hard of hearing young people: A review of the literature and analysis of official statistics in England. *Deafness & Education International, 17*(1), 49–59.

Index

Page numbers in *italics* indicate a figure and page numbers in **bold** indicate a table on the corresponding page.

ABA *see* applied behavior therapy (ABA)
accommodations 78–80
Adaptive Behavior Assessment System 285
additive multilingualism 6, 108
advocacy, for bilingual learners 73
Akamatsu, C.T. 253
Algonquian community 2, 17–18
alphabetic principle 144, **160**
Amadi, Chidinma 142
American Annals of the Deaf 4
American Sign Language (ASL) vii, 9, 14, 49, 51, 115, 175, 265
Amharic language 2
applied behavior therapy (ABA) 236–237
Arabic 277–278
Arc, the, Self Determination Scale 285
Arias, M.B. 37
ASD *see* Autism Spectrum Disorder (ASD)
ASL *see* American Sign Language (ASL)
assessor qualifications 72–73
asset-based approach 16–17, 224
augmentative alternative communication xi, 225, 230
Australian Sign Language (Auslan) 88
authentic assessment models 80, **82–84**
Autism Spectrum Disorder (ASD) viii, x, xi, 220, 222, 231–249, 285

background knowledge 154, **162**
Baker, S. 30, 33, 117, 253
basic interpersonal communication skills (BICS) 6, 114
Becker, S.J. 54
Benedict, K.M. 155
BICS *see* basic interpersonal communication skills (BICS)
bilingualism 7, 8, 67–68, 143, 158
Birth of a Word project 39
Bonds, B.G. 273
Borders, C. 250, 251
Bowen, S.K. 30, 45, 54, 117, 253
Braun, V. 234
Brewster, C. 32
Brisbane, Australia 15
Bristol Deaf Children's Society 8
British Sign Language (BSL) 88, 157
broader community, connecting **192**, 207–209
BSL *see* British Sign Language (BSL)
Butts, Terynce 142

Calderon, R. 42
CALP *see* cognitive academic language proficiency (CALP)
Cannon, J.E. 1, 144, 159, 219, 223, 264
Cantonese 120, 204

CDC report *see* Centers for Disease Control (CDC) report
CEC *see* Council for Exceptional Children (CEC)
CELF *see* Clinical Evaluation of Language Fundamentals (CELF)
Centers for Disease Control (CDC) report 221
cerebral palsy xi, 229, 230
Cheng, L.-R.L. 124
Cherokee 44
child-centered supportive learning 197–198; emotional climate **187–188**, 200–201; physical environments **187**, 199–200
child characteristics 53–54
Cholymay, M. 268
Clarke, V. 234
CLD families *see* culturally and linguistically diverse (CLD) families
Clerc Center 53
Clinical Evaluation of Language Fundamentals (CELF) 121
coaching **189–190**, 202–205
code-mixing 114
cognitive academic language proficiency (CALP) 6, 114
cognitive reserve 110–111
Cole, E. 253
collaboration 36, 224; *see also* leadership, shared
communication 36; assessing skills 89; choices 51–52; school-home 33, 51–52; technology-based approaches 44
community-based instruction 285–286
comprehension 144; and decoding 145; monitoring 155–156
comprehensive language profile viii, 69–85; accommodations 78–80; assessor qualifications 72–73; determining purpose 73–75; informal assessments 80–85, **81–84**; interpreting assessment data 93–96; involving families in assessment 91–93; selecting assessments for DMLs 75–85; specific language assessment 85–91; stages *72*; theoretical framework 68–69; translation 76–78
connections, making 155
content equivalence 77
content integration 19
conversation, and fluency 144
Corbett, C.A. 42
Cote, D.L. 279
Council for Exceptional Children (CEC) 276
criterion-referenced assessment 120, 122
cross-cultural competence **13**, 46
Crowe, K. 106, 111, 112, 127
cultural bias 77
cultural brokers 13–16, 46, **271**
cultural competence 12, 46, 268, **269–270**, 282, 283
cultural humility 49
Cultural Iceberg Model 10, *11*
cultural identity 12–13
culturally and linguistically diverse (CLD) families 31, 37
culturally responsive leadership and pedagogy 127, 128
cultural reciprocity 37
cultural transfer 112
Cupples, L. 111
curriculum based assessment 80, **82**

Dalke, C. 287
DCDT *see* Division of Career Development and Transition (DCDT)
d/Deaf and hard of hearing (d/Dhh) multilingual learners (DMLs) vii, 2–6; assessment 119–121, 124–127; asset-based approach 16–17;

criterion-referenced measures 122; cultural awareness 12–16; dynamic measures 123–124; educational support 127–128; family-centered approach 19; FLP 117–119; language-processing measures 122–123; linguistically and culturally responsive approach 17–19; monolingual *vs.* multilingual perspective 7–10; multilingual development 6–7; norm-referenced standardized measures 121–122; sociocultural approaches 124; statistics and demographics 3–4; understanding multilingualism 107–116

Deaf identity/culture 158, 182
decision-making 36, 282
decodable texts 151–152, **160**
decoding, and comprehension 145
De Lamo White, C. 120
descriptors 274
DesJardin, J.L. 39
developmental delays xi, 227, 230
Developmental Language Disorder 115
disputes, resolving 282
Division of Career Development and Transition (DCDT) 276
DML-D *see* DMLs with disabilities (DML-D)
DMLs *see* d/Deaf and hard of hearing (d/Dhh) multilingual learners (DMLs)
DMLs with disabilities (DML-D) viii, ix–x; collaboration 238–239, 242–243; cultural considerations 239–240; demographic and prevalence data 220–223; eligibility 226–228, 235–236, 250; educators' perspective 240–245, 248–249; and family 235; interventions 230, 237–238, 243–244, 251–252; issues and considerations 226–231; linguistic and communication considerations 230, 246–249, 252–254; methodology 231–234; parent's perspective 234–240, 247–248; placement 228–230, 236–237, 240–242, 250–251; psychosocial aspects 244–245; qualifications 242; theoretical frameworks and approaches 223–226
Down syndrome xi, 86, 225
dynamic assessment 80, **84**, 120, 123–124

educational support 127–128
educational systems 52–53
educators, relationships/trusts 179–180
ELL *see* English Language Learners (ELL)
El Salvador Sign Language 266
ELs *see* English learners (ELs)
embedded assessment models 80, **81**
emergent literacy 50
emotional behavioral challenges 220
emotional climate **187–188**, 200–201
empowering, school culture 19
English, A. 19
English Language Learners (ELL) 221
English learners (ELs) 74, 143
Epstein, J.L. 36
equity pedagogy 19
ESSA *see* Every Student Succeeds Act (ESSA)
Essential Instructional Supports Framework ix; ambitious interactions/instruction **189–190**, 201–205; child-centered supportive learning environments **187–188**, 197–201; families/schools/ community partnerships **191–192**, 205–209; inclusive/instructional

leadership 177–182, **184–185**; recommendations 209–210; routine teacher collaboration 182–197, **186–187**
Ethiopia 15
ethnolinguistic communities 2, 108
European Union 68
Every Student Succeeds Act (ESSA) 31
Ewing, K.M. 250
experiential learning 148, **161**
experiential learning opportunities 145, 148
explicit instruction 145–148, 153–154, **160**

families/schools/community partnerships **191–192**, 205–209
family: characteristics 53–54; programming 181, **191–192**, 206–207; support 158
family-centered approach 19, **191**, 205–206, 231
family-centered early intervention (FCEI) 38–41; emergent literacy 50; needs and concerns 45–51
family engagement/involvement viii, 38–53; availability of resources 54–55; in early intervention 38–41, 45–51; educational considerations for **47–48**; Epstein's spheres of influence 36; Hoover-Dempsey and Sandler method 37; models 36–38; non-traditional models 37–38; in school-age populations 41–45, 51–53; in transition planning 280–282
Family Language Policy (FLP) 117–119, 128
Faroese language 126
FCEI *see* family-centered early intervention (FCEI)
Fishkin, O. 148

FLP *see* Family Language Policy (FLP)
Ford, Laurie 67
formal assessments 274–276
"Functional Math" 286

Gallaudet Research Institute (GRI) 175, 222
Grant, K.B. 32
Greene, G. 268, 281
GRI *see* Gallaudet Research Institute (GRI)
Guardino, C. 1, 144, 159, 219, 223
Guiberson, Mark 106
guiding principles, for transition planning 267–273, **269–271**
Gujarati language 193

Handley, C.M. 156
Hanson, M.J. 268
Henner, J. 126
heritage culture 182, 207–208, 223
high-quality interview techniques 92, 93, 94–95
Hindi 109
home literacy environment 158
home-school communication 33, 36, 51–52
home signs, assessing 89–90
Hoover-Dempsey, K.V. 37, 53–54
horizontal identity 207

Icelandic Sign Language 108
iconicity 78
ICS *see* Intelligibility in Context Scale (ICS)
IDEA *see* Individuals with Disabilities Education Act (IDEA)
IEP team *see* Individualized Education Program (IEP) team
IFSP *see* Individualized Family Service Plan (IFSP)

inclusive/instructional leadership 177–182; establishing vision 178–179, **184**; respectful relationships with educators 179–180, **184–185**; shared leadership practices 180, **185**; teachers and managing resources 181–182, **185**
Individualized Education Program (IEP) team 30, 43, 225, 265, 268, 278, **279**
Individualized Family Service Plan (IFSP) 39
Individualized Plan for Employment (IPE) 283
Individuals with Disabilities Education Act (IDEA) 31, 143, 265
inferencing 155
informal assessments 80–85, **81–84**, 86, 274–276
Intelligibility in Context Scale (ICS) 125
interactions/instruction, ambitious 201–205; coaching/mentoring/supervision **189–190**, 202–205; quality improvement **189**, 202
International Consensus Statement 38
International Guide to Speech Acquisition 126
Inuit Sign Language 126
IPE *see* Individualized Plan for Employment (IPE)

Jackson, C.W. 146
Jaffee, A.T. 148
Jin, L. 120
Jones, T.W. 250

Kieffer, M.K. 146
Kluwin, T.N. 42
Knight, M.G. 287
knowledge construction 19
Korean 231
Kwon, Eun Young 219

language 117: acquisition, multilingual 113–116, *113*; processing assessment 120, 122–123
Leacox, L. 146
leadership, shared 180, **185**; *see also* Essential Instructional Supports Framework
Leake, D. 268
learning: at home 36; opportunities, professional **186–187**, 194–197
learning disability 220
least restrictive environment (LRE) 52
Lenihan, S. 54
Lesaux, N.K. 146
"life contexts" 37
life-skills curriculum 285–286
Limited English Proficiency 221
Linguistically Responsive Teaching (LRT) framework 17–19, 68–69, 127
linguistic diversity 73
literacy instruction 142–164; background knowledge 154, **162**; comprehension and decoding 145; and d/Dhh Learners 153–157; decodable texts 151–152, **160**; ELs with disabilities 151–153; experiential learning 148, **161**; explicit instruction 146–148, 153–154; family support 158; future directions 159; home environment 158; identity/culture of Deaf 158; metacognitive strategy instruction 154–157, **155**, **162**; peer learning 149, **161**; recommendations 159–164; scaffolding 149–150, **161**; US education system 158–159; visual language 158; vocabulary instruction 146–148, 159; word study 153, **161**
LRE *see* least restrictive environment (LRE)
LRT framework *see* Linguistically Responsive Teaching (LRT) framework

Lucas, T. 73
Luckner, J.L. 156
Luckner, John L. 264
Lynch, E.W. 268

MacArthur-Bates Communicative Development Inventories 121
Mandarin 120
Martin, J.E. 279
Mayan Sign Language (K'iche' language) 119
McLeod, S. 127
mediated assessment models 80, **83–84**
mentoring **189–190**, 202–205
metacognitive strategy instruction 154–157, **155**, **162**
Mexican Sign Language (MSL) 3, 9, 34, 88, 147–148, 228, 273
Mini-TCB 276
misidentification 116
Moeller, M.P. 39
Morillo-Campbell, M. 37
morphology 70, **71**
MSL *see* Mexican Sign Language (MSL)
MTSS *see* multi-tiered system of support (MTSS)
multicultural education 18–19
Multicultural Topics in Communications Sciences and Disorders 126
multilingual behaviors 114
Multilingual Children's Speech 126
multilingualism 67–68; additive 6, 108; cognitive pros/cons 110–111; defining 107–110; language acquisition 113–116, *113*; learners assessment 124–127; linguistic pros/cons 111–113; subtractive 6–7, 108
multimedia tools **160**
multi-tiered system of support (MTSS) 17
Musti-Rao, S. 151
Myanmar 35

National Deaf Center on Postsecondary Outcomes (NDC) 287, 289
National Technical Assistance Center on Transition (NTACT) 268, 286
naturalistic assessment 80, **81**
NDC *see* National Deaf Center on Postsecondary Outcomes (NDC)
Nepali 227
Netherlands 68
Newborn Hearing Screening 235
Newcomers Program 33, 35, 54
New Zealand Sign Language (NZSL) 229
non-word/non-sign repetition 123
norm-referenced standardized assessment 120, 121–122
NTACT *see* National Technical Assistance Center on Transition (NTACT)
NZSL *see* New Zealand Sign Language (NZSL)

Oesterrich, H.A. 287
online ASL classes 51
overrepresentation 116

Páez, M. 206
parenting 36
parent participation 30–31
Paul, Peter V. vii
PECS *see* Picture Exchange Communication System (PECS)
Peercy, M.M. 149
peer learning 145, 149, **161**
performance based assessment 80, **82**
Person-Centered Planning 274–278, 283
Philippines 14
Philippine Sign Language 228
phonological features, of languages 70, **71**
physical disabilities 230
physical environments **187**, 199–200

Picture Exchange Communication System (PECS) 237
Pizzo, Lianna 67, 175
placement options 52–53
play based assessment 80, **81**
Pleet, A.M. 281
portfolio assessment 80, **83**
postsecondary education 287–289
Powers, G.W. 42
pragmatics 70, **71**
prejudice reduction 19
psychometrics 75–76

Q'anjob'al (Mayan language) 119
Qualitative Similarity Hypothesis 6
quality improvement **189**, 202
quality of life 268
Quiñonez-Sumner, L. 46

Radical Middle approach viii, ix, 10, 224
Railsback, J. 32
Ray, J. 32
Reed, S. 42
residential schools 53
routine teacher collaboration 182–194, **186–187**, 194–197
Roy, D. 39–40
Russia 43

Sandler, H.M. 37, 53–54
Saskiewicz, J.A. 42
scaffolding 145, 149–150, **161**
school-home communication 33, 36, 51–52
Schwartz, M. 117–118
Scott, Jessica 142
self-advocacy 287
self-determination **272**, 287
self-efficacy 39
semantics 70, **70**, 77
SES *see* socioeconomic status (SES)

shared leadership 180
Sign Bank 51
Signing Times (television program) 51
sign language(s) 2, 51; additional languages in home 88; assessing 87–88; *see also specific entries*
Sign Language Assessment Instruments 126
Sign Language of the Netherlands (SLN) 79
Simple View of Reading 145
SLN *see* Sign Language of the Netherlands (SLN)
SMARTSign app 51
social-emotional development 200–201
sociocultural assessment 120, 124
socioeconomic status (SES) 53
sociolinguistic consciousness 73
SOLOM *see* Student Oral Language Observation Matrix (SOLOM)
SOP document *see* Summary of Performance (SOP) document
specific language assessment 85–91; communication skills 89; home signs 89–90; interpreting data 93–96; involving families 91–93; natural sign language(s) 87–88; spoken language 88–89; written language 90–91
speech perception/production 125
spoken language, assessing 88–89
standardized assessment 120, 121–122, 228
standards based assessment 80, **84**
Stredler-Brown, A. 40
structural equivalence 77
student involvement, in transition planning 276–280
Student Oral Language Observation Matrix (SOLOM) 121, 122, 126
subtractive multilingualism 6–7, 108

Summary of Performance (SOP) document 287
supervision **189–190**, 202–205
Swahili 284
Swanwick, R. 127
syntax 70, **70**
Szymanski, C.A. 222

TAGG *see* Transition Assessment and Goal Generator (TAGG)
TCB *see* Transition Competence Battery for Deaf & Hard-of-Hearing Adolescents and Young Adults (TCB)
TDHH *see* teacher of the d/Dhh (TDHH)
teacher management 181–182; *see also* routine teacher collaboration
teacher of the d/Dhh (TDHH) 150, 237, 238, 243
technology-based communication approaches 44
telehealth 40–41
Tenets of Effective Practice for Learners who are DWD framework 223–226, *223*
Thai Sign Language 229
Tierney, W.G. 287
TPI *see* Transition Planning Inventory (TPI)
Transition Assessment and Goal Generator (TAGG) 275
Transition Competence Battery for Deaf & Hard-of-Hearing Adolescents and Young Adults (TCB) 276
transition planning 264–290, **269–272**; family involvement 280–282; guiding principles 267–273; importance of 265–266; informal and formal assessments 274–276; life-skills and community-based instruction 285–286; postsecondary education 287–289; student involvement 276–280; vocational rehabilitation 282–284
Transition Planning Inventory (TPI) 275
translanguaging 127
translation 76–78
two-way communication 281

UDL *see* Universal Design for Learning (UDL)
underrepresentation 116
Universal Design for Learning (UDL) 285–286
US education system, experiences in 158–159

verbal fluency 123
Verschik, A. 117–118
vertical identity 207
Villegas, A. 73
Vineland-II Adaptive Behavior Scales 285
vision, establishing 178–179
visual accessibility 200
visual language 78, 158
visual learning, and bilingualism 158
visual phonics 144
vocabulary 144, 146–148, 159
vocational rehabilitation 282–284
volunteering 36
Voss, J. 54
Vygotsky, L.S. 149, 223–224

Walker, J.M.T. 37
Wandry, D.L. 281
Wang, Q. 158
Webb, K.W. 268
Wehmeyer, M.L. 250, 268
Westby, C.E. 124
WIDA *see* World-class Instructional Design and Assessment (WIDA)

Wieber, W.B. 46
word study 153, **161**
World-class Instructional Design and Assessment (WIDA) 274
written language, assessing 90–91

Young, R.A. 40

Zaidman-Zait, A. 40
Zehler, A.M. 221
Zimbabwe Sign Language (ZSL) 115
Zone of Proximal Development 149, 224
ZSL *see* Zimbabwe Sign Language (ZSL)